LITERARY SISTERHOODS

Literary Sisterhoods
Imagining Women Artists

DEBORAH HELLER

McGill-Queen's University Press
Montreal & Kingston • London • Ithaca

ISBN 0-7735-2822-9

Legal deposit first quarter 2005
Bibliothèque nationale du Québec

Printed in Canada on acid-free paper that is 100% ancient forest free (100% post-consumer recycled), processed chlorine free.

This book has been published with the help of a grant from the Canadian Federation for the Humanities and Social Sciences, through the Aid to scholarly Publications Programme, using funds provided by the Social Sciences and Humanities Research Council of Canada.

McGill-Queen's University Press acknowledges the support of the Canada Council for the Arts for our publishing program. We also acknowledge the financial support of the Government of Canada through the Book Publishing Industry Development Program (BPIDP) for our publishing activities.

Library and Archives Canada Cataloguing in Publication

Heller, Deborah, 1939–
Literary sisterhoods: imagining women artists / Deborah Heller.

Includes bibliographical references and index.
ISBN 0-7735-2822-9

1. Women and literature. 2. Fiction – Women authors – History and criticism. 3. Women artists in literature. 4. Women authors in literature. I. Title.

PN481.H644 2005 809′.393528 C2004-904805-8

This book was typeset by Interscript Inc. in 10.5/13 Sabon.

Physical Processing **Order Type:** NTAS

Seq No: **39149** **/211**

Cust/Add: 158330000/01 POKC OKANAGAN COLLEGE LIBRARY

Cust PO No. **Cust Ord Date:** 23-Jun-2005

BBS Order No: C325339 Ln:260 Del:1 **BBS Ord Date:** 23-Jun-2005

0773528229-20858570 **Sales Qty:** 1 **#Vols:** 001

Literary sisterhoods

Subtitle: imagining women artists Stmt of Resp: Deborah Heller.

HARDBACK **Pub Year:** 2005 **Vol No.:** Edition:

Heller, Deborah. **Ser. Title:**

McGill Queens University Press

Acc Mat:

Tech Services Charges:

Barcode Label Spine Label Protector US
Base Charge Processing Spine Label BBS US
Property Stamp US
Security Device US

Cust Fund Code: K **Cust Location:**

Stock Category: **Cust Dept:**

250701

Order Line Notes

Notes to Vendor ;

Blackwell's Book Services

Contents

Illustrations

For Jules and Daniel

Acknowledgments

I am pleased to have this opportunity to thank the friends and colleagues who have read parts or all of this book at one stage or another of its progress and who have helped me by their comments, conversation, and intellectual companionship over the years in which the book developed: Gisela Argyle, Henry Auster, Gail Chiarello, Derek Cohen, and Daniel Heller-Roazen. I am grateful to the Jewish Studies Department at Cornell University for their invitation to present to them an earlier version of chapter 2. Special thanks go to Louis Madonna for his support during the last stages of writing this book.

Some of the chapters or parts of them have been published previously in significantly different versions. For their kind permission to republish this material in its new form (in chapters 1, 3, and 4 respectively), I thank the editors of *Papers on Language and Literature*, *Atlantis: A Woman's Studies Journal*, and *Essays on Canadian Writing*. I thank the editors of the University of Massachusetts Press for their kind permission to publish material (in chapter 2) from my chapter in *Contemporary Women Writers in Italy*, edited by Santo Aricò.

LITERARY SISTERHOODS

INTRODUCTION

Women Artists

Exceptional and Representative Lives

The novel's early foregrounding of private experience gave to women in fiction an equality they did not have outside of it. In literary representations a woman's private domestic life was often shown to be as important as a man's struggles in the wider world. Yet this kind of equality evidently proved insufficient for some female writers, who chose to portray women venturing beyond the domestic sphere into the public domain. The exemplary figure of this daring woman is the woman artist. *Literary Sisterhoods: Imagining Women Artists* presents a genealogy of the figure of the woman artist in selected literary works by women authors from Mme de Staël at the beginning of the nineteenth century to the contemporary Alice Munro and Grace Paley. Setting side by side writers and texts from cultures and time periods not normally examined together, the book is composed of chapters on works of French, English, Italian, Canadian, and American women's writing: *Corinne ou l'Italie* (1807) by Germaine de Staël, *Daniel Deronda* (1876) by George Eliot, *Artemisia* (1947) by Anna Banti, and recent collections of short stories by Alice Munro and Grace Paley. No great stretch of the imagination is needed to see the women artists represented in these texts – whether performer, painter, or writer – as some kind of figure for her female creator. I have thus considered the metafictional relation between writer-narrator and her subject in all my chapters, particularly those on the work of the three twentieth-century writers, Banti, Munro, and Paley, where it becomes more pronounced and deliberate. The "sisterhoods" of my title has three distinct meanings. It refers to the relation, whether explicit or implicit, between the author of the text and her woman artist subject; it refers as well to the equally important relation, whether hidden or highlighted, between the fictional artist and the other women in the text. Additionally, the women writers of these novels and stories, grappling in their several ways with fictional representations of women artists, constitute a sisterhood of their own, despite the differences in the cultures and eras to which they belong.

Germaine de Staël's *Corinne ou l'Italie* is the pioneering novel in presenting the figure of the woman artist and had profound reverberations throughout the nineteenth century. Corinne's powerful example, along with Mme de Staël's persuasive delineation of Italy as a country uniquely favourable to female genius, left a mark on successive generations of women, some of whom actually went to Italy in emulation of Staël's fictional heroine. Corinne's talents as an artist are multiple. Following her initial appearance as a woman of genius acclaimed by an admiring multitude, she is subsequently revealed as a poet and playwright who acts, dances, paints, sculpts, sings, plays the harp, and translates. Above all she is an *improvisatrice* – a public improviser and singer of impassioned verses.

George Eliot, who refers to *Corinne* in two of her own novels, began her novelistic career with discursive justifications of her portrayals of humble and rustic life but quickly found her more congenial subject in the depiction of characters of exceptional sensibility. Nonetheless, in her novels such sensibilities are typically exercised within a narrow range, and in the case of her women they rarely find a theatre for expression beyond private life. The charismatic young woman preacher of Eliot's first novel, *Adam Bede*, does assume a limited public role through most of the novel but gives it up at the end when the new Methodist policy bars women from preaching. The heroine of Eliot's historical novel *Romola* assumes for a time a quasi-public role as a sister of mercy in her plague-ridden Florence but lapses into domesticity at the end. Eliot has sometimes been faulted for not allowing any of her heroines to escape constraints that she herself was able to overcome, but clearly she considered her own example too exceptional to merit a place in the kind of realistic fiction about ordinary people that was her professed novelistic aim. However, in her last novel, *Daniel Deronda*, she creates her first and only important woman character to assume a public role – a true vocation that she pursues into adulthood. Though treated with notable ambivalence by her author and marginalized within the novel, where she appears in only two late chapters, this woman artist, the Alcharisi – an internationally renowned opera singer – eloquently defends her right to have pursued a career determined by her exceptional talents, even though it entailed rejecting the role of nurturing mother to her son.

In the twentieth century the Italian novelist Anna Banti has given us a fictionalized account of the seventeenth-century painter Artemisia Gentileschi. Blending fiction with history, and drawing on trial records in the Vatican library, *Artemisia* retells the story of Artemisia Gentileschi's rape at an early age and her emergence from an imagined period of shame and isolation to become a major painter whose works hang today in museums throughout the world. Like the two artist performers in the nineteenth-century novels I discuss, Artemisia too, though at first for reasons other than her talent, is presented as a public figure. The early rape trial, at which her father was the plaintiff and she was tortured, gave her an immediate notoriety. Her public role is subsequently, and more happily, sustained by her work as a court painter in Florence, Naples, and London.

In all three cases, the novelists dwell on their artist characters' great talents and accomplishments, as well as their exceptionality, while at the same time highlighting the ways in which the pursuit of their art comes at a heavy price, costing them dearly as women. Abandoned by her lover, Corinne dies an early death. The Alcharisi first appears in the novel as a dying woman, years after her glorious career has come to an end. Although Banti's Artemisia survives her shame and isolation to become a great painter, she has had to forfeit the love of her husband and daughter. This mid-twentieth-century rendition of the artist's story ends on a more affirmative note, however: not with her death or defeat but with her continued life and health after the death of her father.

In my discussions of *Corinne* and *Daniel Deronda* I have focused on women characters who appear, in each novel, in only two chapters that seem almost detached from the rest of the lengthy narratives to which they belong. In *Corinne*, while the eponymous heroine indisputably holds centre stage, she is contrasted with two other women who are given subordinate roles. Her pale English half-sister, Lucile Edgermond, who marries Corinne's beloved Oswald, is presented as an explicit contrast to Corinne and has received much sympathetic attention from feminist critics, who comment on Mme de Staël's readiness to acknowledge bonds of sisterhood with the "other woman." But there is another "other woman" in *Corinne* who has escaped similar attention; Mme d'Arbigny, Corinne's predecessor in Oswald's affections, appears in two interpolated chapters narrated by Oswald, whose negative presentation of her has been unquestioningly accepted by feminist critics. I point, however, to the striking similarities she shares with both Corinne and her author and argue that recognizing bonds of sisterhood beyond the obvious one between Corinne and Lucile helps deepen our understanding of Staël's attitude to her heroine and, more generally, to the position of women. In *Daniel Deronda*, it is the woman artist who occupies the marginal position. Yet here too, as in *Corinne*, paying attention to the woman on the margins of the main plot and her relation to her more centrally placed "sisters" casts an important – and destabilizing – light on the text as a whole and on the writer's often conflicted attitudes toward gender roles.

In *Artemisia*, the novelist herself chooses suddenly, near the end, to foreground another woman artist whom she has shown only briefly earlier in the book, and with whom Artemisia belatedly recognizes her kinship. Moreover, the kinship between the author and her imagined artist, which in the two nineteenth-century novels is left to the reader to infer, is inscribed within Banti's twentieth-century novel from its opening pages; there, the narrator introduces herself – the woman author of the text – into the narrative as a character who interacts and bonds with her imagined subject, the painter Artemisia Gentileschi. A climactic moment in the novel comes when the writer-narrator imagines her subject, Artemisia, painting the work (now in Kensington Palace) currently held to be a self-portrait; but here this becomes the portrait, painted from memory, of another woman painter, of less renown, whom Artemisia had met earlier in the book. Echoing the initial mirroring of narrator and protagonist, Banti thus sets up a sisterhood of women artists, one famous, one largely forgotten, and one – the writer of the narrative – still aspiring.

The high claims for the achievements of the women artists in the novels of Staël, Eliot, and Banti and their visible public positions set them apart from the more modest treatments of women writer-narrators in the stories of Alice Munro and Grace Paley. Writing is, admittedly, a more private experience than performing before an audience or working as a court painter (especially one who has emerged from a notorious rape trial), and the element of fame never even enters into Munro's and Paley's representations of their writer-narrators. Indeed, one might almost miss the fact that the narrators of many of the stories by Munro and Paley are women writers. These narrators deliberately stress their kinship with other women in the texts rather than their own exceptionality and make no superlative claims for their own talent. Being a writer in the second half of the twentieth century emerges as a less unusual role for a woman and a far less hazardous one than being a performer in the nineteenth century or a painter in the seventeenth. The women writer-narrators of Munro's and Paley's stories are no more likely to suffer or come to a bad end than other women; nor do they feel a special need to justify themselves or to affirm their right to their vocation. It would seem that a contemporary woman writer can dispense with either fanfare or disguise if she wants to construct a narrator who is also a woman writer.

In the shift from earlier representations of the woman artist as an exceptional figure to more recent treatments of her as integrated into the lives of her contemporaries, Virginia Woolf, writing in the early twentieth century, deserves mention for her pivotal role, even though this study does not directly address her work. No one has more eloquently presented the costs to an aspiring woman artist of earlier times than Woolf in her fictional portrait of the doomed Judith Shakespeare in *A Room of One's Own*. With a genius equal to her brother's, Woolf argues, a woman artist living in the Age of Shakespeare could only lead a painful, unfulfilled life, meeting an early tragic death. For Judith Shakespeare, the insurmountable obstacles are both external and internal. In her essay "Professions for Women," Woolf turns to the inner obstacles facing a woman writer in the early twentieth-century, "when the path is nominally open," finding that even when she overcomes the first hurdle and slays the powerfully inhibiting Angel in the House, "she still has many ghosts to fight ... many phantoms and obstacles."[1] In Woolf's idyllic *Orlando*, however, the woman artist is spared these battles. Here Woolf highlights how attitudes toward women have altered over time. Constructing the charmed life of her subject, Woolf shrewdly grants him a male identity when he begins work on his poetry in the Elizabethan period, so that his efforts meet with no greater disapproval than the restrained scorn directed at his aristocratic lineage. Generously allowing several centuries for her protagonist's talent to mature (during which Orlando also changes sexes), Woolf then presents it as quite natural and easy that by "the present moment" – precisely dated at 1928 – the completed poem on which Orlando has been working for centuries wins her both fame and a prize, despite her female gender. In *To the Lighthouse*, which immediately precedes *Orlando* though set somewhat earlier in the twentieth century, Woolf more realistically creates the painter Lily Briscoe. Lily's dedication to painting is, to be sure, presented as somewhat eccentric; she is complemented by the more typically feminine artist-of-life, Mrs Ramsay, who creates beauty and order through harmonious moments. But Lily is the one who survives. Despite her self-doubts and the world's indifference, even at times its hostility, she perseveres. Confronted with the time-honoured misogyny expressed by a character who tediously reiterates that "women can't paint, can't write," Lily succeeds in resisting his potentially debilitating judgment; and other male characters actually listen with interest to her discussion of her painting. While she receives no prizes – and neither the author nor anyone else advances great claims for Lily's talent – her painting is a major unifying thread throughout the novel, which concludes with her completion of the canvas on which she has been working from the book's outset and her triumphant achievement of her "vision." (It is intriguing to speculate about the possible influence of the humble Lily Briscoe on the fictional recreation of Artemisia Gentileschi by Anna Banti, who had translated Woolf's *Jacob's Room*.[2]) The artist's vision is less wholly private in Woolf's last novel, *Between the Acts*, where she creates the contemporary Miss La Trobe, playwright, director, and costumer of the annual village pageant. Although she herself takes only fleeting comfort in reflecting that "for one moment" she "made them [her audience] see," and ultimately concludes "that she had suffered triumph, humiliation, ecstasy, despair – for nothing,"[3] the reader is encouraged to take a more generous view of Miss La Trobe's achievement. We see that she has indeed succeeded in bringing her audience together and in effecting, at least temporarily, some kind of thought-provoking communal vision, however variously its meaning is interpreted. Despite each woman's eccentricity and the fact that neither is fully integrated into her society, Lily Briscoe and Miss La Trobe are in fact less outcast than they sometimes feel. Lily is, after all, a longtime friend and houseguest of the Ramsays, and the villagers appreciate and depend on the dynamism and creativity of Miss La Trobe. Both figures thus contribute significantly to the literary normalization of the woman artist. Their self-confident descendants, the writer-narrators in the fiction of Alice Munro and Grace Paley, are the beneficiaries of this sea change.

My chapter on Munro's *Friend of My Youth* focuses on three stories in particular, of which two have women writer-narrators and one, narrated in the third person, concerns a dying opera singer of decidedly modest achievement and talent, whose life remains unremarkable,[4] and her daughter, a writer only in embryo, who tells stories to herself. While the narrator's role as a writer in both "Friend of My Youth" and "Meneseteung" is important since each is involved in some kind of competition for narrative authority, the fact of their being writers is not presented as in any way exceptional. Indeed, in the latter story, where the narrator is attempting to reconstruct the life of a forgotten nineteenth-century woman poet, her imagination focuses on the difficulties of her foremother's position and the costs her predecessor has had to pay for even her modest deviation from the norm, which contrast sharply with her own unapologetic confidence. In "Meneseteung," as in Banti's *Artemisia*, the effort of a contemporary female narrator to resurrect and reconstruct the life of an artistic foremother gives shape to the structure of her narrative. At the same time, taking the phrase from one of Munro's narrators, I treat *Friend of My Youth* as a collection of stories about the ways the women characters in one way or another "get loose": from the roles expected of them by other characters, from the roles that readers may expect them to play in predictable plots, and from the author's knowledge and control. "Getting loose," these characters often discover unexpected affinities with apparently dissimilar women. Writer-narrators appear elsewhere in Munro's stories, though frequently her female narrators and protagonists are not writers or artists of any kind but simply intelligent, perceptive, and articulate women. They do not sound notably different from their writer or performer "sisters," however, even though they are likely to work in bookstores, libraries, schools, or even businesses.

The chapter on Grace Paley is longer and more wide-ranging than the others, in part because I treat the progress of her recurrent protagonist and narrator, Faith, and the way she is used to illuminate the culture and world she shares with her author, through three collections of stories and one subsequent story, rather than focusing, as I do in the other chapters, on a single text or collection. Like

Munro, Paley refuses to claim an exceptional status for her writer-narrator. Indeed, although there are fleeting indications in a couple of stories that Faith is a writer as well as narrator, Paley does not highlight this fact until the last story of her last collection, when, in a metafictional move, she clearly establishes Faith as the writer of the stories in which she has appeared, most of which she has also narrated. Yet Faith's (belatedly clarified) identity as a writer has in no way set her apart from the other women throughout the stories with whom she shares so many life experiences. Bonds among women – affirmations of sisterhood – are repeatedly emphasized in the stories of Grace Paley, as in those of Alice Munro.

The Canadian Alice Munro and the American Grace Paley are not often examined together. The differences between them – most obviously, the kinds of characters they write about and the backgrounds from which they come – may come to mind more readily than their similarities. One could also contrast Paley's *engagé* political activism with Munro's lack of explicit political involvement, or Munro's prolific narrative output with Paley's much more modest one and the greater variety of forms in which she writes, which include poetry and political, autobiographical and occasional pieces. Yet the similarities between the two writers are at least as significant. On the simplest level, there are thematic affinities. In addition to the decision to present their women artists as representative rather than exceptional, similar situations also appear in their stories, though not all in the stories I discuss here: single motherhood, a woman's chance meeting with an ex-husband, an adult daughter's visit to a hospitalized father, the aftermath of abortion, a mother's coming to terms with unwanted separation from a grown-up child, dealings with impermanent lovers, and friendships among women. Moreover, both show a keen interest in history and the role of broad cultural forces; they write of women's lives, generational changes, and the openness of opportunity in the modern world, the possibility of leading successive lives in one lifetime. Their writings reveal the cross-cultural character of many aspects of modern life. There are also biographical affinities; born within nine years of each other, both began to publish in the 1950s and continue to do so into the present. Additionally, the Canadian Munro has for many years been a regular and widely acclaimed contributor to the *New Yorker*, where the native New Yorker Paley now also publishes.

More important, however, are the similarities of narrative method, structure, and form. The subject matter of unexceptional lives merges with the question of form as their writing often intentionally problematizes the distinction between margin and centre. In the stories I discuss from *Friend of My Youth*, Munro deliberately calls attention to women who are at first seen as marginal but then move to the foreground of her narratives. In Paley's last collection she shifts her frequent narrator and protagonist from the centre to the background of several stories, while focusing on other characters in a displacement that increases our awareness of the fluidity between centre and margin. Munro's and Paley's sensitivity to the openness of possibility in contemporary life also has its formal dimension in both writers' resistance to definitive narrative closure. Their stories are similarly marked by radically non-linear structures, abrupt transitions, careful whittling down to essentials, and rejection of traditional concepts of plot. Notably, too, the prose fiction of each consists almost exclusively of the short story.[5] Both writers trace their initial choice of this format to the demands of motherhood, with its sporadic opportunities for work; subsequently, in response to publishers' urgings, both struggled to produce a novel, at the time considered *de rigueur* for a serious writer. For both, however, such struggles ended in failure and their recognition that the short story was actually their preferred form, not simply preparation for a novel yet to come.

In some sense both are also regional writers. (Both are frequently compared to Faulkner.) Munro's characters are most often geographically rooted in rural southwestern Ontario, though some have settled in British Columbia or move back and forth between the two provinces. Almost all reveal something of their dour Scots Presbyterian background of propriety and self-denial, even if only through their efforts to distance themselves from it. More predictably rooted than Munro's characters, and never straying far from New York City, the first-generation children of middle or east European Jewish immigrants who people Paley's stories come from poor but culturally rich backgrounds, revealing a verbal fluency, an exuberance, ease of impulse, and faith (at least while young) in the American promise of opportunity, which contrast sharply with the deprivation, tight restraint, and curbed expectations of Munro's world. Yet both writers are funny and ironic, though Paley's humour is more apparent, Munro's subtler.

While both Munro and Paley accept the label of regional writer, both take care to qualify its meaning. Writing of her rural southwestern Ontario setting, Munro has specified, "I don't think that I'm choosing to be confined. Quite the opposite. I don't think I'm writing just *about* this life. I hope to be writing about and *through* it."[6] Paley, who readily describes herself as a "regional writer ... an urban writer with a New York focus,"[7] makes the same point in a different way: "The more specific and regional you are, the more you speak to everybody ... if you really speak out of a specific place and time, somehow or another it's interesting to others, and they pull out of it what's close to them."[8] Along with their regional focus goes their evident fascination with ordinary life, though for each of them the ordinary is also the mysterious. Writing of a river, Munro might just as well be describing all her stories: "This ordinary place is sufficient, everything here is touchable and mysterious."[9] Again, Paley's view is similar: "That's what interests me ... ordinary life is sufficiently dramatic." And elsewhere, "What I think is mysterious is life. What I'm trying to do is show how mysterious ordinary life is."[10] While both writers identify ordinary life as their subject, there are metafictional and surrealistic elements in their stories, although these are always placed in the service of writing about real – or better, true – life.

As in their willingness to be seen as regional writers and their commitment to ordinary life which is also mysterious, Munro and Paley are alike in their readiness to integrate their narrator-protagonists into the life of their times. The earlier artist figures of exceptional women portrayed by Staël, Eliot, and Banti illuminate their times in a different way, by their greater difficulty in finding accommodation in them. This reflects the more anomalous position of the woman artist in the earlier texts. "You'll never know what it is to have a man's force of genius in you and to suffer the slavery of being a girl," the Alcharisi says to her son in *Daniel Deronda*, by way of justifying her vocation.[11] "Tengo nel petto un animo di Cesare" (I carry the heart of Caesar in my breast),[12] writes Banti's Artemisia to a patron, paraphrasing a line from the letters of the historical Artemisia Gentileschi, "Ritrovera uno animo di Cesare nell'anima duna donna" (You will find the heart [*animo*; also mind, spirit, courage] of Caesar in the soul [*anima*] of a woman).[13] Not so long ago only genius could justify the vocation of the woman artist, and genius was held, even by many women writers, to be fundamentally a masculine attribute.

Staël allows Corinne to be celebrated as a distinctly *female* genius, invoking the model of the classical Sybil, but this combination exacts a bitter price. Ordinary life is precisely what is denied to these earlier representations of women artists.

Throughout the book I am interested in the vision of human possibility presented by the literary texts I examine, the text's relation to its own culture, and its mode of presentation. With each text I have chosen the approach that seemed most fruitful for these explorations. Whether presented as Everywoman or the magnificent exception, narrator or subject, the situation of the woman artist inevitably reflects that of all women of her age and culture. And beyond that, as the plight of the tragic hero carried implications for all people, so the treatments of women artists examined here also speak more broadly to the rest of us; we too, in our strivings for individual expression, are conditioned by the circumstances of our particular time and place. Viewed together, these writers and their subjects, in their different ways, can help illuminate our own separate and shared worlds.

Corinne au cap Misène (Corinne at Cape Misero) by François Girard (1819–1921), which hung in the bedroom of Mme Récamier. Juliette Récamier, herself the subject of famous portraits by Girard and Jacques Louis David, received it from Prince Henry of Prussia in 1821. Courtesy Musée des Beaux-Arts de Lyon; © Studio Basset

1

Tragedy, Sisterhood, and Revenge

Mme de Staël's *Corinne ou l'Italie*

I

The 1987 translation into English of Germaine de Staël's *Corinne ou l'Italie* made accessible to a North American readership the novel that Ellen Moers, in her early pioneering study of women's literature, called "*the* book of the woman of genius," whose "enormous influence on literary women" she traced throughout the nineteenth century.[1] Coinciding with a burgeoning interest in women's studies and, more specifically, with a revival of interest in the once widely known French woman of letters, Avriel H. Goldberger's translation came at an opportune time. Over forty years ago, Madame de Staël's American biographer was content to write off her novels as period pieces. Comparing Staël unfavourably to her contemporary, Jane Austen, J. Christopher Herold observed that while the problems of Austen's characters "are of the commonplace or eternally human variety ... the problems of Germaine's characters are those of her age and place." However questionable this distinction, it led him to an undeniable truth, which he presented as right and just: "Jane is still read, and Germaine is not."[2] A contemporary American Staël scholar, Madelyn Gutwirth, took a different view of *Corinne* in her back-cover quote for Goldberger's translation: "It will set this building block of women's literature firmly back into the foundation of the edifice, where it belongs."

Which is it, then, to be – a book for scholars only or one that speaks to our contemporary concerns? Despite the best efforts of recent Staël scholars, it has proven difficult for modern readers to embrace *Corinne ou l'Italie* with the enthusiasm of Staël's earlier audience. Yet Mme de Staël's most famous novel still merits our serious attention. For in its fundamental concern with the status of women, it addresses issues that touch us deeply today. Staël challenges female stereotypes that still afflict us and poses problems that remain relevant to our experience. It will hardly surprise, however, if we cannot read *Corinne* in quite the same defiant and self-affirmative spirit in which it was written, or if, in challenging many attitudes and social conventions that were detrimental to female development, the novel nonetheless upholds others that are equally damaging. Our most valiant efforts to achieve critical distance from the intellectual and social climate in which we have developed must, necessarily, remain in some way part of that context. The tension between what is challenged and what is accepted constitutes the hidden drama of *Corinne*.

That Staël was "not only unmilitant but often quite reactionary in her own statements about women" has been aptly demonstrated by Madelyn Gutwirth with regard to the gradual and cautious evolution of Staël's theoretical position.[3] I am concerned here with the complementary issue of the unarticulated logic behind Mme de Staël's dramatic treatment of women in *Corinne*. For while the novel makes extraordinary claims for an exceptional heroine and appears to challenge an ideology that would oppose the flowering of her talent, at the same time it endorses a system of values that proves destructive to that heroine and ultimately calls into question the genius it claims for her.[4]

Explicitly, *Corinne* is presented as a tragedy of a woman of genius who is defeated by the restrictive forces of narrow social conventions and expectations. By now, the story of how female potential is thwarted by the limitations of social possibility is recognizable in fiction – to say nothing of life – as a familiar "woman's plot."[5] This is, to be sure, a variant of a more general pattern in the nineteenth-century novel – the thwarting of individual potential by social constraint; but for the "woman's plot" the social constraints are much greater, the obstacles much more pronounced. Viewed in this context, Staël's novel of 1807 may be seen to prefigure all those subsequent versions of the same general conflict that embody in a manner particular to women a perpetual human dilemma. *Corinne*, however, is immediately distinguishable from the later and more typical nineteenth-century treatments of this theme by its unremitting insistence on the *fulfilled* genius of its heroine; she is already "la femme la plus célèbre de l'Italie" (49),[6] the most famous woman in Italy, when she first enters the novel, seated in a triumphal chariot drawn by four white horses, about to be crowned for her artistic achievement at the Capitol in Rome.

Staël makes plain, however, that such appreciative social recognition of female genius is possible only in Italy. Late in the novel Corinne reveals herself as the daughter of an English lord and a Florentine mother, who from the age of fifteen to twenty-one had lived in a small town in England, where she was made to feel the crushing weight of social disapproval for any activity or interest that departed from the narrowest interpretation of female domestic duty. The best advice her father could give her was to exercise her talents in secret so as not to excite envy. With less conviction he extended the feeble hope that with luck she might be fortunate enough to find a husband who would take pleasure in her talents. But when Corinne spent time alone in order to cultivate her talents, her stepmother became angry and resentful. "A quoi bon tout cela?" (What is the good of all that), she would ask with chilling utilitarian logic, broaching what emerges as an important underlying question throughout the novel: "En serez-vous plus heureuse?" (365; Will you be any happier for it?) Corinne's naive belief that happiness consists in the development of our faculties was met with her stepmother's correction that a woman's role was to care for her husband and children, and all other ambitions could only cause trouble. In Corinne's account, English provincial life appears more wholly suffocating and stultifying than in the novels of Jane Austen or George Eliot, lacking a shred of even the hollow approval for female "accomplishments," such as piano playing or sketching, that are satirized in their work. Hence, when Corinne comes into an independent income after her father's death, recognizing that her energies and enthusiasm need encouragement if she is to develop her talents, she flees the death-in-life of English provincial society and returns to her native Italy. Corinne's past history, then, circumscribed within a single retrospective autobiographical "book" of the novel, presents us only with a tragedy-that-might-have-been, but that is averted by the wise move to a nurturing environment.

Still, Simone Balayé surely reads Staël's intention correctly when she describes the "essential theme" of the novel as "the conflict of the woman of genius with society,"[7] although my reading will suggest ways in which the text that emerges is less simple than the apparent intention behind it. In its broadest outlines the opposition between social requirements and female genius is clear enough. For though Corinne appears to have escaped the asphyxiating influence of English social attitudes, her triumph is short-lived. To summarize a complex plot: at the moment of greatest glory in her career – her coronation at the Capitol – she meets and falls in love with Oswald Lord Nelvil, who unthinkingly accepts all the prejudices of British society from which Corinne has fled. While in Italy and under the direct influence of Corinne, with whom he falls in love, Oswald subjects these attitudes to much scrutiny, concluding each time that the exceptional qualities of Corinne's genius and personality are more desirable than the self-effacing domestic virtues that his society has taught him to value most in women. Nevertheless, he feels bound to do nothing that might go against the wishes of his dead father. Corinne's delayed revelation that his father had met her in England and thought her unsuitable to be his son's wife, preferring her younger half-sister Lucile instead, does not initially alter Oswald's intention to remain faithful to Corinne. But when he is summoned back to his regiment in England, he learns more about his father's disapproval of Corinne, hears her disparaged by her stepmother, and meets the angelic and conventional Lucile. Influenced as well by a series of improbable coincidences and the mistaken belief that Corinne has lost interest in him, Oswald betrays Corinne by marrying Lucile, as his father had wished, and Corinne retires from the world to die. As social forces hostile to Corinne's genius converge to assist her defeat, the novel follows the broad pattern of classical tragedy, dramatizing the fall of a protagonist from her initial position of grandeur, and sidesteps the tragedy *manquée* (which will become more typical of the nineteenth-century novel) of a protagonist whose exceptional sensibilities are inhibited by circumstance from developing fully.

Other embryonic tragedies are also adumbrated in *Corinne* but not pursued. The most important of these is the conflict between the demands of love and genius in a woman. Corinne openly pursues and delights in glory, an attitude commonly regarded as praiseworthy in men but unseemly in women. Yet while it is abundantly clear that her happiness depends on the full and free exercise of her talents, once she falls in love with Oswald his love becomes equally necessary to her. Italy – as much a construct of Staël's myth-making imagination as a product of her powers of observation – is, we have seen, presented as the required sustaining soil for the full flowering of her genius.[8] This fact, implicit in her life history, is made explicit late in the book when we read a letter by Oswald's father to Corinne's father, antedating the action proper of the novel, which underscores the importance of social context in determining identity and possibility: "Des talents si rares doivent nécessairement exciter le désir de les développer ... elle entraînerait nécessairement mon fils hors de l'Angleterre; car une telle femme ne peut y être heureuse; et l'Italie seule lui convient" (Such rare talents must necessarily excite the desire to develop them ... she would necessarily lead my son outside of England; for such a woman cannot be happy here; and only Italy is suited to her). But, the letter continues, whereas English provincial domestic life is entirely unsuitable to Corinne, "un homme né dans notre heureuse patrie doit être Anglais avant tout" (a man born in our happy fatherland must be English above all). In short, the politically responsible male citizen and the woman artist must necessarily prove incompatible: "Dans les pays où les institutions politiques donnent aux hommes des occasions honorables d'agir et de se montrer, les femmes doivent rester dans l'ombre" (466–7; In countries where political institutions provide men with honourable opportunities to act and to prove themselves, women must remain in the shadows). The late Lord Nelvil's letter only confirms the potential conflict that has cast its menacing shadow over the love story all along. A good Englishman, Oswald needs England; an artist and a woman, Corinne needs Italy. What Oswald's father does not predict, however, is that because of her passionate, loving nature, Corinne needs Oswald as well.

Thus, the potential conflicts between Oswald's love for Corinne and his role as a British peer, military man, and devoted son, and between Corinne's needs as an artist and a woman in love are carefully constructed. But they are not sustained, and the focus of the tragedy shifts elsewhere. Once back in England, Oswald wonders how he can reconcile loyalty to his dead father's wish that he not marry Corinne with his sworn fidelity to her. The compromise they have earlier discussed of his returning to her in Italy as a devoted, loving friend hovers unsatisfactorily in his mind as a hazy, ill-defined alternative. But he does not clearly confront the problem of how frustrating such an existence might prove to him in the long run. This is partly because the novel offers no convincing proof that Oswald has any real *work* from which an idle residence in Italy, passed in single-minded devotion to Corinne, would keep him. (His exploits of military bravery after his marriage are presented more as desperate attempts at self-destruction than anything else.) Fundamentally, however, he never gets to face directly the potential love-vocation conflict because his new love for Lucile, the insufficiency of his prior love for Corinne, his moral scruples regarding his father's wishes, and his faulty interpretation of Corinne's silence all combine with his deeply rooted prejudices to lead him, confusedly and almost passively, into his precipitous marriage with her half-sister.

For Corinne, the potential conflict between love and career – in her case, between love and genius – is both more abundantly prepared for and more completely abandoned. Throughout the novel Staël scatters indications of an inherent conflict between Corinne's increasing dependency on Oswald, which characterizes her love, and the necessary independence of spirit required for her artistic creativity. But as long as Oswald remains with her, this embryonic conflict results in no appreciable ill effects. Indeed, as long as she is sure of his love and can enjoy his company, she is perfectly happy and even regards the idea of marriage with distaste, especially when she contemplates that it would force her to leave Italy and live in England. Ultimately, however, she does come to hope that Oswald will want to marry her, as she recognizes "qu'il ne concevait le bonheur que dans la vie domestique, et que s'il abjurait le dessein de l'épouser, ce ne pouvait jamais être qu'en l'aimant moins" (397; that he conceived of happiness only in domestic life and that he could never renounce the plan of marrying her except by loving her less). In fact, she goes so far as to assure him, "s'il vous plaisait de passer vos jours au fond de l'Écosse, je serais heureuse d'y vivre et d'y mourir auprès de vous: mais loin d'abdiquer mon imagination, elle me servirait à mieux jouir de la nature" (366; if you wished to spend your days in the remotest part of Scotland, I would be happy to live and die there by your side; but far from giving up my imagination, it would serve me better to enjoy nature). Yet how can we believe this claim after all we have read? The novel prepares us for the tragic ramifications of irreconcilable conflicts between

Corinne's need for Oswald's love *and* for an environment and state of mind conducive to her uninhibited development as an artist, and between the demands of marriage and those of a woman's creative self-fulfilment; but it does not follow up this preparation. Instead of pursuing the internal dynamics of Corinne's contrasting needs and desires, the focus of the tragedy shifts to Oswald's betrayal, his failure to appreciate adequately Corinne's extraordinary worth and love for him.

The tragedy growing out of a woman's contradictory needs and desires would have conferred a more contemporary, even a more feminist, flavour on the novel, whereas the tragedy of a woman's misplaced affections, her betrayal by an unworthy man, is, sadly, a more conventional as well as conceptually less interesting plot. A particularly dated aspect of the structure Staël develops is that in the contrast between the intensity of Corinne's love and the insufficiency of Oswald's, Oswald is portrayed not only as psychologically weak and indecisive but also as morally culpable. Although Corinne repeatedly affirms that she wants Oswald's love freely given and never seeks marriage as a means of holding him against his will, his failure to reciprocate the intensity of her love is presented, in the context of the novel's moral structure, as objectively blameworthy. This judgment, implicit throughout, is made explicit in several authorial statements on greater female vulnerability – both emotional and social – in love and is reiterated near the end by Prince Castel-Forte, who pronounces definitively on Oswald's guilt by pointing above all to women's greater vulnerability in the world's opinion ("dans l'opinion du monde" [565]). Interestingly, Staël might have bolstered her view of Oswald's culpability by developing the implications of a situation that, again, she first introduces and then declines to pursue dramatically. The point is made repeatedly that Corinne is concealing from Oswald the extent to which she is "compromising" herself when she sets off from Rome to travel alone with him to other parts of Italy. But when she returns from these travels unmarried, though her friends are surprised, her social position has in no way suffered. Even after she is abandoned by the man to whom she has publicly devoted herself, her friends esteem her as highly and remain as eager for her company as before. The issue of Corinne's social vulnerabilty is raised only to be dropped. On the other hand, Corinne's angry reproach near the end, "Hé bien, qu'avez-vous fait de tant d'amour?" (572; So then, what have you done with so much love?), echoes the novel's sustained viewpoint, implicit throughout, that a love as exceptional as Corinne's somehow *deserves* to be returned. It is her emotional, rather than her social vulnerability that proves her undoing. It may be, of course, that the author does not really believe in the idyllic social context she has constructed for her heroine. But as the novel is written, Corinne becomes a victim of her love for Oswald because of forces within herself, not within society.

2

A modern reading of the novel might want to overlook the emphasis placed on Oswald's "fault" and to locate the deeper tragedy in the way all Corinne's extraordinary talents, her intellectual and artistic energy, creativity and achievement, ultimately fail to help her when she is wounded in love. Such a reading would lead us to review, in a sadly ironic light, Corinne's earlier conversations with her stepmother, in which Lady Edgermond questioned the worth of female genius and Corinne expressed unhesitating confidence in the intrinsic value of cultivating her faculties. Not only do these highly developed faculties fail to sustain her when she needs them most; with a logic that recalls Rousseau as it anticipates Stendhal, Staël reiterates that the very power of Corinne's faculties – the richness of her sensibilities, intellect, and imagination – only serves to increase her unhappiness.

However, if we attempt to "update" the novel by ignoring the clearly expressed view of Oswald's responsibility for Corinne's death and considering the profounder tragedy to be the heroine's own emotional vulnerability despite – indeed, in part because of – so many strengths, we come up against an unavoidable difficulty: it is not at all plain that we are being invited to regard Corinne's monomaniacal fixation on Oswald's betrayal and her determined drift toward death as tragic. Rather, her withdrawal from the world and death of a broken heart are presented, finally, more as triumph than as tragedy. How this happens may best be seen by considering the role of the two other women in the novel whose relation to Oswald can be compared to Corinne's. One is her half-sister Lucile, with whom she ultimately develops a strange bond that has been sensitively commented on by feminist critics and that I shall examine shortly. The other is Mme d'Arbigny, Oswald's first love, the other "other woman" in *Corinne*, who typically receives only the briefest possible mention from critics, when they do not ignore her entirely. Yet Mme d'Arbigny deserves considerably more attention if we are to understand the values implicit in *Corinne* – its ideology – and the problems the novel poses for a contemporary reader.

Mme d'Arbigny belongs to the pre-history of the narrative proper, existing only in two chapters in which Oswald gives Corinne an account of his earlier life. The apparent antithesis to Corinne, whose honesty and naturalness are everywhere insisted upon, Mme d'Arbigny is from the first presented as calculating and deceitful. The widow of a rich older husband whom she had married without love at a time of temporary financial hardship, she inveigles herself into Oswald's affections by flattering and always agreeing with him – unlike Corinne, who in a spirit of loving equality readily engages in intellectual disputes. After the death of her brother – Oswald's friend – during the early stages of the French Revolution, Mme d'Arbigny lures Oswald back to France from Scotland by appealing to his sense of chivalry, untruthfully expressing anxiety about her financial plight and pretending to be more friendless than she is. However, her interest in him is not venal, any more than Corinne's is. She is rich and loves him as much as one can love when "l'on conduit les relations du coeur comme des intrigues politiques" (318; one conducts the affairs of the heart like a political intrigue). Moreover, in Oswald's account she is also somehow at fault for failing to resist his overtures of physical passion: "Comme il entrait dans ses projets de me captiver à tout prix, je crus entrevoir qu'elle n'était pas invariablement résolue à repousser mes désirs; et maintenant que je me retrace ce qui s'est passé entre nous, il me semble qu'elle hésitait par des motifs étrangers à l'amour, et que ses combats apparents étaient des délibérations secrètes" (319; As it was part of her plan to captivate me at any cost, I thought I perceived that she was not invariably set on rejecting my desires; and now that I think back over what happened between us, it seems to me that she hesitated from motives that were foreign to love, and that her apparent struggles were secret deliberations). Oswald's observations imply that true love would have fortified her resistance. Afterwards, "Elle me montra plus de douleur et de remords que peut-être elle n'en avait réellement, et me lia fortement à son sort par son repentir même" (319; she showed more unhappiness and remorse than perhaps she actually felt, and bound me tightly to her destiny by her very repentance). She refuses Oswald's entreaties to return with him to England to obtain his father's consent to their marriage, urging him instead to marry her first and threatening to give herself up to assassins if he leaves her. Finally, in response to his sick father's repeated urgent summonses, he is on the point of departing alone when she pretends to be pregnant and claims that his departure would cause the death of her unborn child as well as herself.

Ultimately Oswald is released from his agonizing moral dilemma by the disclosures of M. de Maltigues, a close relative and confidant of Mme d'Arbigny, whom, Oswald learns belatedly, she has been planning to marry if Oswald should leave her, "car elle ne voulait à aucun prix passer pour une femme abandonnée" (321; for under no circumstances did she want to appear as an abandoned woman). An engaging cynic, M. de Maltigues reveals Mme d'Arbigny as "une personne d'une haute sagesse ... qui, lors même qu'elle aime, prend toujours de sages précautions pour le cas où on ne l'aimerait plus" (329–30; a person of great wisdom ... who, even when she is in love, always takes wise precautions for the eventuality that she will no longer be loved). Exposing Mme d'Arbigny's "pregnancy" as a hoax, M. de Maltigues advises Oswald against marrying her ("Elle est trop rusée pour vous" – She is too crafty for you), while relieving him of possible moral scruples: "Elle pleurera, parcequ'elle vous aime; mais elle se consolera, parceque c'est une femme assez raisonnable pour ne pas vouloir être malheureuse, et sur-tout passer pour l'être. Dans trois mois elle sera madame de Maltigues" (330–1; She will weep, because she loves you; but she will recover, because she is a woman too reasonable to want to be unhappy, and above all, to appear to be so. Within three months she will be Madame de Maltigues). M. de Maltigues's prophesy seems to provide a satisfying closure to this episode in Oswald's history. Oswald returns to Scotland but too late to see his father alive; blaming himself for his father's death, he is left with an unassuageable sense of guilt.

Mme d'Arbigny's absence from the rest of the novel is deceptive, for her unacknowledged, invisible presence hovers over much of what follows. While her most obvious dramatic function is to have intensified Oswald's deference toward his father's wishes regarding his marriage choice, structurally and thematically she also serves other functions. Most immediately, her many differences from Corinne throw into relief aspects of the heroine's character – for example, Corinne's simplicity and naturalness and her refusal to try to hold Oswald against his will or scruples by marriage, or indeed by any stratagem or ruse. But at least as significant is the way the physical love affair between Oswald and Mme d'Arbigny highlights the different nature of his romance with Corinne. Although Oswald is forever clasping Corinne to his heart in outbursts of passionate intensity, the novel makes unequivocally clear that their love is a chaste one: "Plusieurs fois il serra Corinne contre son coeur, plusieurs fois il s'éloigna, puis revint, puis s'éloigna de nouveau, pour respecter celle qui devait être la compagne de sa vie. Corinne ne pensait point aux dangers qui auraient pu l'alarmer, car telle était son estime pour Oswald, que, s'il avait demandé le don entier de son être, elle n'eût pas douté que cette prière ne fût le serment solennel de l'épouser. Mais elle était bien aise qu'il triomphât de luimême et l'honorât par ce sacrifice" (288; Several times he pressed Corinne to his heart, several times he moved away, then returned, then moved away again, in order to respect the woman who was to be the companion of his life. Corinne gave no thought to the dangers which might have alarmed her, for such was her esteem for Oswald, that, if he had asked for the full gift of her being, she would not have doubted that this prayer was his solemn oath to marry her; but she was quite glad that he would triumph over himself and honour her by this sacrifice).

Thus, she assures him, "j'en suis assurée, vous respecterez celle qui vous aime: vous le savez, une simple prière de vous serait toute puissante; c'est donc vous qui répondez de moi; c'est vous qui me refuseriez à jamais pour votre épouse si vous me rendiez indigne de l'être" (289; I am confident you will respect the woman who loves you; you know a simple prayer from you would be all-powerful; therefore it is you who are answerable for me; it is you who would refuse me forever as your wife if you rendered me unworthy of being such).

In short, they both subscribe to the familiar double standard whereby female chastity is an unquestioned virtue, while men are thought to have stronger sexual feelings than women and are permitted greater sexual liberties – but not with women whom they truly respect. Tellingly, the story of Oswald's romance with Mme d'Arbigny arouses no feelings of jealousy in Corinne; indeed, having listened to his lengthy tale, Corinne wastes not a word or even a thought on her predecessor in Oswald's affections. By contrast, Corinne's account of her perfectly chaste prior relationships with two suitors arouses considerable jealousy in Oswald.[9] The novel thus implicitly admonishes the reader not to confuse the unabashed public display of female talent, intelligence, and eloquence with emotional lightness or sexual unchastity. Whatever other literary and social conventions Corinne is permitted to violate, female chastity is not one of them. Sadly, it is in part by insisting on a code of sexual propriety much more confining than any Mme de Staël herself followed that the novel seeks to validate Corinne's right to lead the free life of an artist.

That the sexually freer "other woman" is in reality less passionate than the virtuous virgin heroine is not in itself implausible. We may want to recognize, however, that this polarity has appeared particularly congenial to women novelists in a world unreceptive to the unconventional, "unfeminine" public display of talent, eloquence, and emotional intensity that writing necessarily entails. It can be understood as a kind of back-handed defence of passion, a way of demonstrating its compatibility with virtue. We see the same pattern later in the century in *Jane Eyre*, whose sexually chaste heroine is more truly passionate than any of the four "looser" "other women" in Mr Rochester's past – his Creole wife or his three Continental (French, Italian, and German) mistresses. Charlotte Brontë, herself a passionate writer, lived under severely circumscribed social conditions; moreover, the value she placed on Jane's "virtue" corresponded to her own ethical beliefs. Staël's beliefs, as well as her personal conduct, were different. But despite this, and despite the vastly greater social rank and economic independence enjoyed by Staël and her fictional heroine, the pattern of polarities that separates Corinne and Mme d'Arbigny is essentially the same as in Brontë's novel.

Mme d'Arbigny's shallowness is revealed not only in her sexual "looseness" but also, and perhaps chiefly, in her ability to recover from her disappointment in love and transfer her affections to another man, "car elle ne voulait à aucun prix passer pour une femme abandonnée". The pre-defined role of *la femme abandonnée* was to be contemptible, ridiculous, or pathetic. By outliving a lover's rejection and redirecting her affections a woman might escape the stigma of being an abandoned woman – but only at the cost of confirming her fundamental "lightness," compromising the dignity and integrity of her prior feelings of love and, in turn, her own dignity and integrity as a person.

Since Mme d'Arbigny exists only in Oswald's discourse, his is the only direct judgment on her, and it is severe. (We may note that Oswald's reciprocal attraction to Mme d'Arbigny, to which in retrospect he even denies the name of love, does not similarly impugn the integrity or dignity of *his* nature.) Corinne, we have seen, does not even deign to comment on her. Yet in the broadest outlines, Mme d'Arbigny is a kind of prototype of Corinne, despite all the obvious differences already noted. In relation to Oswald, both are enticing foreign women, both in some way too clever for him but also too clever for their own good. Oswald's father disapproves of each as a wife for his son. The most significant similarity, however, is that both are abandoned by him. Oswald's story of Mme d'Arbigny, with its stern assessment of her, might well serve Corinne as a cautionary tale, though we are given no evidence that it does. However, it does serve the reader as a guide to the author's view of the appropriate attitude toward Corinne's willed death. Reminding us of the unflattering associations attaching to *la femme abandonnée* while demonstrating the indignity that, alternately, attaches to a woman who accepts rejection and carries on with her life, the episode helps us to recognize the predicament that Corinne goes on to demonstrate: that only through death can the abandoned woman escape being stigmatized as light, ridiculous, pitiable, or contemptible. A woman who loves unwisely can reaffirm her dignity and worth only by proving the absolute and uncompromising purity of her love, and this proof can be achieved only through her complete and demonstrated inability to sustain its loss.[10] Corinne may come to recognize at the end that Oswald "n'est pas celui que je croyais" (565; is not the man I thought he was). But this discovery only makes it the more imperative for her to prove that her love was and remains "unique en ce monde" (572; unique in this world). Corinne's death distinguishes her from the other "other woman" in the novel. It thus becomes a means of heroic self-vindication, rather than tragic defeat.

The Mme d'Arbigny episode leads as well to other reflections. If Corinne feels no bonds of "sisterhood" between herself and Mme d'Arbigny, it would be strange if the same were true of the author who created them both. On the simplest level, among the cosmopolitan cast that populates *Corinne*, Mme d'Arbigny is the only Frenchwoman. And who could be more French than her Paris-born author (albeit of Swiss parents), who yearned throughout years of exile to return to her native city? Both character and author were the widows of much older husbands whom they married without love; yet both pursued love and were sexually accessible. And while Mme d'Arbigny's approach to her love affair with Oswald, as well as her reaction to his loss, may have been totally alien to Corinne, her conduct cannot have been entirely so to Mme de Staël. Although Staël was not particularly looking for another husband, Oswald's accounts of Mme d'Arbigny's scenes – her tears, hysterics, operatic demonstrations of suffering, her threats of suicide, her swooning at his feet in attempts to renew a cooling lover's ardour – all have a familiar ring to readers acquainted with Staël's biography. Equally familiar is Oswald's account of Mme d'Arbigny's calculated strategies, her attempts to hold a current lover by stressing her dependence, while yet encouraging a future one, and above all, her not wanting to pass for an abandoned woman. Moreover, as has been widely noted only in relation to the author's difference from Corinne, Staël herself survived and recovered from rejection by lovers – indeed, far more often than Mme d'Arbigny.

If aspects of Mme de Staël's experience found their way into the creation of this resilient, unchaste Frenchwoman, however, such an identification is unlikely to have been conscious. Her portrayal is so generally negative as to have not only prevented critics from appreciating her complex function in the novel but also to have rendered her all but invisible to them.[11] Perhaps we need a Jean Rhys to enable us to see this overlooked woman with fresh eyes.[12] In a novel deliberately designed to challenge so many conventional ideas about women, the harsh, dismissive judgment passed on Mme d'Arbigny reminds us how difficult it is for even a writer as boldly unconventional as Mme de Staël to break free from entrenched ways of writing about her own sex.

3

While critics have failed to recognize any kinship between Mme d'Arbigny and her creator, and while Corinne herself experiences not the slightest bond of sympathy with Oswald's first love, the same neglect has not attached to the figure of the more obvious "other woman," whom Oswald does marry.[13] Half-sisters in fact, Corinne and Lucile near the end of the novel establish a bond of spiritual "sisterhood" as well, which benefits them both. Through her bond with Lucile, Corinne assures the triumphant nature of her death. Five years after his marriage Oswald returns to Italy with his wife and daughter. In the final stages of her gradual and deliberate drift toward death, Corinne asks to see her niece, Juliette. In what become daily visits to her aunt, "l'enfant fit des progrès inconcevables dans tous les genres" (the child made inconceivable progress in all fields) as Corinne "se donnait une peine extrême pour l'instruire et lui communiquer tous ses talents, comme un héritage qu'elle se plaisait à lui léguer de son vivant" (575; took the greatest pains to instruct her and communicate to her all her talents, as a legacy she took pleasure in bequeathing her while she was still alive). Thus, the child of her half-sister and her perfidious lover will become the vehicle of Corinne's immortality, the means by which she perpetuates her genius beyond the tomb. Moreover, Lucile, too, takes to visiting her sister, at first out of pique but then to benefit from the manifold talents that Corinne is so generously ready to share.

In passing the legacy of her talents on to niece and sister, Corinne is, of course, ensuring her continued spiritual presence in Oswald's daily life. Corinne teaches Juliette to imitate her on the harp by playing a Scots tune with which, formerly, she had deeply touched Oswald's emotions, and she teaches Lucile to complement her own virtues with those of her dying sister: "Il faut que vous soyez vous et moi tout à la fois" (578; You must be you and me at the same time). While Corinne's pedagogical undertakings ostensibly reflect her generosity of spirit and desire to sweeten Oswald's life with the pleasures she was once able to give him, they also transparently constitute a means of triumphant self-affirmation, a victorious superimposition of her presence on the future lives of niece, sister, and lost lover. Despite the patina of Christian resignation that colours Corinne's last weeks, her generosity, as critics have noted, far from being selfless, can be seen as a form of triumphant revenge.[14]

Here, however, the reader encounters a serious difficulty in reconciling what the novel claims with what it actually shows. It is clear enough how Corinne is able to perpetuate her memory; but just how she might be able to perpetuate her talents and genius (terms used interchangeably) poses an embarrassing question. Corinne has been presented as a universal genius – poet, writer, above all *improvisatrice* in the first definition; as the novel proceeds, her talents multiply. She acts, dances, paints, sculpts, sings, plays the harp, translates, writes plays – the common thread is that she is inspired: "une prêtresse inspirée qui se consacrait ... au culte du génie" (68; an inspired priestess who devoted herself ... to the cult of genius), "une prêtresse d'Apollon" (52), a priestess of Apollo, all the while remaining a perfectly natural and unaffected woman. The superlative nature of the multifaceted talents claimed for Corinne may lead us to wonder how the "legacy" of such genius, or even talents, can be transmitted in a few weeks, or even months, to a five-year-old girl or a young British-educated wife and mother. Of all her many talents, what can – and does – Corinne actually teach?

The text provides some startling answers. Regarding Juliette, here is the whole of a passage cited earlier in part: "En peu de jours, l'enfant fit des progrès inconcevables dans tous les genres. Son maître d'italien était ravi de sa prononciation. Ses maîtres de musique admiraient déjà ses premiers essais." (In a few days the child made inconceivable progress in all fields. Her Italian teacher was enraptured with her pronunciation. Her music teachers already admired her first efforts.) Enrapturing Italian pronunciation and admirable *premiers essais* in music, in addition to learning how to imitate Corinne on the harp, are the only concrete evidence of Corinne's legacy to her niece that the novel provides – along with the more general statement that "des leçons ... ajoutaient à ses agréments d'une manière si remarquable" (575; the lessons ... added to her attractions in a most remarkable manner). The key summarizing word appears to be *agréments* – those attractions, or adornments, that render us *agréable* (pleasing) to others.

Corinne's legacy to Lucile is similar. After his wife's first visit to Corinne, Oswald is struck by the increased interest she shows in conversation, and after several days he observes that his wife "se montrait constamment plus aimable et plus animée qu'à l'ordinaire" (576–7; appeared constantly more likeable and more lively than usual). It is no accident that Lucile's gains are seen through Oswald's eyes, since what we actually watch Corinne teaching her sister is the art of pleasing her man: "Connaissant parfaitement le caractère de celui-ci, elle fit comprendre à Lucile pourquoi il avait besoin de trouver dans celle qu'il aimait *une manière* d'être à quelques égards différente de la sienne ... Corinne se peignit elle-même dans les jours brillants de sa vie ... et montra vivement à Lucile combien serait *agréable* une personne qui, avec la conduite la plus régulière et la moralité la plus rigide, aurait cependant tout *le charme*, tout l'abandon, tout *le désir de plaire* qu'inspire quelquefois le besoin de reparer des torts" (578, emphasis added; Knowing his character perfectly, she made Lucile understand why he needed to find in the woman he loved a *manner* that was in some respects different from his own ... Corinne depicted herself in her days of splendour ... and keenly showed Lucile how *pleasing* a person would be who, with the most proper conduct and the most rigid morality, nevertheless would have all the *charm*, all the abandon, all the *desire to please* which is sometimes inspired by the need to redress errors). The lesson continues in this vein, with Corinne helping Lucile to understand how she should seek "à se montrer plus *aimable*" (to appear more *likeable*) and should recognize "que vos vertus ne vous autorisent jamais à la plus légère négligence pour *vos agréments*" (578, emphasis added; that your virtues never justify you in neglecting in the least bit *your attractions*). Lucile's studies "à ressembler à la personne qu'Oswald avait le plus aimée" (to resemble the person whom Oswald loved the most) are rewarded, as her husband daily observes in her "les graces nouvelles" (579), new grace(s). As her essential legacy, the erstwhile crowned priestess of Apollo and the cult of genius, repeatedly likened to the Sibyl of Domenichino, in her final days seems to be teaching the arts of a geisha.

Staël thus trivializes her heroine's genius and undermines the claims she has made for her. Even when we consider that the art of conversation and the social skills of pleasing a cultivated audience were more highly valued by the eighteenth-century Parisian salon society in which Staël grew up than they are in our own culture, the conclusion of the novel may still come as a shock. While Corinne's need for a receptive audience is integral to her character and has received abundant critical attention,[15] at least she seeks an audience for her *genius*. But that she should choose to privilege her skill in pleasing an audience of one as the essence of the legacy she bequeaths has escaped similar notice and may well find the reader so unprepared as scarcely to absorb the sudden turn the text takes here.

To be sure, if readers have overlooked the strange turn in the dénouement and ignored its implications, this is also a tribute to the imaginative power of Staël's original conception, which succeeded in inspiring generations of female readers.[16] But we may better appreciate the full daring of that conception if we face the extent to which Corinne's legacy – hence her chosen immortality – represents a radical retreat from the novel's earlier bold claims. This finale also adds to the difficulty of any attempt to regard the true tragedy as the failure of all Corinne's talents – her education, intelligence, creative achievements, her sensitivity to art and literature – to sustain her in the face of her loss of Oswald; for if this were the case, then how could her ability to pass on to his wife and daughter the art of knowing how to please and the secret of acquiring "*agréments*" be seen as any kind of adequate, much less triumphant, "revenge"?

Still, there is a disturbing coherence between this dénouement and what the narrative has revealed. Corinne can scarcely transmit her artistic and intellectual attainments as being their own reward, since they have manifestly not proven so to her. At the same time, the fact that her profoundest legacy should be the art of pleasing enables Corinne to effect a specific revenge. In the autobiographical letter in which Corinne discloses her past to Oswald, she describes his father's visit to her home seven years earlier, when he came to look her over as a potential wife for his son, and she speculates on the causes for his disapproval: "Quand lord Nelvil arriva, je désirai de lui plaire, je le désirai peut-être trop, et je fis pour y réussir infiniment plus de frais qu'il n'en fallait; je lui montrai tous mes talents, je dansai, je chantai, j'improvisai pour lui, et mon esprit, longtemps contenu, fut peut-être trop vif en brisant ses chaînes" (373; When Lord Nelvil arrived, I wanted to please him, perhaps I wanted it too much, and I gave myself infinitely more pains to succeed than were necessary; I showed him all my talents, I danced, I sang, I improvised for him, and my spirit, contained for so long, was perhaps too lively in breaking its chains). Her account of her performance as a kind of trained pet is sad to read, as it must be for her to reflect on, especially since it was, she fears, her very eagerness to please that made her seem to his father unsuitable as a wife for Oswald. She goes on to suggest, however, that with her greater age and experience she would actually *better* please Lord Nelvil today, were he alive to see her: "Depuis sept ans l'expérience m'a calmée; j'ai moins d'empressement à me montrer ... Je suis, je le sais, améliorée depuis sept années" (374–4; After seven years, experience has calmed me; I am not so eager to show myself off ... I have, I know it, improved after seven years.)

A pitiable plea, and with cause. For Corinne is caught here in a classic female double bind. Women are supposed to seek to please, but to please only a very restricted few – or, better, a select "one" – and they are not supposed to reveal their intentions too obviously. The transparency of Corinne's youthful efforts to please – and what it suggests about her need for a wide audience – is at fault, not the efforts themselves. Corinne's speculations about Lord Nelvil's reaction in fact prove correct; as he writes to her father, "Sans doute votre fille n'a reçu de vous, n'a trouvé dans son coeur que les principes et les sentiments les plus purs; *mais* elle a besoin de plaire, de captiver, de faire effet" (466, emphasis added; No doubt your daughter has received from you, has found in her heart, only the purest principles and feelings; *but* she has the need to please, to captivate, to make an impression.) Once deemed unsuitable for Oswald because of her excessive zeal in wanting to please, Corinne, through the legacy she bequeaths during her last days, has the satisfaction of passing on to his wife and daughter precisely that talent for which she was too hastily condemned and whose lack in Lucile Oswald has felt painfully for the last five years. The demure, retiring Lucile is encouraged to become a synthesis of herself and Corinne not by assimilating her sister's genius but by learning how to *plaire,* to *captiver*, without falling into Corinne's youthful error of visibly striving to *faire effet.*[17]

Our discomfort with what is presented as Corinne's final triumph is only one more instance of the difficulty a modern reader experiences in responding to *Corinne* in the spirit in which it was written, or even once read. The discrepancies between our contemporary response and the author's intentions, however, may prove instructive, since they clarify important aspects of her world and our own and dramatize the insidious power of the constraints Mme de Staël had to overcome in her bid for a woman's right to lead a full, unfettered existence. Certainly, we can still respond to her concern with the obstacles society places in the way of woman's quest for self-fulfilment. But since Oswald appears so clearly undeserving of Corinne, and since her world apart from him – her Italy – has proved so attractive to female readers precisely because it seems to offer women all but unlimited possibility for self-development, it is easier for us to appreciate *Corinne* for what it suggests about a woman's own inner conflicts and what it demonstrates about the dynamics of her incomplete liberation from the social codes she has internalized, than for what it shows about her struggles with external obstacles. Although we are quick to recognize ways in which women are disadvantaged by society, we are more comfortable in our literature with the tragedy that grows out of internal conflicts and contrasting needs and desires, or that reveals the insufficiency of even great strengths in the face of great needs. On the other hand, the opposition between Corinne's need for the independence necessary to creativity and her counterbalancing need for love, as that between healthy female identity and marriage, though only adumbrated, has a timely ring and finds a ready response in a modern reader. So does the portrayal of Corinne's all-too-human pain and suffering in the face of loss, despite her acclaimed genius and achievement.

By contrast, we are less comfortable with the notion of blame in a failed romance and prefer, at least in theory, to see people take responsibility for their own choices, even for their own mistakes. Implicit in the novel's focus on Oswald's fault and betrayal is a dangerous diminution of Corinne's stature, her uncongenial transformation into a passive victim of someone else's inadequacy. Similarly, her uncompromising rejection of life as a means of remaining "uncompromised" by her unfortunate bestowal of love on an unworthy object is apt to diminish rather than elevate her in our eyes; our instinctive sympathy is with survivors, not with those who seek a source of triumphant revenge in what Dickens was to call the "vanity of sorrow."[18] Nor do we believe – any more than did Mme de Staël in her own life – that a woman must deny her sexuality to preserve her dignity and deserve our sympathy. And we regret, even as we try to understand, Staël's need to uphold in fiction those standards – so demeaning and divisive to women – by which she did not want to live. In Corinne's heroic death and in her failure to acknowledge any spiritual kinship with her resilient, sexually freer predecessor in Oswald's affections, we may recognize the tenacious hold, on both author and heroine, of values that are deeply destructive to women. Corinne's closing bond of sisterhood with her actual sister, on the other hand, would strike us as satisfyingly "modern" were it not for the questionable object of their alliance. However, the final element of Corinne's apparent revenge, in which she and her author choose to trivialize her talent and genius in favour of her *agréments* and ability to please an undeserving lover, can best be appreciated – as can so many disturbing elements in the novel – as an eloquent demonstration of the unconscious imperatives and double binds at work in both author and heroine. Read as the valiant and sadly flawed attempt of two extraordinary women, one real, one fictional, to free themselves from a pattern of internalized sexist demands and inhibitions that ultimately prove too strong for them, the novel may still engage us, move us, and even make us weep.

George Eliot 1860, from a drawing in chalks by Samuel Laurence

2

A Voice from the Margins

George Eliot's *Daniel Deronda*

"Madame de Staël's name still rises first to the lips when we are asked to mention a woman of great intellectual power," wrote Marian Evans in the *Westminster Review*, several years before she became George Eliot. Justly cited as an example of Eliot's admiration for Staël, her esteem is nonetheless notably specific; indeed, this sentence goes on to name George Sand as "the unapproached artist."[1] It is for her intellectual power, then, rather than her literary or artistic talents that the French woman of letters is praised. The novels George Eliot began to write a few years later, moreover, did not follow *Corinne* in directly engaging the situation of the woman artist, as did, for example, the literary works so famously influenced by Staël's novel, *Consuelo* and *La Comtesse de Rudolstadt* by Sand herself, or *Aurora Leigh* by Elizabeth Barrett Browning, two women writers enormously admired by Eliot.[2]

Two female characters in George Eliot's novels refer to Corinne in passing, but both highlight her role as a romantic heroine rather than a woman artist. In *The Mill on the Floss*, Maggie Tulliver returns Philip Wakem's copy of Mme de Staël's novel, agreeing with him that Corinne "would do me no good" – presumably the French heroine's conduct appears somewhat dubious to English eyes; but Maggie also rejects his supposition that she "should wish to be like her." While Philip seems pleased to infer that Maggie concurs "in not liking Corinne," her reaction leads him to express surprise that she "wouldn't ... like to be a tenth muse." Maggie's disapproval, however, is directed at the plot rather than the character. "As soon as I came to the blond-haired young lady reading in the park I shut it up and determined to read no further. I foresaw that the light-complexioned girl would win away all the love from Corinne and make her miserable." Maggie's response reflects her awareness of established literary conventions, as her subsequent references to other heroines illustrate. But it is striking how exclusively Corinne's anticipated romantic defeat overshadows her early artistic triumph in Maggie's eyes.[3] Mary Garth's reference to Corinne in *Middlemarch*, though much briefer, is also directed only at the novel's romantic plot.[4]

If Corinne is viewed by George Eliot's female characters chiefly in terms of her romantic experience rather than her artistic role, this may reflect Eliot's reluctance to explore the figure of the woman artist in her own novels, at least prior to *Daniel Deronda*.[5] Indeed, as has been widely observed, Eliot's fictional women rarely succeed in making a life for themselves outside of the domestic sphere. Her gallery of female heroines contains a number of young women of exceptional sensibility, but none, with the exception of Dinah Morris in *Adam Bede*, seems to have any particular talent for a specific vocation, and even Dinah settles into domesticity at the end of the novel, as she acquiesces to the new Methodist prohibition against women preachers and abandons her public role. Typically, when these young women, such as Dinah or Dorothea Brooke (in *Middlemarch*), grow past early womanhood (as, for example, Maggie Tulliver in *The Mill on the Floss* does not), the reader is asked to accept that they find a qualified fulfillment of their exceptional natures through a happy marriage and motherhood. Romola is something of a quirky exception to this pattern, assuming for a limited time a public role – though still not a vocational one – as a sister of mercy, first in a distant plague-stricken village and then in her native plague-stricken Florence. But she too retreats to domesticity, though of a less usual sort, at the end.

Only in her last novel, *Daniel Deronda*, does Eliot construct an exceptional woman who has a concrete vocation at which she excels and which she has pursued into adulthood. The mother of the book's eponymous hero, Eliot's only important "career woman" is also the only major woman artist in her novels. She first enters the story as the Princess Halm-Eberstein but in earlier days achieved international renown as the Alcharisi, a supremely talented lyric actress, or opera singer. (Lydgate's first love, the actress Laure in *Middlemarch*, is an interesting early prototype, though she is more suggestive than developed.) Though Deronda's mother appears in just two late chapters, her presentation holds important implications for our understanding of Eliot's treatment of both women and Jews, who are an intended focus of the novel. Her delayed appearance in the book and her apparently marginal status in its structure are deceptive – or better, they are revealing. For as much as any successfully conceived minor character in fiction she raises issues and questions that expand far beyond the limited space she occupies in the text, issues and questions that seem to sweep backward over the novel in which she appears and to the whole body of George Eliot's work as well.

Most obviously, in her construction of Leonora Halm-Eberstein (frequently referred to simply as "the Princess"), George Eliot shows an awareness of the position of women in Jewish culture and tradition that is sharply questioning, if not actually critical. Her presence in the novel suggests that Eliot's treatment of her Jewish material is more complex and problematic than has usually been allowed. In her, Eliot has created an original, uncharacteristic, independent, talented, angry, "unfeminine" – we might almost say "modern" – woman, who is in rebellion against the constraints imposed on her by traditional Judaism and the role it allots to women. If not quite a feminist, she is at least a protofeminist figure. And while she is by no means held up as a model, her undeniable charisma and eloquence help to make the traditional "feminine" submissive virtues of the apparently idealized Jewish heroine, Mirah, seem questionable indeed. Through the construction of this remarkable woman from an alien culture, Eliot permits herself to raise directly some questions about womanhood, or as we would say, gender construction, that she has not raised earlier.

Though we meet her only after her life as a great opera singer is over, the Princess Halm-Eberstein is presented as having been a truly great artist who placed her artistic vocation before all else. To be free to pursue her calling in the face of her father's disapproval, she married her weak adoring cousin, though she had not wanted to marry at all. After the death of her husband, in order to devote herself more freely to her career and to liberate her son from what she considered the bondage of his Jewish identity, she arranged for Daniel to be raised by an English baronet, in ignorance of his true parentage. She married again (thus acquiring her title) only once she had begun to fear that her voice was going bad and that her career as an artist was coming to an end.

Deronda's mother is a foil to Gwendolen Harleth, the heroine of the English half of the novel, as well as to the virtuous Jews Mirah and Daniel. Her contrast to Gwendolen and Mirah is most apparent, however, as both the Jewish and the Gentile young women are presented, in their different ways, as aspiring singer-actresses as well. Gwendolen is a morally fallible, though potentially redeemable, representative of the corrupt, narrow, philistine, Victorian English society, which is juxtaposed with the artistically – particularly the musically – rich, intellectually broad, cosmopolitan Jewish world of the novel. From the narrative's initial focus on Gwendolen at the gambling table in the first paragraphs of the book, through her successive appearances – on horseback, at the archery meet, in the drawing-room – she is repeatedly presented as the object of the viewer's fascinated gaze. In the early part of the novel especially, she is always somehow on stage, conscious of her audience, and in moments of solitude is apt to fulfill the dual roles of absent admirer as well as admired object, feasting on her own reflection in the glass. "She had never acted," the narrator makes plain, "only made a figure in *tableaux vivans* [*sic*] at school; but she felt assured that she could act well, and having been once or twice to the Théâtre Français, and also heard her mamma speak of Rachel, her waking dreams and cogitations as to how she would manage her destiny sometimes turned on the question whether she should become an actress like Rachel, since she was more beautiful than that thin Jewess."[6] If Gwendolen's narcissistic self-regard reveals a blithe ignorance of the nature of the great French actress's artistic talent, this has surely been fostered by the doting admiration of Gwendolen's benighted mother, who assures her, "You have better arms than Rachel ... your arms would do for anything, Gwen" (85).

Gwendolen, we are early told, "having always been the pet and pride of the household, waited on by mother, sisters, governess, and maids, as if she had been a princess in exile ... naturally found it difficult to think her own pleasure less important than others made it." (53). And the refrain of Gwendolen as a princess in exile is sounded several times – for example: "Always she was the princess in exile, who in time of famine was to have her breakfast-roll made of the finest-bolted flour from the seven thin ears of wheat, and in a general decampment was to have her silver fork kept out of the baggage" (71). With a society girl's ability to sing a little and the good looks and poise to participate at social gatherings, as she had at school, in *tableaux vivants* – "an entertainment which, considering that it was an imitation of acting, was likely to be successful, since we know from ancient fable that an imitation may have more chance of success than the original" (90) – Gwendolen, when her family falls on hard times, fancies she might instantly make a living as an actress, only to be bitterly humiliated by the unbiased judgment of the great musician Klesmer ("a felicitous combination of the German, the Sclave, and the Semite" [77]). Gwendolen has neither the talent nor the training of an artist; nor has she the discipline or temperament necessary to acquire such training. A princess in exile only by virtue of her own and her family's sense of her entitlement, she might even be said to conform to the negative stereotype of the "Jewish Princess" today, to whom somehow all shall be given and from whom nothing asked. However, Gwendolen is set, finally, in sharp contrast to the real Jewish princess, the Princess Halm-Eberstein, who has willingly sought to sacrifice her life to her art. Literally too, the Princess Halm-Eberstein, now married to a Russian nobleman and bearing a German name, is a princess in exile. Her dramatic appearance – in Genoa – toward the close of the book offers the reader a dazzling image of all that the English heroine can never expect to be.

Along with her disciplined artistry and exceptional talent, the Alcharisi's daring rebellion against the norms of her culture and, more immediately, the demands of her father may well remind the reader of the narrative's earlier ironic description of the "inwardly rebellious" Gwendolen: "She rejoiced to feel herself exceptional; but her horizon was that of the genteel romance where the heroine's soul poured out in her journal is full of vague power, originality, and general rebellion, while her life moves strictly in the sphere of fashion" (83). In the world of *Daniel Deronda*, Gwendolen is central and the Alcharisi peripheral. But the world that the princess's appearance suddenly opens up to the reader's imaginative view – the world suggested by the text but lying beyond the confines of the story it chooses to narrate – momentarily destabilizes the dominant narrative perspective. Daniel's long-deferred meeting with his mother gives the reader a brief glimpse of a world in which the Alcharisi has been "the greatest lyric actress of Europe" (703), while Gwendolen is merely a spirited and engaging provincial young lady. The princess's entry into the narrative thus prefigures Gwendolen's dislodgement from "her supremacy in her own world" at the end of the book, when Deronda's revelation of his historic Zionist mission results in "the world ... getting larger round poor Gwendolen," as, faced with "the bewildering vision of these wide-stretching purposes ... she felt herself reduced to a mere speck" (875).

The presence of the Alcharisi, the professional lyric actress, also helps underscore the difference between Gwendolen and Mirah, Gwendolen's successful rival for Deronda's love. From an early age Mirah has been groomed for the stage by her father who, despite his many faults, has provided her with excellent voice instruction. Although Mirah lacks the Alcharisi's powerful voice and presence and so appears to be destined for performances only in small, select drawing-room settings (also a more modest, maidenly venue for her talents), she resembles her future mother-in-law in similarly recognizing art as a disciplined and serious calling. This shared recognition distinguishes both Jewish women from Gwendolen, who readily assumes, initially, that her charm and good looks can carry her through to theatrical success.

Like Gwendolen, however, Deronda's mother married for freedom, never an admirable motive for George Eliot, who felt that virtue consists rather in responding to the duties life confronts us with. Yet the Alcharisi's quest for freedom appears less reprehensible than Gwendolen's because although she sought freedom from the bondage of being a Jewish woman – an impulse George Eliot can hardly endorse – she also sought freedom to pursue the larger life of art, an expansive, non-egoistic motive that we are encouraged, at least to some extent, to admire. In the presentation of Daniel's mother George Eliot's language is revealing. According to her father, the princess tells Daniel, "I was to care forever about what Israel had been; and I did not care at all. I cared for the wide world, and all that I could represent in it ... I wanted to live a large life ... and be carried along in a great current" (693). The words "wide" and "large" are key positive terms for George Eliot, and "currents," likewise, are almost always good. Maggie Tulliver is the big exception to this; more frequently, to be carried along in a current symbolizes the praiseworthy submergence of self in some higher, wider identity.

The virtuous Daniel, for example, has been repeatedly characterized by his "yearning after wide knowledge" (217). He welcomes the revelation of his Jewish origins because it offers him an identity larger than the merely personal – a national, racial, or (as Eliot puts it elsewhere) corporate existence, which links him to the shared historic past of his people and points the way to a greater-than-individual future, his destiny as the leader of a revived and revitalized nation.[7] The mission that Daniel embraces at the end of this nineteenth-century novel – at the time only a vague hope for the future – remains hazy in its detail, though unassailably worthy in its intention.[8] Moreover, Daniel's Jewish identity will enable him to marry the Jewish heroine, Mirah, thus allowing "the very best of human possibilities [to] befall him – the blending of a complete personal love in one current with a larger duty" (685). Forgiving his mother for his upbringing as an English gentleman, Daniel says, "I think it would have been right that I should have been brought up with the consciousness that I was a Jew, but it must always have been a good to me to have as wide an instruction and sympathy as possible" (725).

Similar imagery characterizes the presentation of the contemporary Jewish prophet Mordecai's visionary imagination, which is objectified by his love for "far-stretching scene[s]; his thought went on in wide spaces; and whenever he could, he tried to have in reality the influences of a large sky" (530). By contrast Gwendolen's narrow egoism is symbolized by her fear of wide spaces. "Solitude in any wide scene impressed her with an undefined feeling of immeasurable existence aloof from her, in the midst of which she was helplessly incapable of asserting herself" (94–5). Her narrow horizons are contrasted explicitly with the wide horizon of the world of art, in which she dabbles only as an amateur. When she is rebuffed for her singing at a social evening by the great musician Klesmer, who then asks her to "sing ... something larger," Gwendolen declines "with a sinking of heart at the sudden width of horizon opened round her small musical performance" (79).

Thus it is too simple to dismiss the princess as selfish, though she is that too in some sense, and too simple to dismiss her as the character "who most clearly articulates the position of the assimilationist,"[9] though she does do that as well. The more striking point about her is that all that Daniel finds by embracing Judaism – large horizons, wide vistas, submergence in an existence greater than himself – his mother could find only by rejecting Judaism ("I cared for the wide world ... I wanted to live a large life"). The aspirations of mother and son are remarkably similar. Yet the fate of Deronda's mother serves to illustrate, whether intentionally or not, how very different are the roles, status, and options that Judaism offered to men and women. Speaking of her father, the princess tells Deronda:

> I was to be what he called "the Jewish woman" under pain of his curse. I was to feel everything I did not feel, and believe everything I did not believe. I was to feel awe for the bit of parchment in the *mezuza* over the door; to dread lest a bit of butter should touch a bit of meat; to think it beautiful that men should bind the *tephillin* on them, and women not ... You are not a woman. You may try – but you can never imagine what it is to have a man's force of genius in you, and yet to suffer the slavery of being a girl. To have a pattern cut out – "this is the Jewish woman; this is what you must be; this is what you are wanted for; a woman's heart must be of such a size and no larger, else it must be pressed small, like Chinese feet; her happiness to be made as cakes are, by a fixed receipt." That was what my father wanted. He wished I had been a son; he cared for me as a makeshift link. (692–3, 694)

The princess's outrage at the limitations placed on the development of female potential gives her speech a distinctly modern, even feminist flavour. On the other hand, her unquestioning assumption that "force of genius" is generally a masculine preserve marks her as a woman of an earlier era. We may recognize, further, that what Daniel's mother has rejected here is not so much Judaism as the traditional role of the Jewish woman. Moreover, in not wanting to have her "heart ... pressed small, like Chinese feet," the princess presents herself as a contrast to Mirah as well as Gwendolen; for Mirah, who embodies an ideal of dutiful, unassertive – almost Dickensian – female virtue, is characterized not merely by her "small" voice but also by feet so small that even in the compact, doll's-house sized home of the diminutive Meyrick women, "there were no shoes in the house small enough for Mirah" (249).

In her speeches to Daniel, the princess's passionate rage and hurt at the subordinate, constricting role allotted her as the Jewish woman seem scarcely to have abated through all the intervening years of artistic and social triumph: "My father had tyrannised over me – he cared more about a grandson to come than he did about me: I counted as nothing. You were to be such a Jew as he; you were to be what he wanted" (698). Though she seems perplexed that the Jewish identity, which was bondage to her and from which she therefore thought to save her son, should come instead as liberation to him, the difference is entirely in keeping with her own account of the different roles offered to men and women by the religion she has rejected. Showing Daniel a portrait of herself in her youth she asks,

"Had I not a rightful claim to be something more than a mere daughter and mother? The voice and the genius matched the face. Whatever else was wrong, acknowledge that I had a right to be an artist, though my father's will was against it. My nature gave me a charter."

"I do acknowledge that," said Deronda, looking from the miniature to her face, which even its worn pallor had an expression of living force beyond anything that the pencil could show. (728–9)

But in embracing Judaism Daniel will be much more than a "mere" son and father; he will have a vocation as well in political leadership, a legitimate outlet for *his* living force.

The subordinate position of women exists in the English as well as the Jewish part of the novel, of course. Gwendolen's tragic marriage comes about in part because social attitudes unanimously support her mother's reiterated contention, "Marriage is the only happy state for a woman" (58), and Gwendolen's aunt and uncle fully share her own disparaging view of her sisters: "it [was] a pity there were so many girls" (61). Gwendolen's cousin, Anna Gascoigne, described as the sister of "a brother whose pleasures apart from her were more than the sum total of hers" (87), feels herself "much at home with the Meyrick girls, who knew what it was to have a brother, and to be generally regarded as of minor importance in the world" (717). It is simply in the order of things that the dutiful Mr Lush "has stinted his wife and daughters of calico in order to send his male offspring to Oxford" (165). We learn also, in a repeated refrain, that "Lady Mallinger felt apologetically about herself as a woman who had produced nothing but daughters in a case where sons were required" (267), and we see how social norms confirm her self-image "as the infelicitous wife who had produced nothing but daughters, little better than no children, poor dear things" (498).

Far crueller than any of these instances is the outcast position of Grandcourt's cast-off mistress, Lydia Glasher, whose appearance in Gwendolen's life comes with the force of "some ghastly vision … in a dream ... [saying] 'I am a woman's life'" (190). George Eliot certainly makes the reader aware of the injustice of the double standard governing society's very different treatments of Mrs Glasher and Grandcourt. As a potential husband for Gwendolen, Grandcourt is regarded quite genially by her rector uncle, Mr Gascoigne: "Whatever Grandcourt had done, he had not ruined himself; and it is well known that in gambling, for example, whether of the business or holiday sort, a man who has the strength of mind to leave off when he has only ruined others, is a reformed character" (125).

But while exposing these inequities, George Eliot's narrative persona never frontally challenges them. In fact, the tone with which woman's inferior status is treated throughout the English sections is urbane, ironic, and at bottom one of resigned acceptance; it therefore differs radically from the tone of the princess's impassioned, angry, unforgiving outbursts, which, notably, are scarcely mediated by any authorial comment.[10] Refuting the judgment of Eliot's near contemporary Henry James that "all the Jewish part is at bottom cold" and drawing a contrast between the irony and controlled satire characteristic of the English parts of the novel and the emotional idealizing treatment of the Jewish theme, F.R. Leavis suggested more than half a century ago that George Eliot's more "mature" imagination was at work in the English sections, whereas her more "immature" emotionalism, not properly under the control of her intelligence, surfaced in the Jewish parts.[11] For Leavis, as for James, "the Jewish part" referred simply to Daniel, Mordecai, and Mirah, an emphasis that has continued to mark more recent treatments of the novel in post-colonial criticism.[12] Once Deronda's mother ceases to be invisible, however, Leavis's view of Eliot's idealization of Jewish life and his claim that in its presentation George Eliot's "intelligence and moral insight are not engaged"[13] become particularly quaint, as does his use of the standard of "maturity." Which, after all, is the more "mature," "appropriate" perspective on the inferior status of women? Subdued irony, or impassioned rage?

George Eliot's relation to the feminism of her own day has become an issue of some dispute. Challenging Ellen Moers's confident assertion that "George Eliot was no feminist," for example, Gillian Beer points to Eliot's support for the Married Women's Property Bill and notes that all the women with whom she was intimate from the 1850s were actively involved in the women's movement and that her novels engaged with the vocabulary and issues of that movement.[14]

It remains true, however, that if we limit ourselves to Eliot's letters we can read views that are disturbing to our present-day sensibilities. While she supported educational opportunities for women who could benefit from them (her gift of 50 pounds sterling toward the establishment of Girton College is often cited in this connection) and endorsed the Napoleonic ideal of "'La carrière ouverte aux talen[t]s,' whether the talents be feminine or masculine," she also repeatedly expressed reluctance to undertake "specific enunciation of doctrine on a question so entangled as the 'Woman Question'"[15] and was dubious about the enfranchisement of women, writing, "Woman does not yet deserve a much better lot than man gives her."[16] Her observation that "Woman seems to me to have the worse share in existence" even leads her to suggest that "in the thorough recognition of that worse share, I think there is a basis for a sublimer resignation in women and a more regenerating tenderness in man."[17] On the other hand, Eliot's novels repeatedly show the harm that comes from girls' limited educational opportunities and suggest the injustice and folly of many of the obstacles society places in the way of the development of female potential. The relation between theoretical pronouncements, life, and work is always a slippery one. Still, it is hardly likely that Eliot considered the princess's assault on the role of the Jewish woman powerful enough to vitiate the novel's dominant respectful and admiring attitude toward Jews, which was, after all, George Eliot's clear, conscious intent.

I am suggesting, instead, that one has to recognize a certain ambivalence of judgment, uncharacteristic of George Eliot, in her presentation of the Alcharisi. Certainly, any assessment of the princess has to accommodate the fundamentally disquieting fact of her having given her child to be raised by another, as of her admitted inability to love, both of which cannot help but qualify our sympathy with her, if not with her feminist indignation. Neither of these aspects of her experience, it should be said, is presented as particularly Jewish, and referring to them the princess deliberately extends her attack from the ideal of the Jewish woman to more widely diffused ideas about the uniform nature of womanhood itself, a uniformity that George Eliot herself often questioned:[18] "People talk of their motives in a cut and dried way. Every woman is supposed to have the same set of motives, or else to be a monster. I am not a monster, but I have not felt exactly what other women feel – or say they feel, for fear of being thought unlike others. When you reproach me in your heart for sending you away from me, you mean that I ought to say I felt about you as other women say they feel about their children. I did *not* feel that. I was glad to be freed from you. But I did well for you, and I gave you your father's fortune" (691). Although the princess may be suggesting that our concept of gender identity is a convenient fiction, and that her failure to find self-fulfillment in motherhood is less unusual than it appears, what remains unquestionably unique about her and prevents any easy generalization of her experience to that of other women is her artistic gift, her "force of genius," which, as the conversation with Deronda implies, she believes entitles her to claim a special privilege. Then too, the laws of poetic justice under which George Eliot habitually operates suggest that Daniel's mother – whom we meet only years after her glorious career has ended, as an unhappy dying woman driven by forces almost beyond her control to reveal to her son the secret of his birth, which she had worked so hard to conceal – is, despite all her eloquence and charisma, probably intended to be more strongly judged than applauded.

Yet George Eliot was certainly aware of the subordinate position of women both in Victorian English society and in traditional Judaism, as of some of the differences between the two, and it may be that she found it easier to attack such subordination – or at least to allow one of her characters to attack it – when it appeared in an alien culture and when the attack was placed in the mouth of a character of whom we are not, nominally, encouraged to approve. The white heat of the princess's unremitting articulate resentment at the bondage imposed on her by her gender is strikingly without parallel in any of George Eliot's other female – and English – characters. (And while she is the only woman in Eliot's fiction to express the conflict between creative self-fulfillment and motherhood, she may lead some readers to speculate whether Eliot's own decision not to have children might have had sources beyond her "irregular" relationship with Lewes.)

George Eliot's awareness of the subordinate position of women in traditional Judaism finds its way into the novel in quiet, unobtrusive ways as well. One of the Meyrick girls, for example, "who was much of a practical reformer" and has visited a synagogue with Mirah, "could not restrain a question. 'Excuse me, Mirah, but *does* it seem quite right to you that the women should sit behind rails in a gallery apart?'" (410). George Eliot herself reported of one of her many visits to a synagogue, this one in Amsterdam: "In the evening we went to see the worship there. Not a woman was present, but of devout *men* not a few, curious reversal of what one sees in other temples."[19] And Ezra Cohen refers to the traditional Jewish prayer in which "a man is bound to thank God, as we do every Sabbath, that he was not made a woman; but a woman has to thank God that He has made her according to His will" (636) – a clear error on George Eliot's part (as an early Jewish critic pointed out) for this thanksgiving is in fact part of the *daily* morning prayer.

Welcoming his Jewish identity at the end, Daniel "will not say that I shall profess to believe exactly as my fathers have believed" (792). But there is no suggestion that he has in mind revitalizing Judaism in any way that would affect the position of women or accommodate the princess's artistic and cosmopolitan aspirations. Daniel's chosen bride, Mirah, with her preternaturally small feet, dismisses Amy Meyrick's question about the synagogue's gendered seating arrangement with the pious reply, "I never thought of anything else" (410) and willingly embraces the life of a Jewish woman. But both Gwendolen Harleth and the Alcharisi are more interesting and convincing women than Mirah, and neither can be so automatically "capable," as Daniel says of Mirah, "of submitting to anything when it takes the form of duty" (494; see also 617). Daniel submits to a wider duty at the end, but as I have suggested, it is clear that this duty promises him far greater scope than the duties of a Jewish daughter, wife, and mother, as presented in this novel, can offer any woman. In George Eliot's text, comparable human scope can be found by a Jewish woman only through denying her Jewishness. This may suggest that when one ponders the role of Daniel's mother and the "Woman Question" in general in *Daniel Deronda*, the novel may emerge as somewhat less idealizing of Jewish life than it is generally taken – and was consciously intended – to be. Additionally, by using the Jew as other, Eliot allows herself to express an anger about woman's subordinate position in society that she expresses nowhere else, an anger she saves for the end of her last novel.

Self-portrait as La Pittura (The Art of Painting) by Artemisia Gentileschi.

3

History, Art, and Fiction

Anna Banti's *Artemisia*

The name of the seventeenth-century painter Artemisia Gentileschi has become increasingly familiar beyond the borders of her native Italy. While she has long been recognized for her artistic achievement, as a "pittrice valentissima fra le poche che la storia ricorda" (woman painter of most excellent abilities, one of the few whom history remembers),[1] her dramatic life, which includes her rape at an early age and a public trial at which she was tortured, has certainly contributed to her fascination for contemporaries. In recent years she has received particular attention from British and American art historians as well as historians of early modern Europe, and she has also proven an appealing subject for film, drama, and fiction in North America and France. More than half a century ago, however, she was already brought to life and celebrated in an important novel by the Italian writer Anna Banti. When Banti died in 1985, it was above all as the author of *Artemisia* (1947) that she was remembered and honoured. "Addio, Artemisia," ran the headline in *La Nazione*, the daily paper of her native Florence. Anna Banti – the literary pseudonym of Lucia Longhi Lopresti – had written other novels, as well as short stories, art criticism, and drama; the recipient of various prestigious literary awards, she had also been for many years the editor of the review *Paragone*, founded by her husband, the art historian Roberto Longhi, and was president of the Foundation for the Study of Art History "Roberto Longhi" (Fondazione di Studi di Storia dell'Arte "Roberto Longhi"). But it was Banti's fictionalized biography of Artemisia Gentileschi, "una delle prime donne che sostennero colle parole e colle opere il diritto al lavoro congeniale e a una parità di spirito fra i due sessi" (4; one of the first women to maintain with words and achievement the right to fulfilling work and spiritual equality between the two sexes) that established her literary reputation and remained her most enduring achievement.[2]

Banti's construction of the painter's life and character is interwoven with her account of the novel's own genesis. The narrative opens with the author-narrator seeking refuge in the Boboli Gardens from the exploding mines and machine-gun fire accompanying the German retreat from Florence in August 1944. In the midst of the disasters of war, her imagination conjures up Artemisia as a living presence, who is eager both to console and to be consoled. "Non piangere" (Don't cry) – the first words of the novel, spoken by the hallucinated protagonist to the author-narrator – set the tone for the narrative that is to follow, which is marked, structurally, by a dynamic interchange between protagonist and author-narrator and, thematically, by the rejection of despair.

In the opening scene, the author-narrator's grief at the violent destruction of her city is subsumed within her deeper grief at a more immediate, personal loss – that of an almost completed manuscript story, entitled "Artemisia," destroyed, as Banti tells us in her preface, by the events of the war, "che non hanno, purtroppo, nulla di eccezionale" (3; which, unfortunately, are not at all exceptional). "Sotto le macerie di casa mia," the author-narrator laments, "ho perduto Artemisia, la mia compagna di tre secoli fa" (6; Beneath the rubble of my house I have lost Artemisia, my companion of three centuries ago). But the author-narrator's anguish quickly merges with that of her suddenly hallucinated companion, who now becomes more real to her than the historically reconstructed figure buried with her manuscript. Together, author-narrator and protagonist begin to reconstruct anew the life whose retelling becomes a shared, almost compulsive need. From the outset, then, the narrative presents itself as something other than simple historical reconstruction, something at once more personal, more imaginative, and more arbitrary. In various instances, as I shall show, Banti deliberately alters known facts about the life of the historical Artemisia Gentileschi. Moreover, throughout the narrative she invents what no historian can ever know – a complex, consistent, and rich inner life for her protagonist, thereby conferring a sense of reality on Artemisia's imagined moment-to-moment thoughts, motives, and actions, as she interacts with her world.

This, of course, is the very stuff of realistic fiction. But if Banti frankly invents the psychology and many details of Artemisia's private experiences, she also incorporates certain salient public facts about the real Artemisia Gentileschi's life into her narrative, thereby tying her protagonist unmistakably to her origins in the world of history. Banti follows historical records that chronicle Artemisia's birth and childhood in Rome, her rape at an early age and the all-too-public rape trial at which she was tortured as her virtue was publicly placed under attack, her marriage to Antonio Stiattesi and her subsequent separation from her husband, an interval of work as a painter in Florence, her role in running an academy of painting in Naples, and her trip alone to join her father, the painter Orazio Gentileschi, at the English court in 1638 or 1639. Above all, Banti calls our attention to the most important historical data about Artemisia Gentileschi, that is, her paintings. Detailed accounts of two paintings in fact constitute the dramatic high points of Banti's narrative and frame much of the protagonist's psychological development in the course of the novel.

The narrative's status, then, while not easily defined, may nonetheless be illuminated by locating its antecedents in realistic psychological fiction on the one hand and, to a far lesser extent, art history and criticism on the other. At the same time, any account of the narrative's idiosyncratic status must also consider the crucial interaction between author-narrator and protagonist, which self-consciously violates the more "traditional" narrative convention of self-sustaining illusion. To be sure, from the very beginnings of the modern realistic novel in the eighteenth-century, such brilliant fictional works as Sterne's *Tristram Shandy* or Diderot's *Jacques le Fataliste* deliberately undercut the illusion of the fictional world's autonomy. While it is therefore historically inaccurate to view as a recent development the emergence of narrative that calls attention to the arbitrariness of its own construction, reminding the reader that its design depends on the writer's act of will and could just as easily have been different, this type of fiction is nevertheless often seen as distinctively "modern," or more accurately, "post-modern." Banti's novel belongs to this "modern/postmodern" – if not new – tradition.

In the interactions between author-narrator and protagonist, moreover, we naturally recognize that we are dealing with not one but two fictional constructions, for the persona and experiences of the author-narrator are themselves, necessarily, part of the fiction, whatever their original basis in fact. Within this frame of Banti's fictionalized autobiography, then, Artemisia's story unfolds, told variously by Artemisia in her own voice, by the narrator to Artemisia in the second person, by the narrator who assumes the first person in passages where her identification with Artemisia becomes almost complete, and, finally, by the narrator in the more conventional mode of the third person, which becomes the dominant voice after the first fifth or so of the novel. During the initial several days that mark the German retreat and Allied liberation of Florence, however, the tone of the exchange between Artemisia and the narrator is fluid and volatile, shifting erratically from playfulness, even mischievous teasing, to urgency and relentless compulsion. As the narrator moves among the Boboli Gardens, the lawn in front of Fort Belvedere, and the indoor refuge of the Palatine Gallery in the Palazzo Pitti, by turns she finds Artemisia, loses her, and then finds her again. The thread of their mutual (re)construction of Artemisia's history is picked up, dropped, and taken up again. Past and present interweave, mirroring the chaos and disorder around them. Artemisia herself passes through a series of rapid changes, her age oscillating backwards and forwards, as she is envisioned, kaleidoscopically, in different phases of her development. At times, the narrator is frankly arbitrary and fanciful, inventing aspects of Artemisia's history. The protagonist listens, sometimes attentive and docile, seeking to reassure the narrator of her credulity, at other times impatient, demanding that the narrator retell a particular episode, and at still others correcting the narrator and interrupting to take over the narration herself. Then the situation is reversed and it is Artemisia who requires the narrator's assurance of belief and the narrator who, variously, gives the desired assurance or else corrects the protagonist's faulty memory. While the dynamic interplay between narrator and protagonist becomes less prominent as the narrative gradually focuses more sharply on Artemisia's own story, the relationship between the two women continues to resonate through the novel, even when not directly in view. The narrator's involvement with her protagonist's story is crucial not only to the way in which Banti presents her material but also to the reader's final understanding of the narrative's wider significance.

What broader vision, then, do these structural pyrotechnics help to establish? This basic question is closely related to another: what is the nature of the bond between the narrator and Artemisia? While answers to both questions evolve gradually over the course of the novel and will be fully clarified only near the end, from its opening a variety of impulses is apparent in the interactions between narrator and protagonist. The Artemisia whom the narrator's imagination conjures up in the first lines of the novel offers her creator/resuscitator words of comfort for both her individual and her more general loss. She will help the narrator to reconstruct and even improve the story contained in her lost manuscript. At the same time, Artemisia's emergence from the ruins of the war suggests the emergence of the narrator's enduring cultural heritage – as an Italian and a woman – in the face of the present destruction of her homeland following two decades of Fascist rule that have led to this debacle. In turning to Artemisia as "anziana nella morte che ci sta intorno" (8; an elder in Death which is all around us), the narrator is seeking both a distraction from the surrounding realities of death and destruction and also a means of transcending them through her identification with that positive past in which she can take pride and find sustenance. Artemisia is one who has suffered and died and yet, we shall see, triumphs and lives. Although the full scope and meaning of the narrator's purpose become clear only late in the novel, through her resuscitation of Artemisia she will ultimately come into possession of the inheritance for which there is, tellingly, no adequate word in English or Italian: her rightful *female* patrimony. (It is perhaps interesting to reflect how far beside the point is "matrimony" in this context.)

The relationship between narrator and protagonist, moreover, is reciprocal. While the narrator depends on Artemisia for a complex of motives – to give her comfort, pride, purpose, inspiration, distraction, and transcendence – Artemisia depends no less on the narrator – also to give her comfort and sympathy, to bring her to life, to tell her story, to justify her, and allow her to justify herself in the eyes of history. "E che cos'altro ha fatto Artemisia se non giustificarsi, dai quattordici anni in su?" (18; And what else did Artemisia do if not justify herself, from the age of fourteen onwards?) The mutual dependence of narrator and protagonist implies, in turn, an ideal of female friendship, the giving and receiving of mutual aid and support.

In the early part of the novel, as the narrative approaches the experiences responsible for Artemisia Gentileschi's historical notoriety – her rape and the subsequent trial – the bond between the two women appears overwhelmingly as one of suffering and mutual support in the face of enormous upheaval and loss. It is, moreover, a bond forged on the basis of a distinctively female vulnerability. "La nostra povera libertà si lega all'umile libertà di una vergine che nel milleseicentoundici non ha se non quella del proprio corpo integro e non può capacitarsi in eterno di averla perduta. Per tutta la vita essa si adoprò a sostituirla con un'altra, piú alta e piú forte, ma il rimpianto di quell'unica restò: mi pareva, con quei fogli scritti, d'averlo quietato" (23; Our own meager freedom is linked to the humble freedom of a virgin in 1611 who has nothing if not that of her own intact body, and who can never ever accept the fact that she has lost it. For her entire life she strove to substitute another, higher and stronger kind of freedom, but her regret over that single loss remained; with the pages I had written it seemed to me that I had soothed that regret). Locating a source of her early identification with Artemisia in their shared female vulnerability, the narrator suggests as well a motive both for her current retelling of Artemisia's story and for Artemisia Gentileschi's historic achievement as a painter.

The character of Artemisia is developed through a series of vignettes, moving from her childhood friendship with a wealthy paralytic in Rome at the age of ten to the initial stages of her return from England, where she had gone to join her father at the age of forty. From the opening pages of the book Banti establishes a firm footing for Artemisia's life in the fictional universe, where the author's imaginative constructions assume the status of reality: "Le avevo regalata un'amica" (8; I had given her a friend). Reflecting on her wholly arbitrary creation in her lost manuscript of a childhood friend for Artemisia, the author-narrator now brings the invented character back to life as a demonstrated proof both of her sympathetic friendship toward her subject and of the power of her autonomous imagination. Through this invented girlhood episode, moreover, Banti lays the foundation for Artemisia's personality as it will emerge in the course of the novel – her bold impetuousness, her vivid imagination that makes itself felt in boastful exaggerations and inventions, and her stubbornness and pride, her tenacious concern for her own dignity and sense of worth. The fabricated childhood is also important in making palpably vivid the innocence that will be violated by the historically documented rape.

In her presentation of this brutal act of force and the resulting trial, Banti makes use of the actual trial records. In 1612 Orazio Gentileschi petitioned the pope, complaining that his daughter had been raped by Agostino Tassi, a friend and fellow painter whom he had engaged to teach her perspective. At the trial, Orazio gave Artemisia's age as fifteen, on the basis of which historians established her date of birth as 1597.[3] Banti appears to have allowed herself a minor novelistic liberty here, in the interest, it would seem, of greater pathos. In her preface, she gives Artemisia's date of birth as 1598, and hence in her novel, which leaves the date of the historical trial unchanged, Artemisia is able to reiterate plaintively, "Avevo quattordici anni" (20; I was fourteen years old). R. Ward Bissell's more recent chronology, which establishes Artemisia's birth date as 8 July 1593, suggests that Orazio deliberately understated his daughter's age by four years in order to make her "conveniently, younger than what appears to have been the seventeenth-century age of majority."[4] This correction, however, postdates Banti's novel.

At the time of the rape, Artemisia testified, she attempted to defend herself, wounding Tassi, as Banti also describes, with a knife – but to no avail. Afterward, he promised to marry her. Orazio's petition stated that the sexual offence had been repeated "più e più volte" (many successive times), a fact that has led most male historians to sneer at the charge of rape.[5] However, Banti (who has been joined by recent feminist art historians) finds no inconsistency in this account. Her narrative convincingly shows how Tassi's original rape and subsequent promises of marriage combined to make Artemisia feel bound to him as a wife, even against her inclination.[6] Presumably, Orazio initiated proceedings when it became clear that Tassi was not going to make good his repeated promises. Banti quotes from the trial records Artemisia's flash of grim wit as, under cross-examination, she was tortured by thumbscrews in front of Tassi: "Questo è l'annello che tu mi dài, queste sono le promesse!" (21; This is the ring you give me, these are the promises!) Banti also follows the historical account in showing Tassi first imprisoned, then released, his defence resting chiefly on his contention that he was not the first, nor the only one.

After closely following the historical sources that document Artemisia's trial, Banti reverts to her own sympathetic imagination to recreate the emotional texture of Artemisia's response to her public humiliation: "Oggi si sente colpevole, colpevole come ciascuno vorrà ... Se la trattano così, devono aver ragione" (32; Today she feels guilty, as guilty as anyone could want her to be ... If they treat her like this, they must be right.) As Artemisia prepares to seek lonely comfort in "l'alterigia fanciullesca e un po' smargiassa della sua natura" (the girlish and somewhat boastful pride of her nature), promising herself, "Vedranno chi è Artemisia" (33; They will see who Artemisia is), it is no longer the known, public life that Banti undertakes to convey but rather, once again, the private, invisible one of moment-to-moment experience. Artemisia, "un personaggio ... di fama illustre ... dalla biografia ovvia, anno per anno" (a figure ... of illustrious fame ... whose biography is clear, year by year), is also someone "che val la pena di risuscitare ora per ora, proprio nei giorni in cui la sua storia tace" (whom it is worth resuscitating, hour by hour, precisely in the days about which her history is silent). Agostino Tassi's acquittal, Orazio's withdrawal of love and esteem, "Artemisia ridotta da una effimera scandalosa celebrità a una solitudine riottosa e insidiata: ecco fatti che mi valgono – e non se arrossirne – come una seconda guerra punica" (33–4; Artemisia reduced from an ephemeral, scandalous celebrity to an intractable and menaced solitude – these are facts which are as important to me – and I don't know if I should blush at this – as a second Punic War). Might there be here an echo of Virginia Woolf (whom Banti had translated), who had earlier challenged the prevailing "masculine values" that held wars more important than the private creative experiences of women?[7] Woolf had referred to the historical moment when "middle-class women began to write" as "a change ... which, if I were rewriting history, I should describe more fully and think of greater importance than the Crusades or the Wars of the Roses."[8] And here is Banti, beginning to imagine the formation of Artemisia as an artist, following her loss of social respectability and her consequent self-imposed isolation behind closed, shuttered windows: "Si può ben congetturare cosa mangiassero gli elefanti africani in Italia; si può ben pensare alle serate di Artemisia nell'estate milleseicentoquindici" (34; One can easily conjecture what the African elephants ate in Italy; one can easily imagine Artemisia's evenings in the summer of 1615).

So compelling, in fact, is the imagined experience that follows that it is a jolt to learn how sharply it diverges from historical fact. Bissell's chronology tells us that in November 1612, one month after the end of the trial, Artemisia was married in Rome to Pietro Antonio di Vincenzo Stiattesi, a Florentine. Bissell adds, "Stiattesi may have taken Artemisia to Florence almost immediately" as "they are documented there in November 1614."[9] Banti may well have been working with a less accurate chronology; at any rate, her Artemisia remains in her father's home for almost three years of painstaking solitary apprentice work after the rape trial, as she hides from the world and grows as a painter, partially compensated for the love and recognition her father withholds by the devoted admiration of her younger brother, Francesco. In Banti's account, Artemisia's marriage takes place at the end of this period, a marriage at first in name only, hastily arranged by Orazio so that he can take his newly respectable daughter with him to Florence, leaving the husband behind.

In Florence, where her much adored father abandons her almost at once, heading off for Pisa, Artemisia paints what Banti presents as her first great painting, "Judith Beheading Holofernes" (now in the Uffizi). One among several treatments of Judith painted by Artemisia – the subject was common enough among paintings of the era – this version, which presents the murder itself, is striking for its gory violence. Assisted by a maid-servant who helps pinion the naked Holofernes to a bed, Judith grasps the helpless general's hair with one hand while the other plunges a sword into his neck as jets of blood spurt forth in many directions. The late French critic Roland Barthes observed that to the modern viewer of Gentileschi's painting, the scene, whose traditional significance was religious and patriotic, here appears to embody the ideology of "*la revendication féminine*" (female protest, or demands). He saw the painter's "first stroke of genius" in "having put two women on the canvas rather than a single one, whereas in the biblical version the servant waits outside: two women, associates in the same work, arms interlaced, combining their muscular efforts on the same object – subduing an enormous mass whose weight exceeds the strength of one woman: might one say, two women workers in the act of slitting a pig's throat?"[10] Barthes' remarks gain a particular poignancy when we consider that the other woman present at the time of Artemisia's rape – according to both the court records and Banti's narrative – was her nurse Tutia (or Tuzia), who, far from assisting the motherless girl as might have been expected, was implicated instead as an accomplice of Tassi. The prominence of Judith's maid-servant in Artemisia Gentileschi's painting may well reflect the painter's wish for the unrealized female solidarity that could have prevented Tassi's act of violence.[11]

Banti's treatment of this painting, however, ignores the role of the maid-servant (a figure who is equally important in Artemisia's other, more serene versions of Judith). Banti concentrates, instead, on Artemisia's identification with her heroine, hypothesizing that the painter has modelled Judith's features on her own. The novelist thus goes one step beyond the widely accepted view that "Judith's decapitation of Holofernes appears to provide a pictorial equivalent for the punishment of Agostino Tassi."[12] More intriguing and original than this hypothesis, however, are the circumstances Banti constructs surrounding the composition of "Judith." In Florence Artemisia is befriended by a handful of court ladies who come to watch her as she paints, taking a voyeuristic interest in her independence, her professional competence, and, above all, her confident command over her powerful male model. Their feelings toward her are a mixture of social superiority, envy, and prurient fascination. Also prurient is their fixation on "tutto quel sangue" (57) – all that blood – in the painting that takes shape before their eyes. Though distrustful of one another, they are nonetheless unwittingly drawn into sharing dark confidences, as their conversation obsessively reverts to men – those they live with, those they know – revealing attitudes of which they are unaware: contempt, resentment, fear, hatred. These are impulses that Artemisia recognizes all too well but that, through her mastery of her art and the sense of self-esteem this earns her, she is able to overcome and reject. Whatever the original motives behind the composition, the process of painting itself is envisioned as a "working through," hence a purgation of her rage and shame; the achievement of the finished work liberates Artemisia from anger and self-denigration, freeing her energies so that she may become the great painter she became: "La vendetta era consumata, scontata la lunga vergogna di Roma. Gli uomini ritornavano uomini" (61; The vendetta was consummated, the protracted humiliation of Rome expiated. Men once more became men).

"Spento ogni rancore, le pareva di stender la mano verso la violenza pentita, lei forte e senz'armi" (63; All hatred spent, it seemed to her that she was extending her hand toward repented violence, she was strong and unarmed).

After this crucial point in Artemisia's development, she returns to Rome to join her husband when Orazio leaves for England. A wholly invented, unexpected love idyll then follows between Artemisia and her husband, a whimsical peddler. But when the exigencies of Artemisia's career lead the couple to relocate in more fashionable surroundings, the husband suddenly looks awkward and out of place, and Artemisia, despite her love for him, cannot keep herself from driving him away. Her unfading memory of this lost love nonetheless persists throughout the novel, contributing to the continuity of Artemisia's consciousness and giving unity to the episodic structure. From Rome, Artemisia moves to Naples, where she runs an academy of painting, bears a daughter, and gains in fame. Accompanying her mounting achievements in these years, Banti imagines, is an unassuageable uneasiness at the indeterminacy of her social position. What must it have been like for a woman of such exceptional abilities to make her way in the total absence of what we so casually refer to today as "role models"? Banti has Artemisia reflect that "una madre priva di marito, madre di famiglia non è. Quale sia, di preciso, la sua condizione, nessun confessore ha saputo spiegarglielo, per quanto abbia insistito: come, del resto, per meditar che faccia, non le è ancor riuscito di riconoscersi e definirsi in una figura esemplare e approvata dal secolo ... Questa è donna che in ogni gesto vorrebbe ispirarsi a un modello del suo sesso e del suo tempo, decente, nobile; e non lo trova" (125; a mother without a husband is not the mother of a family. Precisely what her status might be, no confessor had been able to explain to her, no matter how much she had insisted; as, moreover, however much she pondered it, she had not yet succeeded in recognizing herself and finding self-definition in any exemplary and approved figure of her century ... This is a woman who in her every gesture would like to find inspiration in a model – decent and noble – of her own sex and era; and she does not find it).

During these years in Naples Artemisia's intense love for her only daughter emerges as yet another source of pain. The fictional daughter, in the course of her convent education, refuses to learn drawing, even from the nuns, and she emerges from the convent with deep respect for propriety and order, and strong repugnance for her mother's unconventional way of life. The historical Artemisia's experience was different. She had two or three daughters, at least two of whom were painters, suggesting a possible mother-daughter *camaraderie* through work that Banti denies to her fictional heroine.[13]

In her account of this period, Banti paraphrases comments from Artemisia's letters of a decade or so later, revealing her keen sensitivity to the importance of her gender in the eyes of her patrons: complaints that they are sceptical about her abilities or want to pay lower prices for her canvases because she is a woman, and defensive affirmations of her ability to prove herself – though, as I indicated in my introduction, Banti somewhat softens the most memorable line from the letters, "Ritrovera uno animo di Cesare nell'anima duna donna"[14] (You will find the heart [*animo* – also mind, spirit, courage] of Caesar in the soul [*anima*] of a woman) to "Tengo nel petto un animo di Cesare" (134; I carry the heart of Caesar in my breast).[15] Banti also cites almost verbatim the closing lines of a letter of 1637 to a patron: "Si compiaccia, Vossignoria, darmi nuova di vita o morte di mio marito" (122; Could your lordship please give me news of the life or death of my husband.)[16]

In 1638–39 Artemisia leaves Naples to join her father in England, moving up the Italian coast and across France in a beautifully imagined odyssey in which the painter's consciousness registers a shifting variety of experiences and visual impressions. While the historical Artemisia reported in 1635 that she had received an invitation to England from King Charles I, the cause of Banti's heroine's decision to leave for England is simply the painful news that her husband has a new woman and now wants a legal divorce.

Banti's inventions and distortions of the historical record all seem designed to emphasize Artemisia's solitude and the pain and vulnerability she will have to overcome, while sometimes suggesting as well sources of future strengths. As we have seen, the author creates an Artemisia who is a year younger at the time of her rape and trial than even Orazio had claimed. She postpones Artemisia's (in fact hasty) marriage after the trial, thereby giving her three years in which to hide from the world and study painting in isolation. Moreover, Banti postpones Artemisia's cohabitation with her husband until after her Florentine period and her painting of Judith, through which she overcomes her hatred and distrust of men. Banti also provides Artemisia with a husband whom she comes to love and then, uncontrollably, drives away. In contrast to the historical record, Banti gives Artemisia only one daughter, who rejects her mother's way of life, thus giving Artemisia cause for a new sense of loss, this time maternal. Finally, Banti has Artemisia's trip to England determined not by her renown as an artist or the desire to be with her ailing father but by the familiar motives of pride and hurt feelings. Even in the years of Artemisia's growing fame in Naples, Banti dwells on her social blunders and personal humiliations, which are often shown as the accompaniment of her successes. And while the historical Artemisia appears to have collaborated with her father both at the beginning of her career and during her brief stay in England, Banti's Artemisia only paints alone.[17] Yet in the end, the solitude, loss, vulnerability, and pain so tangibly felt throughout the book will be seen as necessary preparation for Artemisia's final affirmation and sense of achievement.

Although the historical Artemisia's stay in England was brief (she probably left to return to Italy shortly after Orazio's death in 1639), and though she lived until at least 1651, it is in England that Banti brings the novel to a satisfying climax. Artemisia at last gains the long-desired recognition of her father and they are able to relate as equals: "Due spiriti, non un uomo e una donna, non un padre o una figlia ... Non importa esser stata donna, piú volte sconsigliata, due volte tradita. Non c'è piú dubbi, un pittore ha avuto nome: Artemisia Gentileschi" (231–2; Two spirits, not a man and a woman, not a father or a daughter ... It doesn't matter having been a woman, many times discouraged, twice betrayed. There is no longer any doubt, a painter has earned a name: Artemisia Gentileschi.) This reconciliation and affirmation free her to think of her husband without bitterness, of her daughter with renewed maternal love, and of her devoted brother with fresh appreciation. The most important consequence of this new sense of self, however, is the painting many consider to be her greatest, that of a woman painter (hanging today in Kensington Palace). Seen in three-quarter view, her left hand holding a palette and the right one, at the end of a foreshortened arm, reaching a brush upward toward a canvas awaiting her imprint, the painter appears wholly absorbed in the act of painting; a medallion hangs casually over the front of her dress, and a few straggling locks of hair escape from a bun tied at the nape of her neck, falling loosely over her forehead and cheek. The painting was posthumously entitled "Self-Portrait as La Pittura." A recent study has confirmed the appropriateness of both designations, and feminist studies in particular have pointed to the work's ingenuity in reconciling hitherto conflicting female roles.[18] The abstract personification of La Pittura, of the art or allegory of painting, was invariably conceived of as a woman, as was the artist's muse. On the other hand, as most artists were men, the artist's realistic self-portrait was most frequently male.[19] As a woman, Gentileschi's figure is able to integrate the symbolic embodiment of muse and personification with the realistic representation of a female painter seriously engaged in practising her craft.

Whether as inspirational muse, allegorical representation of painting, or simply model, the female figure has typically been viewed as the object of a male painter's creativity, rather than as a possible creator in her own right. Gentileschi's portrait of a woman painter confutes and subverts this expectation within the medium of painting itself. Banti's novel echoes this challenge to conventional stereotypes through the medium of fiction, while setting up some further reverberations with traditional associations between women and painting in literature. Of course, as we noted at the outset, Banti's choice of a great woman painter as fictional protagonist distinguishes her narrative from the tradition of the realistic (above all, nineteenth-century) novel on several grounds, the most obvious of which is the historical authenticity of Artemisia Gentileschi. According to the conventions of the realistic novel, protagonists were to be fictional creations, unknown to history; where actual historical figures do appear in the nineteenth-century novel (as, for example, in Manzoni or Stendhal), they play minor rather than major roles. For the traditional novelistic hero(in)es may be exemplary only to the extent that they remain typical, or at least broadly representative. However much greatness of spirit they may possess, these hero(in)es are invariably limited by constraints of custom and opportunity – time and place – and, usually, by flaws in their own character as well; hence another of the realistic novel's underlying conventions, that even potential greatness can never result in great achievement.

Banti's Artemisia, then, triumphing against overwhelming odds and not forgotten by history, belongs, as we have observed, only in part to the tradition of the realistic novel, diverging from her literary predecessors as much because of her substantial artistic achievement as because of her historical prototype. Still, Banti's fictionalized historical heroine may be more fully appreciated if we pause to reflect on the familiar limitations of the traditional relation between women and painting in literature, from which Banti's Artemisia so conspicuously departs. Certainly, in the novel, as in the history of painting, women have frequently served as models, muses, or the symbolic embodiment of an art form itself, for the male artist.[20] Additionally, women in nineteenth-century novels are often presented as pursuing drawing and painting amateurishly, as one item in a package of feminine "accomplishments" that were supposed to distinguish the properly educated young lady. Even more serious fictional treatments of women's creativity tend to focus on the meaning of their artistic efforts as a key to the psychological depths and complexity of their souls, or as a reflection of a certain inner liberation, rather than on their work as substantial objective achievement, as independent, self-justifying artifacts.[21]

Probably the most notable break from the dominance of this fictional tradition (which in turn reflects a broader cultural one) comes with the creation of Lily Briscoe in *To the Lighthouse* by Virginia Woolf, an author admired and translated by Banti. Though Lily will never achieve fame, she nonetheless takes her work seriously, as does her creator (though not most other characters in the book, one of whom repeatedly maintains, "Women can't paint, can't write)."[22] In fact, the novelist Woolf quite transparently shares her fictional painter's concern with art as objective achievement and even shares Lily's articulated view of the desired nature of that achievement – the transformation of the moment into something permanent, of chaos and fluidity into enduring form. The woman novelist, mirroring her artistic aspirations in those of a painter protagonist, who similarly upholds art as a serious vocation for a woman practitioner – here, some two decades before *Artemisia*, we see an earlier and kindred treatment of a woman painter, which also evokes and subverts older, more entrenched expectations. But where Lily's canvases exist chiefly as verbal suggestion, in terms of a professed theoretical goal, and are not described in great detail,[23] the extra-literary existence of Artemisia Gentileschi's paintings adds a new dimension to Anna Banti's narrative. At the same time, reverberations of earlier literary treatments of women and painting help enrich the significance of her climactic discussion of Artemisia's boldly innovative portrait of a woman painter.

Moreover, Banti takes a radically innovative step in choosing to present this painting – so repeatedly designated as Self-Portrait as the Art of Painting – as a portrait, from memory, of another woman, one Annella de Rosa. In the novel, Annella is a gifted younger artist whom Artemisia meets in Naples, a battered wife whose early death will prevent her from fulfilling her promise. In a briefly sketched episode that becomes significant only retrospectively, Annella rejects Artemisia's overture of friendship, causing her to speculate at the time on the impossibility of friendships between women in a world created by men for their use and convenience. Yet Artemisia's later painting of the younger artist emerges as a triumphant affirmation of female solidarity. Earlier, during her painting of Judith, Artemisia had refused the female intimacy based on shared fears and hatreds that the court ladies offered her. Here, at last, as an accomplished artist, she makes actual the ideal of female friendship through a painting that celebrates the creative spirit in another woman: "Che una donna si faccia onore è il suo onore" (248; That a woman achieves honour, honours her as well.)

As Banti's Artemisia, in celebrating Annella and giving her life, finds that another woman's honour becomes hers as well, so too Anna Banti, in celebrating and resuscitating Artemisia, finds honour for herself in another woman's creative achievement. Thus the novelist-narrator commemorates Artemisia Gentileschi, the woman painter whom history remembers, by imagining her as commemorating Annella de Rosa, the woman painter whom history has forgotten. This vision brings us back to the initial mirroring of narrator and protagonist, so crucial to the novel's structure. The fundamental truth of this reciprocal relationship remains, even if Banti's fanciful redesignation of the painting as a portrait of Annella is fiction: "Ritratto o no, una donna che dipinge nel milleseicentoquaranta è un atto di coraggio, vale per Annella e per altre cento almeno, fino ad oggi. 'Vale anche per te' conclude, al lume di candela, nella stanza che la guerra ha reso fosca, un suono brusco e secco. Un libro si è chiuso, di scatto" (251–2; Portrait or not, a woman who paints in 1640 constitutes an act of courage; this applies to Annella and to at least a hundred others, down to today. "It applies to you, too," concludes a brusque, dry sound, by candlelight, in a room darkened by war. A book is closed, abruptly.) Contemplating the painting, the narrator decodes there a vital message for herself. Through her undying work of art, Artemisia reaches out from her century to ours, to teach and inspire Banti – and through her, her readers – by her enduring, shared affirmation of female courage and achievement.

Alice Munro   Courtesy of Jerry Bauer, photographer

4

Getting Loose

Women and Narration in Alice Munro's *Friend of My Youth*

In two of the stories in Alice Munro's *Friend of My Youth*, a female writer-narrator is self-consciously engaged in reconstructing the life of a woman predecessor. In "Meneseteung," as in Anna Banti's *Artemisia*, a writer-narrator combines research and invention to bring to life an artistic foremother. In Munro's tale, however, the foremother is a fictional forgotten poet, rather than an actual acclaimed artist. In the title story, "Friend of My Youth," a writer-narrator imaginatively reconstructs the life of a woman known to her only through her mother's oral narrative while seeking at the same time to reconstruct her mother's early adult years. Neither reconstructed woman in this story is an artist; still, the writer-narrator's imaginative efforts lead her to recognize a deeper kinship with both her dead mother and the friend of her mother's youth – recognitions very much in the spirit of solidarity among women, living and dead, envisioned in Banti's *Artemisia*. Another story in Munro's *Friend of My Youth*, "Goodness and Mercy," narrated in the third person, concerns a dying opera singer – of limited talents, unlike George Eliot's Alcharisi – and her daughter, who may be seen as a writer in embryo. Munro not infrequently makes use of female artist protagonists (typically writers, sometimes performers) in her work; yet in contrast to the artists we have seen in the novels of Staël, Eliot, and Banti, they are not presented as essentially different from the many non-artist women who also people her narratives. Hence I find it most fruitful to approach Munro's treatment of women artists in this collection through a broader exploration of her treatment of women and of the mother-daughter conflict familiar to readers of her earlier stories.

About mid-way through *Friend of My Youth*, the protagonist of "Oranges and Apples," recalling his mother's disparagement of his wife, reflects on the phrase, "loose woman": "When he heard people say that, he'd always thought of an unbuttoned blouse, clothes slipping off the body, to indicate its appetite and availability. Now he thought that it could also mean just that – loose. A woman who could get loose, who wasn't fastened down, who was not reliable, who could roll away" (132).[1]

Most of the stories in *Friend of My Youth* are about characters – principally, but not exclusively, women – who in one way or another "get loose," are not "fastened down." They get loose from the roles expected of them by other characters in their fictional lives and from the roles readers may expect them to play in predictable plots. In crucial instances, characters also seem to be getting loose from the narrator's knowledge and control. The image of the "woman who could get loose" is thus a suggestive one for the collection as a whole, hovering as it does at the intersection of substance and technique, subject matter and the manner of its narration.

The openness of Munro's characters to metamorphosis and change, as well her own refusal of closure in favour of open-ended narrative structures, have received considerable critical attention.[2] This essay is concerned more specifically with Munro's new departures in her sixth collection of stories and with how, even as she revisits familiar situations, structures, and concerns, she develops them in fresh ways. The opening story, "Friend of My Youth," immediately points in several directions at once, introducing strategies and motifs – including that of getting loose – that will be picked up throughout the eponymous collection, while also returning to material familiar from earlier "autobiographical" stories, notably "The Peace of Utrecht" in *Dance of the Happy Shades* and "Winter Wind," "Memorial," and "The Ottawa Valley" in *Something I've Been Meaning to Tell You*: the mother's unattractive, debilitating illness, the young daughter's inability to respond adequately to the challenge of her mother's needs, her youthful shame and her adult guilt, experienced as especially powerful and tenacious in retrospect.

While critics have commented on the broad similarity between the mother-daughter situation in "Friend of My Youth" and earlier versions of Munro's treatment of what appears to be the same material, none has noted how the crucial framing dream in "Friend of My

Youth" echoes and reworks an earlier account of a dream in "The Peace of Utrecht," the story in which she "first tackled personal material."[3] In both stories these are presented as recurrent wish-fulfilment dreams, revealing a narrator-daughter's fantasy that if only the mother had not been so ill, not made the demands she made, it would have been simple to be a better daughter – and her wish to have been that better daughter, not to have had to be guilty. In the early story, the account of the dream is brief, momentarily emerging out of the adult narrator's reflections about her mother on her first visit home after her mother's death. Moving from painful memories of her long suffering mother and her failures to meet her mother's demands, the narrator recalls how "the disease is erratic and leisurely in its progress; some mornings ... she wakes up better ... tries to make up for lost time, tidying the house, forcing her stiff trembling hands to work a little while at the sewing machine. She makes us one of her specialities, a banana cake or a lemon meringue pie. Occasionally since she died I have dreams of her ... in which she is doing something like this, and I think, why did I exaggerate so to myself, see, she is all right, only that her hands are trembling" (*Dance*, 200). The dream breaks off and, even though the story is concerned with the two sisters' different ways of coping with the aftermath of their mother's illness and death, we do not hear of it again.

Until, that is, it resurfaces in the framing dream of "Friend of My Youth":

> I used to dream about my mother, and though the details in the dream varied, the surprise was always the same. The dream stopped, I suppose because it was too transparent in its hopefulness, too easy in its forgiveness.
>
> ... Sometimes I would find myself in our old kitchen, where my mother would be rolling out piecrust on the table, or washing the dishes ... But other times I would run into her on the street, in places where I would never have expected to see her ... She would be looking quite well – not exactly youthful, not entirely untouched by the paralyzing disease that held her in its grip for a decade or more before her death, but so much better than I remembered that I would be astonished. (3)

But when Munro returns after more than twenty years to the recurrent dream of the daughter's wish to find her mother alive again and almost well, in the very early stages of her illness, she does so in order to use it in a much more purposeful and deliberate fashion. Prominently placed at the opening of the story, the dream is virtually deconstructed before it is recounted by the narrator's unsparing explanation of why the dream stopped. Having acknowledged this, however, the narrator is free to develop the dream fantasy more amply and leisurely, revealing its comfort value directly after she has denied its legitimacy. "I recovered then what in waking life I had lost – my mother's liveliness of face and voice before her throat muscles stiffened and a woeful, impersonal mask fastened itself over her features ... the casual humor she had ... the lightness and impatience and confidence" (3–4). The "recovered" dream-mother does more than forgive her daughter; she renders superfluous any apology or guilt.

> I was sorry I had kept a bugbear in my mind, instead of this reality – and the strangest, kindest thing of all to me was her matter-of-fact reply.
>
> Oh, well, she said, better later than never. I was sure I'd see you someday. (4)

Although offering an already discredited comfort, the recounted dream, by helping her recapture the youthful mother, then serves as a springboard from which the narrator launches into a story told to her by her mother, stemming from her mother's single days teaching in a one-room country schoolhouse and boarding with the Grieves family, whose tangled lives form the substance of her tale. In the narrator's recounting of her mother's story, we witness successively the apparent self-effacement of two storytellers, as the narrator seems to disappear in giving voice to her mother's tale, and then the mother is lost to view within *her* story, which constitutes the bulk of "Friend of My Youth." Just when the reader has all but lost sight of any storytelling presence, however, the apparent self-sufficiency of the tale is abruptly undercut by a series of codas that jolt us into an awareness of the mediating role of the narrative voice. The codas provide glimpses of successively shifting stages in the narrator's own development and her relation to her mother, each constituting a different attempt at understanding the recalcitrant mother-material. The last coda returns to the dream, which now upstages the story it frames. The closing dream provides a new "take" on the mother-daughter drama at the same time that it offers suggestive avenues of approach to the stories that follow; for these will ring their own variations both on Munro's familiar albatross story and also on the wider issues raised in the codas to "Friend of My Youth" – issues of women's relation to one another and of "relation" itself, in the sense of narration.

The central story in "Friend of My Youth," which concerns the strict Cameronian Flora, twice betrayed by her one-time fiancé Robert, has been pieced together by the narrator's mother from her first-hand experience and from gossip and letters telling of events before and after her stay in the community. The account ends with an exchange of letters between the mother and Flora in which the mother writes from afar to express sympathy and profess outrage and Flora replies to reject the sympathy and outrage and, essentially, to tell her former friend to mind her own business. At this point the apparent neutrality of the account comes to a sudden end. The original narrator, temporarily lost to view, re-emerges, offering successive codas, or exegeses, to the interpolated story we have just read. First, reminding the reader of the source of the story, the narrator resentfully recounts her mother's attempt to package it as a moral tale: "In later years, when she sometimes talked about the things she might have been, or done, she would say, "If I could have been a writer – I do think I could have been; I could have been a writer – then I would have written the story of Flora's life. And do you know what I would have called it? 'The Maiden Lady'" (19). *If I could have been a writer ...* the mother's wistful evocation of her unfulfilled potential highlights the fact that the lively, often comic rendition of the sad tale we have been reading is the achievement of the narrator-daughter, the real writer after all. The story of Flora's life emerges as a site of contestation between the narrator and her mother, implicitly posing the question of who will give it definitive voice, and to what end. The narrator then recalls her teenage rejection of her mother's admiring, reverential account of Flora as "a noble figure, one who accepts defection, treachery, who forgives and stands aside, not once but twice" (19). More than Flora is at stake in the narrator's dismissive youthful response to her mother's moralizing. "In her own plight her ideas had turned mystical, and there was sometimes a hush, a solemn thrill in her voice that grated on me, alerted me to what seemed a personal danger. I felt a great fog of platitudes and pieties lurking, an incontestable crippled-mother power, which could capture and choke me ... I had to keep myself sharp-tongued and cynical, arguing and deflating. Eventually I gave up even that recognition and opposed her in silence." While recognizing the vulnerability and impulse to self-preservation behind her teenage rejection of her mother's "reading" of Flora's tale, the adult narrator nonetheless judges her former self harshly, immediately undercutting the sympathetic presentation of her adolescent self she has just written: "This is a fancy way of saying that I was no comfort and poor company to her when she had almost nowhere else to turn" (20).

Still, this unsparing mature judgment on her younger self does not keep the narrator from relating that self's competing construction; in scornful contrast to her mother's wistful evocation of unfulfilled potential, the adolescent daughter "didn't think that I could have written a novel but that I would write one. I would take a different tack." As if anticipating the narrator's literary practice in "Meneseteung," she tells us, "I saw through my mother's story and put in what she left out" (20). The narrator then provides an account of her own youthful imaginings, which lead to an altered ending in which Flora emerges as a Presbyterian witch who gets her come-uppance in a lurid gothic finale.

The mature narrator of "Friend," however, now rejects the competition of codas she has just sketched, seeking instead a more dispassionate and deeper comprehension of their conflict. "What made Flora evil in my story was just what made her admirable in my mother's – her turning away from sex" (22). Moving beyond guilt and self-recrimination, the narrator meditates on the different worldviews inherent in their different exegeses, seeing in them attitudes beyond conscious individual choice. "My mother had grown up in a time and in a place where sex was a dark undertaking for women. She knew that you could die of it." Indeed, within the mother's story Ellie *does* seem to have died of it (though by a logic that is clearer morally than physiologically). "So she honored the decency, the prudery, the frigidity, that might protect you. And I grew up in horror of that very protection, the dainty tyranny that seemed to me to extend to all areas of life ... The odd thing is that my mother's ideas were in line with some progressive notions of her times, and mine echoed the notions that were favored in my time. This in spite of the fact that we both believed ourselves independent, and lived in backwaters that did not register such changes." Her meditation concludes with a stunning image for the *Zeitgeist*: "It's as if tendencies that seem most deeply rooted in our minds, most private and singular, have come in as spores on the prevailing wind, looking for any likely place to land, any welcome" (22–3). Words of remarkable generosity and humility, which enable the narrator to transcend the mother-daughter competition for narrative authority through an understanding of the wider context of their conflict.

The narrator does not, however, bring her story to a close on this note of understanding and wisdom. Like the narrator of "The Ottawa Valley" in *Something I've Been Meaning to Tell You*, she pushes beyond the easier ending, adding yet another coda to the Grieves story. The mood of harmony as well as the competing codas that precede it are now all displaced by the narrator's revelation that years later her mother received a letter from "the real Flora" (23), telling of her move to town and her clerking job in a store, and, in an inversion of roles, offering sympathy to the mother for her debilitating illness. Flora's letter leads the narrator to memories of her stricken mother's inability to get beyond writing beginnings of letters (one of which started with "Friend of my youth") and her own "impatience with [her mother's] flowery language, the direct appeal for love and pity" (24).

Inevitably, the adolescent's impatience becomes guilt when recalled by the adult narrator. But the guilt is addressed by a circuitous route, which imperceptibly leads back to the opening dream. Although at the time of Flora's letter and her mother's illness the narrator "had lost interest in Flora," she has "thought of her since," imagining another, happier ending to Flora's story. In the narrator's more recent speculations, Flora is no longer the hateful, sex-rejecting witch of her youthful fantasies; her new alternative ending springs Flora loose from her predictable stoic fate and the rigidities that defined and confined her in her mother's tale. The older narrator recreates the formerly alien Flora as someone with whom she might even discover affinities. She spins an open-ended fantasy of Flora's progressive liberation, in which Flora, now working in a store, "might have had to learn about food blenders or chain saws, negligees, cosmetics, even condoms" (24). Each image suggests another, leading to a Flora who might "get a permanent, paint her nails, put on lipstick," or even "go on holidays ... eat meals in a restaurant ... where drinks were served. She might make friends with women who were divorced. She might meet a man" (25).

From this fantasy of open-ended possibility the narrator slips into a more personal one: "I might go into a store and find her." Immediately recognizing the impossibility of this ("She would be dead a long time now"), she nonetheless persists: "But suppose I had gone into a store – perhaps a department store," where she imagines meeting Flora, wanting to tell her she knew her story, indeed, "trying to tell her. (This is a dream now, I understand it as a dream)" (25–6). Whether or not we hear an echo in this of the opening sentence of "The Ottawa Valley" – "I think of my mother sometimes in department stores" (*Something*, 227), the dream of meeting a transformed Flora clearly echoes the opening dream of "Friend of My Youth" and quickly merges with it, as the narrator now conflates the two long-dead women. When the dream-Flora responds to the narrator's claims with a mocking smile, "weary ... of me and my idea of her, my information, my notion that I can know anything about her," the narrator recognizes that, "of course it's my mother I'm thinking of, my mother as she was in those dreams, saying, It's nothing, just this little tremor; saying with such astonishing lighthearted forgiveness, Oh, I knew you'd come someday. My mother surprising me" (26).

But the surprise surprises further by not being altogether pleasurable. Seeing her mother's "mask, her fate, and most of her affliction taken away," the daughter, though "relieved" and "happy," is also "disconcerted": "I felt slightly cheated. Yes. Offended, tricked, cheated, by this welcome turnaround, this reprieve. My mother moving rather carelessly out of her old prison, showing options and powers I never dreamed she had, changes more than herself. She changes the bitter lump of love I have carried all this time into a phantom – something useless and uncalled for, like a phantom pregnancy" (26). In springing Flora loose from her fixed role in the mother's story, the narrator has opened the way for the mother, too, to get loose from "her old prison" – her illness and the narrator's fixed memories of her,[4] which in turn places the daughter in a new position. For with her new freedom and independence, the dream-mother also seems to have got loose from the narrator's knowledge and control. That this "turnaround," which destabilizes all that has preceded it, should prove disconcerting as well as "welcome" forces the reader to ponder: Why does a part of the narrator suddenly seem to prefer the rigid, demanding mother? Why does she feel "cheated" at having to relinquish "the bitter lump of love" – presumably, the guilt with which she has lived for so long? (The lump is also an image that, within the story, looks back to Ellie's "growth" and unsuccessful – phantom? – pregnancies,[5] and, elsewhere in the collection, forward to Barbara's lump in "Oranges and Apples.") Is it that by transforming her mother's story into narrative, the narrator has automatically opened it up to the possibility of other directions that threaten the rigidity of her own mechanisms for dealing with the past? Or is it due to the threatened loss of narrative control once she begins to give free reign to her fantasies?[6] Or does her sense of being tricked and cheated point, as Carol Shields suggests, to a painful recognition of the fundamental unknowability of the mother, "her steadfast resistance to the notions of others"?[7] In any case, as the mother is imaginatively freed from "her old prison," the narrator reveals needs and potentialities that we (and she) see for the first time. Perhaps most intriguingly, the destabilizing fantasy calls into question the truth value and stability of any narrative, whether imagined or remembered, reminding us that, as both memory and storytelling are constructions, creative acts, their content is always in some sense problematic and open-ended. There is always another way of coming at the same material.[8]

The mother in the closing dream of "Friend of My Youth" may seem reminiscent of the mother at the end of "The Ottawa Valley," who "is indistinct, her edges melt and flow." But while in the earlier story the mother "weighs everything down ... has stuck to me as close as ever and refused to fall away" (*Something*, 246), the self-sufficient dream-mother of "Friend of My Youth" eludes the narrator's grasp, seeming, on the contrary, simply to slip away. Ultimately, her getting loose is experienced as more unsettling than liberating. Hence, while the narrator of "Ottawa Valley" understands the final "purpose" of her (narrative) "journey" as an effort to "*get rid*" of the mother (246), the narrative of "Friend of My Youth" appears, instead, as an effort to recapture the mother, to bring her back.

The daughter's desire to recapture the mother in "Friend of My Youth" suggests another function of her tale. I have looked at the Grieves story as a site of competition between mother and daughter for narrative (and hence, moral) authority. Additionally, though, we can see the story as a collaborative, co-operative effort, even a kind of homage to the mother, whose early illness and death perhaps prevented her from fulfilling her potential. In "Winter Wind," the daughter relates that her mother's "vocal cords were partly paralyzed," so that "sometimes I would have to act as her interpreter, a job that made me wild with shame" (*Something*, 195).[9] In the later

"Friend of My Youth," the daughter finds a different, more affirmative way to give more permanent voice to the mother whose own voice was prematurely silenced.

Munro has, of course, always been interested in the process of storytelling, and her stories abound with fragments of stories and contradictory versions of characters and events. *Friend of My Youth*, however, viewed in its entirety, shows a newly focused interest in the construction of collaborative, shared, narratives.[10] In addition to the complex title story, this interest is notable in the two other stories that directly treat a mother-daughter relation – "Meneseteung" and "Goodness and Mercy." Before turning to them, however, we should dwell a moment further on the destabilizing dream as well as on the fantasy that introduces it and the unexpected affinities that fantasy suggests, for they illustrate motifs that reverberate through the collection. Just as the mother "moving ... out of her old prison" points to characters in other stories who get loose from the bonds of predictable narratives, so too the narrator's fantasy of meeting an altered Flora and her desire to construct an alternative happier ending for a woman whose fate has been presented to her as sealed in inescapable resignation or gloom are echoed in the impulses of other female protagonists in the collection.

In "Five Points," Brenda refuses to accept as final the dismal end for the adolescent Maria on which Neil's story from his past concludes. (After stealing money from her parents' cash register to pay boys to have sex with her, Maria was "sent to a place for young offenders"; *Friend*, 40). Brenda doggedly wants to know "what happened to Maria? ... The story won't leave Brenda alone," and she goes on to imagine a more generous conclusion: "Well, maybe she got married ... Lots of people get married who are no beauties ... She might've lost weight and be looking good even" (42). Brenda's insistence on pushing beyond the known ending of Maria's incarceration to more open-ended subsequent possibilities provides the occasion for her first fight with her lover Neil. Although it is not clear that he intends his account of Maria's humiliating sexual need to humiliate the attractive, sexy Brenda, Brenda's response, her insistent desire to see Maria get loose from Neil's confining narrative, shows an instinctive identification with the pathetic young woman whom she knows only from her lover's story.

A female protagonist's recognition of affinity in unexpected quarters and her impulse to write an alternate, more open ending through which an apparently dead-ended woman can get loose from what was presumed to be a foreclosed destiny reappear in "Hold Me Fast, Don't Let Me Pass." Having met the beautiful young Judy, whose illegitimate daughter, Tania, seems to confine her to a long dreary future looking after an isolated semi-invalid, Hazel speculates aloud (to Antoinette, Judy's older, successful rival for Tania's father), "It must be a lonely life for her," adding, "She might like to get married." Just as Neil in "Five Points" rejects Brenda's hopeful imagined scenario for Maria, so too Antoinette dismisses Hazel's generous thoughts about a happier future for Judy. And like Brenda, Hazel stubbornly refuses to back down: "It doesn't matter so much nowadays ... Girls have children first and get married later. Movie stars, ordinary girls, too. All the time" (97).

As suggested earlier, it is not only characters and narrators within the stories who offer liberating endings to predictably foreclosed plots presented to them in interpolated tales; the characters themselves also get loose from expected, constricting storylines.[11] For example, Hazel is not simply the sympathetic imaginer of a more open future for Judy than her limiting circumstances might suggest. Hazel is also someone who herself, years earlier, "broke open the shell of her increasingly doubtful and expensive prettiness; she got out." Paradoxically, for her this means that she found a way, while remaining in a dreary marriage, nevertheless to "[take] hold of her life" (82). In *Friend of My Youth*, unlike most of Munro's earlier collections, some women are able to get loose from confinement – Hazel and Brenda, also Barbara in "Oranges and Apples" – even though they remain within their flawed marriages. (It is perhaps puzzling, but an example of the force of optimism, that both Brenda and Hazel, who have not exactly found marriage liberating themselves, should nonetheless construct it as such for others in their imagined narratives.) At the same time, we also see the situation more familiar to Munro readers of a woman breaking free from her marriage,[12] described in ways that tie in with motifs present elsewhere in the collection. Joan in "Oh, What Avails," heeding the call of "a person not heard from in her marriage, and perhaps not previously heard from in her life" (199), "feels herself loosed" and "knows that she cannot go back to the life she was living or to the person she was before" (200). Georgia in "Differently," who similarly discovers that she "contained another woman" (233), is seen as confuting more conventional expectations familiar in literature (and life): "You would have thought that after such scourging she'd have scuttled back into her marriage ... That was not what happened" (241). In "Wigtime," the divergent youthful paths of Anita and Margot seem early to cast them as contraries in a traditional "good woman/bad woman" dichotomy; but their later choices invert and then effectively dissolve this opposition (a staple of more predictable plots). The story ends with their renewed friendship, allowing Margot to tell of her frequent friendly visits to the now-institutionalized ex-wife she has displaced. A similar rejection of clear divisions between recognizable types of women is present in "Hold Me Fast," in the feelings of female loyalty and solidarity with which Hazel responds to both her dead husband's former lover, Antoinette, now a respectable hotel owner and *soi-disant* widow, and the publicly stigmatized Judy.

"Meneseteung" is another story in which a protagonist gets loose from narrative expectations engendered by familiar, predictable plots; it too presents unexpected affinities among three dissimilar women. Moreover, if, in Woolf's much-quoted words, "a woman writing thinks back through her mothers,"[13] then this story of a female narrator seeking to recover a forgotten woman writer of the past may also be read as another version of the mother-daughter drama. Such recoveries have become a frequent subject of both fiction and historical research for contemporary women writers. Here, as in "Friend of My Youth," the narrator's treatment of material deriving from a (literary fore)mother may be viewed as both competition and homage.[14]

"Meneseteung" opens with a discussion of Almeda Joynt Roth's book of poetry, *Offerings*, and excerpts from that volume provide epigraphs heading each of the story's six sections. At the same time, the researching writer of "Meneseteung" – more successfully than the adolescent narrator of "Friend of My Youth," who "saw through [her] mother's story and put in what she left out" (20) – portrays a much denser and imaginatively richer world than that suggested by the pretty, sanitized poetry of her nineteenth-century foremother. Moving from Almeda's book of verse to her world in the second section of the story, the narrator, aided by old issues of the local *Vidette*, evokes a raw frontier town in which "cows are tethered in vacant lots or pastured in back yards, but sometimes they get loose. Pigs get loose, too, and dogs roam free ... animals ... leave horse buns, cow pats, dog turds that ladies have to hitch up their skirts for," young rowdies trundle a drunken Queen Aggie all over town in a wheelbarrow, "then dump her into a ditch" (54), and Almeda's bedroom window overlooks the disreputable Pearl Street at the edge of the swamp, to which "no decent woman ever would ... [walk]" (56). Implicitly underscoring the greater authenticity of her own recreation of Almeda's world, the writer reminds us that "the countryside that she [Almeda] has written about in her poems actually takes diligence and determination to see. Some things must be disregarded. Manure piles ... and boggy fields ..." (61).

The various texts uncovered by the narrator – Almeda's poems, with her author's introduction and photograph, supplemented by *Vidette* entries – suggest a character recognizable from familiar plots: first, the decorous nineteenth-century maiden lady poetess, modest, if not downright apologetic about her literary ventures, baker of "fancy iced cakes and decorated tarts" (58); next, the not entirely over-the-hill spinster, embarking on a budding romance with her neighbor, Jarvis Poulter, presumably hoping for the closure of the marriage plot. The final *Vidette* entry fits Almeda into yet another female plot, that of the increasingly eccentric old maid, who meets an ignoble end. Navigating among the "facts" and "documented" innuendo (supplied by the author of "Meneseteung"), however, the narrator enables Almeda to get loose from these familiar plot lines, inventing for her a story of far greater drama and an inner life of far wider imaginative scope than any that one could hope to find in the pages of the *Vidette* or the work of a nineteenth-century poetess.[15]

The crucial imagined scene of the audible "ball of fire rolling up Pearl Street, shooting off sparks," followed by sounds of "a woman ... being beaten" (63) and the imperfectly glimpsed grappling figures at Almeda's back fence, with their "confused ... gagging, vomiting, grunting, pounding" and the "choking sound of pain and self abasement, self-abandonment," suggest to Almeda that she has witnessed "the sound of murder" and pose the question of her personal responsibility – "What is to be done, what is she to do"?[16] Although her immediate response is that "she must go out into the yard" (64), she succumbs instead to the medically (patriarchally) prescribed "nerve medicine" (62) and falls asleep. Waking, she imagines "a big crow sitting on her windowsill," telling her, "Wake up and move the wheelbarrow! ... and she understands that it means something else by 'wheelbarrow' – something foul and sorrowful" (64). While Almeda's gloss on "wheelbarrow" is certainly apt, if the narrator has found the account of Queen Aggie's treatment in the *Vidette*, might not Almeda have read it there too? A wheelbarrow is, additionally, often used to cart away rubbish, but the woman's body "heaped up" at the back fence is neither rubbish nor ready to be carted away, though it appears to Almeda's horrified gaze in dehumanized, brute animal – and vegetable – terms: "a bare breast let loose, brown nipple pulled long like a cow's teat, and a bare haunch and leg, the haunch showing a bruise as big as a sunflower. The unbruised skin is grayish, like a plucked, raw drumstick" (65). Fearing that her hesitation has been responsible for the woman's death, Almeda hastily summons Jarvis, who "looks down at" the body and "nudges the leg with the toe of his boot, just as you'd nudge a dog or a sow." In response, sustaining its closeness to brute animal life: "The body heaves itself onto all fours, the head is lifted – the hair all matted with blood and vomit – and the woman begins to bang this head, hard and rhythmically ... As she bangs her head, she finds her voice and lets out an openmouthed yowl, full of strength and what sounds like an anguished pleasure" (66).

Whether or not we accept Dermot McCarthy's description of this woman as "Life itself in all its obscene splendour,"[17] she certainly serves as a graphic reminder of the animal nature of human – if not, indeed, specifically female – life. After his encounter with the beaten, bruised woman and the dishevelled, agitated Almeda, Jarvis Poulter may still wish to preserve the fiction of two types of women, though he now "speaks to her [Almeda] in a tone of harsh joviality that she has never before heard from him" (67). Almeda, however, consciously or unconsciously, recognizes her bond with this other woman,[18] hitherto so remote from her fenced-in world and representing all that has been excised from her poetry; and Jarvis's contemptuous treatment of *her* signals the end of Almeda's romantic interest in *him*.

In a series of interlocking images, the blood that has congealed in the woman by the fence begins to flow in Almeda, as her menstrual flow merges with the grape juice overflowing its container, and both with the flow of words in her mind, staining the kitchen floorboards with a "stain [that] will never come out" (70). Almeda's newly recognized kinship with the other woman has irrevocably changed and stained her. The "little jars of grape jelly" that Almeda has planned as "fine Christmas presents, or offerings to the sick" (62) are rather like her earlier literary *Offerings* – discrete units, attractively packaged and carefully contained. But Almeda and her new vision can no longer be contained so neatly. Like the genteelly crocheted roses in her tablecloth, which she soon imagines escaping into "floating independence" (70), Almeda has gotten loose from her previous moorings. Resembling another nineteenth-century fictional woman poised to rebel against patriarchal confinement, who obsessively watches the patterns of the wallpaper, seeing figured in these domestic surroundings her own imprisonment and then a promise of her escape,[19] Almeda "[surrenders] to her surroundings," watching the "garlanded wallpaper," curtains, floral carpet, and "sideboard spread with embroidered runners and holding various patterned plates and jugs ... For every one of these patterns, decorations seems charged with life, ready to move and flow and alter. Or possibly to explode. Almeda Roth's occupation throughout the day is to keep an eye on them. Not to prevent their alteration so much as to catch them at it – to understand it, to be part of it." As the "glowing and swelling" in Almeda "begins to suggest words ... a flow of words" (69), she has a Whitmanesque vision of "one very great poem that will contain everything," including "the obscene racket on Pearl Street and the polished toe of Jarvis Poutler's boot and the plucked-chicken haunch with its blue-black flower." Judging that the violence of climate and life can be "borne only if it is channelled into a poem," she decides, "the name of the poem will be – it *is* – 'The Meneseteung.' The name of the poem is the name of the river. No, in fact it is the river, the Meneseteung, that is the poem – with its deep holes and rapids and blissful pools under the summer trees and its grinding blocks of ice thrown up at the end of the winter and its desolating spring floods" (70).[20]

As the story has progressed, the narrator has gradually seemed to lose herself in Almeda, moving into her mind and shedding the cool detachment of the first section, with its almost pedantic observations about masculine and feminine rhymes. But here, a glaring cliché suddenly reminds us of the distance between Almeda and the narrator through whose mediation we have been reading her story, as we are shown Almeda's vision in what must surely be her own words: "Almeda looks deep, deep *into the river of her mind* and into the tablecloth, and she sees the crocheted roses floating" (70, emphasis added). Almeda is presented as a foremother who is granted a vision that, due to the limitations of her time, place, and culture, she lacks not simply the courage and encouragement but also the adequate linguistic resources – the language – to express. Unlike the woman by the fence, Almeda does not, finally, "[find] her voice." Yet while Almeda's all-embracing cosmic vision remains unwritten, the narrator's imagined rendering of decisive moments in Almeda's life and thought constitute her own "offerings" to a literary foremother. The narrator's story can be viewed as a collaborative creation in which a more privileged literary daughter gives voice to a disadvantaged predecessor who did not, ultimately, succeed in finding her own.

The final scene, as in "Friend of My Youth," brings us back to the frame. The narrator now distances us from Almeda through the *Vidette*'s report of her ignominious end, allowing the reader to draw ironic parallels between this and the earlier accounts of Queen Aggie and the woman by the fence. But though we are brought back to the narrator as researcher, the detachment of the first section is gone. Looking for Almeda's gravestone, the narrator passionately begins "pulling grass and scrabbling in the dirt with my bare hands" (73), seeking to affirm her conjecture that the "Meda" mentioned in one of the poems is indeed Almeda Roth, author of the poems. The narrator on her hands and knees in the dirt (how else can we envision the scene?) suggests by her posture her own closeness to the animal life that she has imagined Almeda recognizing in herself on seeing the woman by the fence. Thus, the narrator's identification with Almeda is completed by her own final bodily identification with this other, unnamed woman.[21]

At the same time, there is a certain play in this frantic search, for the narrator's bold leap of imagination does not lie in her intuition that Meda was Almeda's nickname. The Almeda Roth who has come to interest the narrator – and us – is no longer primarily the Almeda Roth of the early book of poems and of the *Vidette* accounts but rather the author of the wholly imagined poem that remains unwritten – though the story we have just finished reading may be seen as a prose approach to it. No sooner has the narrator prided herself on "scraping the dirt off gravestones, reading microfilm, just in the hope of seeing this trickle in time, making a connection, rescuing one thing from the rubbish," than she concedes radical doubt: "I may have got it wrong. I don't know if she ever took laudanum. Many ladies did. I don't know if she ever made grape jelly" (73). These final sentences, added after the published *New Yorker* version, may be seen as part of Munro's increasingly characteristic refusal of definitive closure, and in light of issues raised earlier in this chapter the disclaimer also provides another example of a character escaping authorial control. But, of course, it is not the "facts" of laudanum or grape jelly that are in question, any more than whether Almeda was called Meda in her family. The narrator's apparently meticulous concern for historical accuracy is belied – even ignoring for a moment the fundamental fictionality of Almeda Roth – by the "fact" that even the (constructed) "record" gives no justification for the crucial events of the fracas on Pearl Street, the woman by the fence, the voice of the crow, and, indeed, all of Almeda's vibrant inner life in response to these experiences, including her unwritten poem. However, because the constructed "record" – *Offerings*, the *Vidette* – *has been* invented, we cannot help but return at the end to the implied author behind the narrator who can never be wholly erased from the reader's consciousness. So we are left at the end with a series of refracting and related women, a sisterhood encompassing the invisible author, the narrator, Almeda/Meda, and the other woman.

Where "Meneseteung" presents a daughter generously reaching out across the gulf of historical time to resuscitate a forgotten foremother, "Goodness and Mercy" reworks the mother-daughter drama as a wish-fulfilment idyll. Here, it is the mother rather than the daughter who is the artist, an opera singer (of very modest achievement) rather than a writer, though the daughter can also be seen as a writer in embryo, as she "often told herself stories – the activity seemed to her as unavoidable as dreaming" (169). In contrast to Maddy's "ten-year's vigil" caring for a mother whose "bizarre" disease inflicted "such unnecessary humiliation" on her daughters in "Peace of Utrecht" (*Dance*, 195), or, in "Friend of My Youth," the "decade or more" during which "the paralyzing disease" held the mother "in its grip ... before her death" (3), the companionable ocean voyage of Bugs and Averill, for which Averill has generously paid out of "money left to her by the father she had never seen" (156), lasts a mere ten days. Behind the figure of the "charming," witty Bugs (160), minimizing her illness, continuing to jest, uncomplainingly absenting herself gradually from one meal or social occasion after another, yet still able to sing "with unimpaired – or almost unimpaired – sweetness" (167), we may see the shadows of other ailing mothers, far less attractive and easy to love: the mother in "Peace of Utrecht," barely able to articulate, who "demanded our love ... without shame or sense" (*Dance*, 199), or the mother in "Friend of My Youth," who, with her "direct appeal for love and pity," refused "to withdraw with dignity, instead of reaching out all the time to cast her stricken shadow" (24). And unlike the daughter-narrator in the earlier story, left to lament that "the resources of love we had were not enough, the demand on us was too great" (*Dance*, 199), or the daughter-narrator in the later story who "was no comfort and poor company to her [mother] when she had almost nowhere else to turn" (*Friend*, 20), Averill is unwavering in her devotion to her dying mother, the exemplary, loving, dutiful, daughter – except in her own eyes, as we learn when the captain tells "her perfectly secret story" aloud, the story she "had been telling herself night after night." Here, it is Averill's story itself that seems to get loose: "She had made it, and he had taken it and told it, safely" (178). For in telling it "safely," the captain, the embodiment of "peaceable authority" (167), who is "alert to everything on the ship" (166), acknowledges Averill's hidden fantasies and absolves her from guilt.

"Goodness and Mercy" hovers at the borders of magic realism. The captain's wisdom and knowledge of human nature may, of course, suffice without supernatural powers to tell him that even a love as true and freely given as Averill's must have its ambivalent dark side. Still, the story shared by Averill and the godlike captain seems to emerge as a mysterious collaboration, one that stands out from the collaborations between and among women that we have been looking at. Told by the captain, then amended (with his acceptance) by Averill, who recognizes it as her own, it slips loose from any fixed form, changing through successively shifting versions in Averill's fluid imagination, and ultimately proving capable, through the captain's authority and participation, not only of absolving Averill from guilt but also of legitimizing the plenitude of her desires even in the face of loss and death.

The daughter's ambivalent feelings for the mother, implicit in the combination of competition and homage in "Friend of My Youth" and "Meneseteung," are revealed here by the presence of the secret liberating deathwish that Averill harbours toward Bugs alongside her profound love and solicitude. Except perhaps in Averill's free-floating fantasies or in the grace with which Bugs is dying, neither woman can be said to get loose from expected roles, as in other stories we have considered; nor does either escape authorial control or discover surprising bonds with other women. Rather, "Goodness and Mercy" may be viewed as an idyllic replay of Munro's albatross story, creating a charmed space that corresponds to "the thing she [Averill] always felt, when her mother sang. The doors flew open, effortlessly, there was the lighted space beyond, a revelation of kindness and seriousness. Desirable, blessed joy, and seriousness, a play of kindness that asked nothing of you ... It was a gift that Bugs was obliged to offer" (168). In contrast to Almeda Joynt Roth's poetic *Offerings* to an unreceptive audience, Bugs's art is invariably greeted by Averill's loving appreciation. And unlike the mother's generous words in the opening dream of "Friend of my Youth," whose "transparent ... hopefulness [and] too easy ... forgiveness" (3) the daughter is forced to deconstruct, Bugs's "gift," though first presented as lasting only as long as her singing, seems endorsed at the end as "Averill accepts the captain's offering." Within the idyllic space created by the story, "Averill is absolved and fortunate" (179), and the hope expressed in her hymn – "Goodness and Mercy all my life/Shall surely follow me" (169) – seems almost attainable. But Munro never wholly abandons her ironic edge. Underscoring the tenacity of the bond between daughter and mother, Averill first marries one man "chiefly because Bugs would have thought the choice preposterous," and then a second, who, with his "offhand, unsettlingly flippant and ironical manner ... either charmed people or aroused their considerable dislike" (179) – just like the flippant, ironic Bugs, whom "people either think [charming] or ... can't stand" (160) – a sure indication of the daughter's abiding loyalty to the first friend of her youth.

Grace Paley © Nancy Crampton

5

The Work of Faith in the Stories of Grace Paley

THE LITTLE DISTURBANCES OF MAN AND *ENORMOUS CHANGES AT THE LAST MINUTE*

Early Faith

When Grace Paley's most frequently recurring character and narrator first appears in her earliest collection of stories, *The Little Disturbances of Man*, her name is simply Faith. The two husbands to whom Faith is serving the unappreciated breakfast in that memorable opening sentence of "The Used-Boy Raisers" ("There were two husbands disappointed by eggs"[1]) are also each given only a single name, immediately derived, by antonomasia, from the adjectives that register their disappointment: Livid and Pallid. The naming of Faith's husbands here constitutes the only authorial suggestion of allegory in the Faith stories. Still, in Paley's third and last collection, *Later the Same Day*, Faith meets the Chinese woman Xie Feng, who is visiting New York: "The two women said each other's strange name and laughed. The Chinese woman said, Faith in what?" (374). While it would be foolish to view the Faith of Paley's three volumes of stories as a simple or consistently allegorical character, the antonomastically named husbands with whom she is juxtaposed in the first Faith story and Xie Feng's question about her name two books later cannot but whet the reader's curiosity about the status of the figure who appears with increasing frequency throughout Paley's three collections of stories.

In answer to frequent interview questions about her narrator/heroine, Paley's own comments are limited. To the query, "Does she have a faith, do you see her as faithful?" Paley has replied, "No she doesn't. She did when she was younger, sort of a faith, but not really."[2] In answer to questions about the possible self-referentiality of her literary creation, she has repeatedly stressed that she is not Faith, that her own life has been very different from Faith's, she was not a single mother but lived with her children's father for 22, 23, or 25 years (the numbers vary), and she did not have two sons but, rather, a daughter and a son. Paley has also said that in the initial Faith story, Faith was her friend Sybil, an identification she repeats in her epigraph to the *Collected Stories*. Additionally, Paley has qualified this, saying that over time, Faith "wasn't Sybil either. She began to just take on characteristics of at least four friends ... she's a collective us really ... an invented person who lived in circumstances similar to most of the women I knew – which were not my circumstances."[3] Bearing in mind a distinction Paley has made between writers and critics, leading her to advise that "the poor writer ... really oughtn't to know what he's talking about,"[4] I have found most helpful Paley's succinct reiterated description of her relation to Faith: "Faith is the one who does the most work for me"; or again, "she lives within a few feet of my head ... She does a lot of work for me";[5] and yet again, "she does all this work for me ... she works for me."[6]

There have been critical studies of Faith's psychological and ideological growth and development over the course of Paley's stories, and others that treat Faith as a spokeswoman, either direct or oblique, for Paley's own values.[7] Here I would like to shift the focus somewhat to consider the various ways in which Faith "works for" Paley – how she works as a literary, dramatic figure in the stories, the functions she serves and the roles she plays, as narrator, narratee, and storyhearer, straightman and comedian. While this will sometimes lead me to consider links between the Faith stories and the others with which they are interspersed, and between the Faith stories and Paley's other writings – her poetry and political and occasional pieces – viewed as an ensemble the Faith stories have a coherence of their own. Not until the last story of Paley's second collection, *Enormous Changes at the Last Minute*, is Faith first revealed as a writer; but even there, the disclosure is so fleeting that the reader might well miss the clue. At the end of an early story in *Later the Same Day* Paley again lets the reader glimpse another indication that Faith is fabricator as well as narrator. But only in the final story of this third and last collection does Paley at last highlight Faith's identity as a writer, and moreover, in a clear metafictional move, as the writer of the stories in which she has appeared, most of which she has also narrated. If Faith's writerly identity is deliberately muted, however, she is a skillful storyteller throughout. Even where Faith is not the narrator, Paley's deft command of different linguistic registers, apparent in the range of narrative voices in her entire corpus, is displayed with particular virtuosity within the narrower body of the Faith stories. Focusing on the Faith stories and how Faith "works for" her author can help shed light on Paley's humour and the modulations of her tone and styles of narration, on the culture and world shared by author and protagonist, and, finally, on Paley's wider vision, its evolution and continuity.

Xie Feng's question "Faith in what?" may seem naive, but it is not entirely beside the point. Still, it is generally less easy to answer than in the quasi-allegorically flavoured debut story, where the husbands' abstract designations suggest that Paley is also playing on the meaning of her heroine's name, a suggestion immediately strengthened when, as if in response to her husbands' disappointment, Faith reaches "under the kitchen table for a brown paper bag full of an embroidery which asked God to Bless Our Home," a motto she is "completing ... for the protection of my sons" (81). The element of play, of course, is much in evidence here, as always in Paley, for though "one man was livid, the other pallid," one the original father, the other a used-boy raiser, the livid/pallid distinction quickly evaporates in the face of their shared attitudes and attributes – their joint criticisms of Faith's homemaking abilities and her upbringing of her two sons (Livid criticizes the eight-year-old's deficient reading skills and Pallid, Faith's choice of a public, rather than parochial, school)[8] and their shared Catholic background (leading easily to Pallid's line, "When you married us ..."). Faith is presented somewhat more individually, as a woman trying to make a viable life for herself and her two children in a context of precarious relationships between men and women, as manifested both by the presence of her ex-husband and by the two husbands' dialogue about Faith's ex-boyfriend from the period between her marriages to them. She seeks to deflect their criticism with apologies, her talismanic embroidery of the Norman Rockewellesque cushion, and the ironic affirmation that her "destiny ... is to be, until my expiration date, laughingly the servant of man" (85). To her husbands' joint astonishment, she expresses one serious opinion, a defence of her brand of liberal secular Judaism (though that term was not yet current in the 1950s). Countering Pallid's ignorant appeal to her knowledge of Jewish tradition – as a Jewish *woman*, she rightly points out, "what do I know about Kaddish?" – she affirms, "I believe in the Diaspora, not only as a fact but a tenet" (84), and then voices her disapproval of the creation of the state of Israel. Faith's positive credo, set in the context of her implicit belief in the 1950s American dream of the happy home, with mother in the kitchen, cooking and serving, responsible for the children, and ultimately seeing her "attractive, shiny men" off (after a final apology for the eggs) "on paths which are not my concern" (87), points to her embrace of the similarly American promise of a multicultural, non-sectarian society in which a Jewish woman named Faith can marry two Catholic husbands (neither of whom appears troubled by the problem of divorce) and still express her belief that Jews *are* the "chosen people," who best fulfill their moral/social role by remaining "a splinter in the toe of civilizations, a victim to aggravate the conscience" (85).

Only in this first Faith story does Paley sound such a quasi-allegorical note. In later stories, Faith at times appears as a character who has faith in something, but the object of that faith is generally less easily articulated than in "The Used-Boy Raisers." In the companion piece to this story, "A Subject of Childhood," in which Faith recounts an earlier episode in her life from the period between her two marriages – her break-up with Clifford – rather than personifying any specific attribute, she becomes an image of all harried loving mothers. In the much-praised closing image, after hurling an ashtray at her lover, who has accused her of doing "a rotten job" of raising her sons, Faith cradles her (only moderately traumatized) younger son in her lap, strikingly illustrating the mother love that transfigures and exhilarates, even as it binds and imprisons: "The sun in its course emerged from among the water towers of downtown office buildings and suddenly shone white and bright on me. Then through the short fat fingers of my son, interred forever, like a black-and-white barred king in Alcatraz, my heart lit up in stripes" (96).[9] Those water towers are pure New York, Alcatraz a more widely recognized reference, but the mother's sudden recognition of the restricted yet radiant kingdom over which she reigns, as her heart paradoxically "[lights] up in stripes," is an image of universal resonance.

Faith acquires her first surname, Darwin, in Paley's second collection, *Enormous Changes at the Last Minute*, in a story that shows her visiting her parents in the Children of Judea ("Faith in the Afternoon"). And here, in the Jewish context of her parents' retirement home (her married name has not yet been mentioned), it becomes even more tempting to ask, what's in a name? In interviews Paley consistently ignores an occasional question about the relation between "Grace" and "Faith." But it is hard for readers not to see a similar impulse behind the naming of both the American-born Grace and Faith by immigrant parents newly arrived from the Old World ghettos of Europe. It is not simply that Grace and Faith are not traditional Jewish names. Both are also names with specific Christian resonances. If we cannot know how clear this was to the parents of Grace Paley (*née* Gutzeit, or, as it was anglicized, Goodside), Paley makes the Christian resonances of Faith unambiguously clear when she places her in a family of three children, named Faith, Hope, and Charles. Subsequently Paley has commented, "Some of that stuff I did early and it was pretty stupid. I got stuck with it. I thought it was a big joke to have characters named Faith, Hope and Charlie. Now I think it's awful, but there's nothing I can do about it."[10] Though Paley may have come to regret the heavy gag of Jewish children named after the three (Christian) theological virtues, the name Faith is by itself sufficient to suggest her parents' effort to distance themselves from the closed world of a previous culture as they eagerly embraced a more open new one. To be sure, the Darwin parents, like their daughter, unquestionably identify themselves as Jewish, so these onomastics imply no denial of their Jewish identity; but whether Christian or secular, Faith is a name that unmistakably suggests the parents' assimilationist faith in a New World promise quite different from the culture they have chosen to leave behind.[11]

Like Faith, the surname Darwin is hardly Jewish. On the realistic level, we are free to suppose, variously, that the family chose this name as more readily recognizable or pronounceable than their original "foreign" one, or that they viewed it as a shortened anglicized form of an original name – practices common among Jews and other immigrant groups (as the transformation of Gutzeit into Goodside may remind us), or – in keeping with Paley's early jokiness – that they selected it in the manner of many revolutionary figures who chose entirely new names to indicate new identities. Since Paley offers no explanation for the family name, however, the reader is left only with the popular associations to Charles Darwin as one of the fathers of the modern scientific era, best known for his pivotal theory of evolution. He may thus have been a particularly congenial namesake for Faith's parents in their own evolution from the Old World to the New, from one language to another, and from a culture based on religion and tradition to one in which they felt themselves invited to embrace a secular, non-religious, rationalist, left-wing social and political ideology. Moreover, the family name shared by parents and daughter may additionally call attention to the generational evolution that many of the Faith stories dramatize.[12]

Paley gestures toward establishing consistency between the Faith of "The Used-Boy Raisers" in *The Little Disturbances of Man* and the Faith of "Faith in the Afternoon" in *Enormous Changes at the Last Minute* by referring to the absent Ricardo in the later story as "Faith's first husband" (148); but the Ricardo described here and in subsequent stories (in which he never actually appears) bears little relation to Livid of "The Used-Boy Raisers" other than his probable Catholic background, and in later stories there is no further mention of a second husband for Faith.[13] This suggests that Paley subsequently decided to change the facts of Faith's life to enable her to "work for" her author in new ways, while in the bridging "Afternoon" Paley is keeping her options open.

More directly than "The Used-Boy Raisers," "Faith in the Afternoon" engages the question of the position of Jews, especially first-generation native-born Jews, in American society. By their premature retirement to the Children of Judea, the Darwins have chosen to enter an even more coherent Jewish community than the old neighbourhood of Faith's childhood, which it nonetheless recalls. Their move thus suggests a certain abandonment of the earlier assimilationist ethic indicated by the choice of their children's first and their own last names. In her wisecracky prose, Paley charts the erratic course of Faith's family's relation to the wider culture through more twists than we need follow here. But we learn that Faith's "grandmother had been planted" in Yorkville (at that time a German neighbourhood in Manhattan) by Faith's grandfather, with whom presumably she had emigrated from Europe, and that the Darwins (who most probably accompanied their parents to the US as children) had moved from there to Coney Island "for the air." "Her grandmother pretended she was German in just the same way that Faith pretends she is an American. Faith's mother flew in the fat face of all that and, once safely among her own kind in Coney Island, learned real Yiddish … and … took an oath to expostulate in Yiddish and grieve only in Yiddish, and she has kept that oath to this day" (147–8). While the second sentence tells that Faith's mother, in contrast to her grandmother – whose impulses were to assimilate to the wider host culture – and to her own younger self, has become more self-consciously Jewish with age (a not uncommon experience among her generation), the bitterly jokey first sentence may require a gloss. It appears to mean that just as Faith, born in America, thinks of herself as American, her grandmother, born in Germany, thought of herself as German (a reading confirmed later in the story: "their grandmother, who thinks she's German" [157]) – but that in the eyes of the "German Nazis" among whom she lived in Yorkville, to say nothing of the greater number who remained in Germany, her sense of German identity appeared as mere pretence. (And indeed, in the light of the subsequent history of the German Jews who shared Faith's grandmother's view of herself, it was to appear as tragic blindness.)[14] But what is the meaning of the ironic narrative claim, "Faith pretends she is an American"? This claim is immediately followed by what first appears to be a contradiction but may instead be an elucidation: "Faith has only visited her parents once since she began to understand that because of Ricardo she would have to be unhappy for a while. Faith really is an American and she was raised up like everyone else to the true assumption of happiness" (148).

This highly ironic "true assumption" may recall the idyllic domestic scene Faith was embroidering in the earlier story but is here specifically linked to her "really" being "an American." The distinctively American faith in happiness, whose pursuit and attainment are considered a natural human entitlement, appears to have replaced Faith's earlier stated belief in the Diaspora. Hence, when instead of successfully achieving her birthright Faith "is absolutely miserable," the very foundations of her American identity seem, albeit jokingly, to be called into question. Faith is "ashamed … before her parents," and they "are ashamed of her willful unhappiness" (148). Confuting the "true assumption" of American culture, Faith's unhappiness can only be understood as "willful," not just painful but a source of shame.

In the only Faith story in Paley's first two collections that Faith does not narrate herself, Paley presents her heroine's suffering ironically, neither sentimentalizing nor dismissing it, while nonetheless making a very funny story out of Faith's real pain. Part of the humour lies in the fact that Faith finds unhappiness so surprising. Faith and her family are, after all, heirs to a tradition – historical, cultural, and literary – in which unhappiness and even disaster are the norm rather than a perverse exception, as the Children of Judea setting may help to remind us. But whereas the stories of Sholom Aleichem, to whom Paley has sometimes been compared, in dramatizing the lives of the shtetl Jews of eastern Europe, often derive their ironic humour from the protagonists' escalating misfortunes, the humour of Faith's situation lies partly in her naive American belief in her distance from the assumptions of the Old World, where misfortune was always to be expected. Paley nonetheless brings that world of excessive suffering into her story, providing different linguistic registers to highlight the contrasting viewpoints of different generations. Faith's question "Well, Ma, what do you hear from the neighborhood?" (152) prompts Mrs Darwin to embark on three tales of disaster that move us into a very different tonal space. Marianne DeKoven, who has made the most serious effort to account for the varying registers of Paley's humour, describes the first of these stories as an example of "the comic grotesque," which she distinguishes from the "comic bizarre" language and imagery through which Paley subsequently describes Mrs Hegel-Shtein's tears, the main focus of her impressive analysis of Paley's use of language to distract the reader from pathos.[15] DeKoven, however, is only minimally interested in the stories of misfortune befalling Faith's friends from "the neighborhood," though her passing attention to the mode of their narration at least implicitly acknowledges their comic effect, an aspect of these tales not considered by the thematic readings of other critics who describe them simply as recounting "losses" that "overshadow her [Faith's] own disappointments,"[16] or "sad news ... told so as to awaken Faith to her own comparatively less unfortunate state and to the community of suffering women,"[17] or "stories of disappointments, failed expectations, deceit, and loss not unlike her own."[18] In fact, the three tales of woe that Mrs Darwin, egged on by Mrs Hegel-Shtein, tells her daughter constitute a kind of throwback to an earlier kind of Jewish black humour, which achieves comedy through its very extremity, even as it sometimes mixes the trivial and the catastrophic. They cannot easily be summarized, as their meaning lies largely in the mode of their narration. First come the physical or health disasters befalling Tess Slovinsky: "'You know about the first tragedy, Faith? The first tragedy was she had a child born a monster. Nobody saw it. They put it in a home. All right. Then the second child ... This one was born full of allergies. It had rashes from orange juice. It choked from milk. Its eyes swoll up from going to the country. All right. Then her husband, Arnold Lever, a very pleasant boy, got cancer. They chopped off a finger. It got worse. They chopped off a hand. It didn't help. Faith, that was the end of a lovely boy'" (154).

If this first story narrates a series of escalating natural disasters for which no one can be blamed, the next one, concerning Faith's friend June Braun, intimates a pattern of retribution for overmuch success: "'Junie's husband, an engineer in airplanes. Very serious boy ... He was in the movement. They bought a house in Huntington Harbor with a boat, a garage, a garage for the boat. She looked stunning. She had three boys. Brilliant. The husband played golf with the vice-president, a goy. The future was golden. She was active in everything. One morning they woke up. It's midnight. Someone uncovers a little this, a little that. (I mentioned he was in the movement?) In forty-eight hours, he's blacklisted. Good night Huntington Harbor. Today the whole bunch live with the Brauns in four rooms'" (155). An old pattern: "The black Furies stalking the man/fortunate beyond all right/wrench back again the set of his life/and drop him to darkness."[19] Whether for Aeschylus's Agamemnon or Sholem Aleichem's Enchanted Tailor, good fortune is temporary or illusory, in either case a mere prelude to disaster. Although the effective cause of June's family downfall is political activism, there appears to be another, covert moral to this tale. Playing golf with the vice-president, a goy, June's husband has overstepped, Mrs Darwin intimates, not only through buying his house, boat, and two garages but also in his profounder abandonment of the old closed neighbourhood and his own people there.

Assimilation as a marker of overweening pride becomes more pronounced in the last of Mrs Darwin's tales, concerning Anita Franklin, who "was married way ahead of you and Ricardo to a handsome boy from Harvard ... Arthur Mazzano, you know, Sephardic. They lived in Boston and they knew such smart people. Professors, doctors, the finest people. History-book writers, thinking American people. Oh, Faith, darling. I was invited to the house several times. Christmas, Easter. I met their babies. Little blondies like you were, Faithy. He got maybe two PhD's in different subjects'" (155–6). The golden aura surrounding the Mazzano family before the fall is created not only by Arthur's personal achievements (his "maybe two PhD's" and intellectually distinguished friends) but also by more subtle distinctions. He is Sephardic, a term designating Jews of Spanish origin, who were wealthier and considered to be of higher caste than the multitude of poor Jews of East European origin, the bulk of Jewish immigration to America, or even than the German Jews, themselves somewhat higher on the social ladder; he is "from Harvard" (rather than, say, City College), and lives in Boston (rather than New York City). The casually mentioned occasions of Mrs Darwin's visits ("Christmas, Easter") underscore his success.

Such excessive good fortune encounters its predictable peripeteia. One day "Anita finds out ... he is fooling around with freshmen. Teenagers. In no time it's in the papers, everybody in court, talking talking talking, some say yes, some no, he was only flirting, you know the way a man flirts with youngsters. But it turns out one of the foolish kids is pregnant." Here, as in the preceding stories, Paley's wonderful attention to language, her brilliant ear, contributes to the hilarity of Mrs Darwin's account. But just when we think nothing can top "one of those foolish kids" being pregnant, we get the unexpected punchline: "'Spanish people,' said Mrs Hegel-Shtein thoughtfully. 'The men don't like their wives so much. They only get married if it's a good idea'" (156).

Mrs Darwin, at first reluctant to tell these tales, is bullied into doing so by the overbearing Mrs Hegel-Shtein, an embittered busybody, whom Mr Darwin describes as having "a whole bag of spitballs for the world" (159). Though her eagerness for Faith to hear these stories may be whetted by a personal *Schadenfreude*, Mrs Hegel-Shtein also carries with her the age-old wisdom of her culture; she knows that the seemingly boundless promise of America is not to be trusted. Hence she sees it as her duty to ensure that Faith hear these cautionary tales to remind her of truths obscured by her American upbringing: misfortune, unhappiness, calamity are not aberrations but the norm, as every Jew should know. ("Life is life. Everybody today is coddlers" [153].) This assumption about the world, carried over from an earlier time, is conveyed by Mrs Darwin in an appropriate earlier voice and mode of "Jewish humor."

The oscillations among tones that also exist elsewhere in Paley's stories are particularly pronounced here, where this appropriation of an earlier comic voice and mode can be understood as a tribute, even homage, to a kind of Jewish humour that was virtually passé by the time of this story. Faith herself, audience and straightman within the comic routine, does not, of course, join the reader in finding these stories funny. But Paley employs quite another, ironic and yet compassionate, language to capture Faith's empathy with Anita Franklin. As she sorrowfully identifies with her friend's loss, "the thumb of Ricardo's hovering shadow jabbed her in her left eye, revealing for all the world the shallowness of her water table. Rice could have been planted at that instant on the terraces of her flesh and sprouted in strength and beauty in the floods that overwhelmed her from that moment on through all the afternoon. For herself and Anita Franklin, Faith bowed her head and wept" (156). If our attention is deflected from Faith's sorrow here by the imaginative wit of the image, the narration comes closer to pathos, though never at the expense of humour, when, having taken leave of her mother, Faith "tried to keep her father behind her until she could meet the commitments of her face" (157). The closeness between father and daughter, absent in Faith's more comic interactions with her mother ("Be something, don't be a dishrag" are Mrs Darwin's parting words), is revealed in brief snatches of dialogue, including Mr Darwin's proud recitation of his recent verses on the passage of life. Faith's goodbye at the subway entrance, as she hastens home to relieve a friend who is looking after her kids, prompts her father's unthinking enthusiastic outburst,

> "Wonderful invention, babysitters. With this invention two people could be lovers forever."
>
> "Oh!" he gasped, "my darling girl, excuse me ..." Faith was surprised at his exclamation because the tears had come to her eyes before she felt their pain.
>
> ...
>
> "Faith, he called, "can you come soon?"
>
> "Oh Pa," she said, four steps below him, looking up, "I can't come until I'm a little happy." (159–60)

But even this delicate interchange, which skirts pathos by understatement, is undercut by the grotesque tragicomic pathos of the last paragraph, in which Mr Darwin reaches for Faith's fingers through the rail, touches them to her wet cheeks, and then turns away from her in "an explosion of nausea, absolute digestive disgust" (160).[20]

The mixture of linguistic registers, often as appropriate to different generations and their world views, along with a remarkable ear and sense of humour, from which, increasingly, pathos is never entirely absent, characterizes many of Grace Paley's stories, but it is particularly evident in this one. "Faith in the Afternoon" is the last story, however, to concern itself directly with the place of Jews in America, and the last in which Paley evokes the slapstick world of a familiar tradition of Jewish humour. Still, we may want to keep in mind Faith's pivotal role in this story that engages the twin issues of happiness, presented above all as an American expectation, and Jewish identity and tradition. For in Paley's most recent separately published story, "Midrash on Happiness," she once again uses Faith to explore both happiness and Jewish tradition in the same narrative space.

Single Mothers: Living with Friends and Children

Faith appears in four more stories in *Enormous Changes at the Last Minute*, as narrator and at least one of the protagonists. In addition, she narrates "Northeast Playground," in which her identity is so muted that we do not realize Faith is the teller until she refers to the episode in a later story. In "Living," "Faith in a Tree," "The Immigrant Story," and "The Long-Distance Runner," Paley creates a more mature and self-confident Faith, no longer striving to please the men in her life or grieving for the absent Ricardo. After "Faith in the Afternoon," peers replace parents, husbands, and live-in lovers as the important people in her life, and even with her children and lover(s) she is on a more egalitarian footing. This tougher, more resilient, wisecracking Faith is now able to view the world with a degree of irony and detachment that previously had belonged almost exclusively to her author.

Several critics have pointed to "Faith in a Tree" as marking the character's decisive turn from personal to wider social and political concerns. But while the end of that story does record a significant turning point, we have already been shown a more socially and politically engaged Faith in "Living," first published two years before "Faith in a Tree" and placed ahead of it in *Enormous Changes at the*

Last Minute. In barely three pages in the earlier story, Faith tells of a five-week period on either side of Christmas when she and her friend Ellen both think they are dying. Ellen does die, but Faith recovers. Still, her terror is real enough; she is hemorrhaging, and her doctor's laconic response is, "You can't bleed forever. Either you run out of blood or you stop bleeding" (165). Faith gives no explanation for her bleeding, though her description of her recovery, "I was in such first-class shape by New Year's, I nearly got knocked up again" (166), suggests that it resulted from an abortion or a miscarriage.

Paley retells this part of Faith's story (originally published in 1965) in two different versions published many years later (both in 1991) to make a political, feminist point. In "The Illegal Days" in *Just as I Thought* (13–21), she tells of her own and a friend's experiences of irregular, uncontrollable bleeding similar to Faith's. Paley knew she was having a miscarriage, but her doctor advised her to call someone in her family and to get a particular drug, adding, "*Don't come*." After she continued to hemorrhage for three or four more days, "was really in terrible shape," and "couldn't get anyone to take care of me ... my doctor finally said, 'Come over.' He had to do a D&C." When she later told her father (a doctor) this story, he surmised, "That doctor was being watched" (17). In her friend's case, the doctors in the emergency room at a Catholic hospital refused to examine her until they could determine, through a rabbit test involving a wait of several days, whether she was pregnant. She was not. "It turned out she had a tumor. It was an emergency – she had to be operated on immediately" (18). In "Two Old Stories" (*Long Walks and Intimate Talks*), she tells a more compressed version of two women whose experiences are identical to those in "The Illegal Days," without identifying herself as one of them. She makes the same points in both stories. First, that this is what "happened frequently to women before *Roe v. Wade*, and can't have legally happened since." And also, that the stories are "not about abortion" but about male power and the control of women's bodies and lives. "That deep proprietary interest is in the womb, the cervix, the belly, the vagina, the entire female body, which once it's stolen from us will end probably for decades all our new, free womanly rights to those good companions sex and love" (*Long Walks*, 73).[21]

While it is instructive to see how Paley draws on the kernel of "Living" a quarter of a century later to make a feminist political point, the earlier, more literary story has another focus and is told in a very different way. Sharing the prospect of imminent death, Ellen asks, "What'll we do? About the kids. Who'll take care of them, I'm too scared to think." And Faith records, "I was frightened too, but I only wanted the kids to stay out of the bathroom. I didn't worry about them. I worried about me." Faith's unheroic candour lends a personal immediacy to her terror that is absent from Paley's later reportorial accounts. "I could hardly take my mind off this blood," Faith continues graphically: "Its hurry to leave me was draining the red out from under my eyelids and the sunburn off my cheeks. It was all rising from my cold toes to find the quickest way out." She interrupts her phone conversation with Ellen when "I felt a great gob making its dizzy exit" (166). Humour and hyperbole blend with *Todesangst* to create an account that is intimate while free from sentimentality or polemical purpose.

But above all, in "Living" Paley uses Faith to articulate and celebrate the friendship between two women, forged in "the million things we did together in these scary, private years. We drove the kids up every damn rock in Central Park. On Easter Sunday, we pasted white doves on blue posters and prayed on Eighth Street for peace. Then we were tired and screamed at the kids ... For a joke we stapled their snowsuits to our skirts and in a rage of slavery every Saturday for weeks we marched across the bridges that connect Manhattan to the world. We shared apartments, jobs, and stuck-up studs. And then, two weeks before last Christmas, we were dying" (167). This concluding recollection is an affirmative reworking of Faith's assessment as she faces death earlier in the story: "Life isn't that great Ellen ... We've had nothing but crummy days and crummy guys and no money and broke all the time and cockroaches and nothing to do on Sunday but take the kids to Central Park and row on that lousy lake. What's so great, Ellen? What's the big loss?" (166). But finally, living – cockroaches and all – *is* what it's all about, and death *is* a terrible loss. As Faith grieves for the loss of her friend, her catalogue of memories merges frustrations and disappointments with the fun of their shared times together; and – wonderfully! – praying on Eighth Street for peace coexists with screaming at the kids, sharing apartments, jobs and stuck-up studs. For during those "scary, private years" Faith has also been well aware of the scariness of the world. She observes on the story's first page that "wherever you turn someone is shouting give me liberty or I give you death. Perfectly sensible, thing-owning, Church-fearing neighbors flop their hands over their ears at the sound of a siren ... You have to be cockeyed to love, and blind in order to look out the window at your own ice-cold street" (165). And yet, without being blind, to death or human cruelty, Faith does love – her children, her friend Ellen – and perseveres with buoyancy, humour, and a resilience of spirit that is far from simple optimism (a term too often used to describe Paley and her characters). Here, as in all her stories – unlike her specifically political pieces – Paley foregrounds personal interactions, while setting them carefully in a complex social and political world.

"Faith in a Tree" is as meandering as "Living" was compact. The leisurely structure gives wide scope to the more fully developed figure of Faith as an ebullient, ironic, free-associating member of a community of single mothers and their children, which she observes from a branch on a sycamore tree in Washington Square Park, Greenwich Village. In contrast to her somewhat self-effacing role in "Faith in the Afternoon," she not only narrates this story; she dominates it. The specifically Jewish context of "Afternoon" is here replaced by a more cosmopolitan New York that, viewed through Faith's eyes, seems to encompass much of the world – flora, fauna, and people – within its wide embrace. "Oh what a place in democratic time!" she muses, identifying with the One God, "who can look down from His Holy Headquarters" and see "south into Brooklyn how Prospect Park lies in its sand-rooted trees among Japanese gardens," then "north to dangerous Central Park" and "far north" to "the deer-eyed eland and kudu ... grazing in the open pits of the Bronx Zoo" (175). She reflects proudly on her brilliant son Richard who, in a "third-grade class of learned Jews, Presbyterians, and bohemians," is eclipsed only by the "Chinese – Arnold Lee, who does make Richard look a little simple, I admit it," and expresses satisfaction at their living "on this wonderful block with all the Irish and Puerto Ricans though God knows why there aren't any Negro children" (181) – a telling indication of the naive limits of Faith's social understanding; indeed, her well-intentioned description of Chinese, Irish, and Puerto Rican children without at least a hyphenated American identity lends the whole passage a somewhat antiquated flavour.

She is given her married surname, Asbury, here for the first time but evinces only a limited interest in Ricardo's current activities. The old romantic vulnerability is gone. She opens the story complaining about the absence from her life of "at least one brainy companion who could translate my friendly language into his tongue of undying carnal love" but is not diminished or incapacitated by this lack. Her thoughts range freely over the life of the city, incidents from her past, her friends, their children and her own. Despite a fleeting sexual interest in a new man in the park, she accepts his marked preference for a more glamorous friend with good, if ironic, grace. Her acceptance, in fact, marks the end of the first version of the story, originally published in *New American Review* in 1967 as "Faith: In a Tree," leading Neil Isaacs to describe "Faith in a Tree" as "actually two stories," the first, "a brilliant evocation of the young-single-mother-in-the-park scene, in which ongoing concerns with child raising and PTA-related politics are constantly being undercut or conflicted by ongoing sexual urges" and the second, a "little political demonstration, Faith's son Richard's response to it, and Faith's epiphanic decision to change her life – in her children's behalf – to become active in the larger struggles of the world."[22]

Isaacs' analysis has the merit of calling attention to the way in which the final form of the story in *Enormous Changes at the Last Minute* has been constructed from an earlier version, but (ignoring for the moment his view, to which I shall return shortly, that the "ongoing concerns" of Faith's daily life are "undercut" or "conflicted" by her sexual urges) his claim that the story is "actually" or "literally" two stories seems to ignore Paley's own repeated dictum that she doesn't really have a story until she has two stories.[23] Still, noting the story's first format should give pause to those critics who suggest a more unitary reading of "this story as Faith's awakening to political activism."[24] After all, we read for some seventeen pages before the anti-war demonstrators arrive – fewer than three pages before the ending that does not even appear in the earlier version. Faith's meandering reflections, memories, and interactions with others should not be written off as mere preparation for an ending that repudiates them; they are absolutely essential in creating the complex texture of her life as a single mother in this community – this culture – which is surely a good part of what the story is all about. This is not to minimize the ending in which the story all at once opens out, promising a new departure, in keeping with the openness implied by the collection's title and the ending of the title story, and by Paley's memorable phrase "the open destiny of life," so central to "A Conversation with My Father," probably the collection's most discussed story. Richard's anger at his mother's failure to stand up to the policeman who disperses the anti-war demonstrators does mark the pivotal moment when Faith is "turned ... around ... and directed out of that sexy playground by my children's heartfelt brains" so that she "thought more and more every day about the world" (194). Nonetheless, the story must be seen as a whole. Even if we did not have access to Paley's aesthetic views that a story should be "two stories working against each other and in connection with each other,"[25] "one story sort of half-contradicting another or corroborating another,"[26] we should recognize that in Paley's world the politics of everyday life is not separate from the wider world but of a piece with it.

For example, what Isaacs describes, rather too succinctly, as "PTA-related politics" refers to a vignette that is actually quite significant, though Faith narrates it seemingly at random ("I digressed and was free"), in a comic, even farcical key. She tells of "a cross-eyed man with a red beard" who became president of the Parent-Teacher's Association, "appointed a committee of fun-loving ladies who met in the lunchroom and touched up the coffee with little gurgles of brandy," and "had many clever notions about how to deal with the money shortage in the public schools," a real issue that serves to introduce a matter of even greater seriousness to Paley, the place of public and private schools in a democratic society. In contrast to many left-leaning New Yorkers, who go to considerable expense to keep their children from attending what they regard as inferior public schools along with children of parents less fortunate and enlightened than themselves, Paley maintains, in an essay she includes in her collection *Just as I Thought*, "I'm obsessed with the notion that the children of radicals belong in the public elementary-school system. There, they and their parents and teachers can take part in the great social struggle for sensible education for *all* the children. The school is the event: the school and its citizens are the education" (205). Paley acknowledges the worthy motives of parents (including friends) who want the best for their children but is ultimately unsparing: "Even when the local public school was fairly good, the class decision was to extract its children from among the others. In some cases this turned the local school into a ghetto. In other cases, an array of exclusive schools was established. (We wrote lots of angry articles about that kind of thing when it happened in the South [206])."

In "Faith in a Tree," as in "Living," we again see how differently Paley treats crucial issues in her stories from her essays. In "Faith in a Tree," which has some of the farcical elements we saw in "Faith in the Afternoon," though without their specifically Jewish context or the black humour of Mrs Darwin's tales of disaster, Faith tells of the PTA man's plan

> to promote the integrated school in such a way that private-school people would think their kids were missing the real thing ... He suggested that one month of public-school attendance might become part of the private-school curriculum, as natural and progressive an experience as a visit to the boiler room in first grade ... Actually something did stir. Delegations of private progressive-school parents attacked the Board of Ed. for what became known as the Shut-out, and finally even the parents-and-teachers associations of the classical schools ... began to consider the value of exposing children who had read about the horror at Ilium to ordinary street fights, so they could understand the Iliad better. Public School (in Manhattan) would become a minor like typing, required but secondary. (185–6)

The downfall attendant on too high aspirations is gentler here than in "Faith in the Afternoon." "Mr Terry Koln, full of initiative, energy, and lightheartedness," growing marijuana on the windowsills of his tiny office, "was the joy of our PTA. But it was soon discovered that he had no children and Kitty and I have to meet him now surreptitiously in bars" (186).

Although it may seem that this vignette has nothing to do with anything, it actually plays an important role in thickening the texture of Faith's life and her subculture. If the story itself seems too farcical to be taken seriously, the issue is not; and Faith's role as one of the fun-loving ladies drinking coffee touched with brandy in the lunchroom and later meeting Terry Koln surreptitiously in bars may remind us of the alliance between irreverent hippies and peaceniks that was an important part of American radical life in the 1960s and 1970s. Faith's irreverent local activities thus help prepare for her turn to international politics at the story's end. Moreover,

Faith's participation in the PTA helps establish her as a socially active member of her community. Though the key is lighter here, Faith's narrative looks forward to her recollection in the later "Friends" (*Later the Same Day*) of how "Our PTA had decided to offer some one-to-one tutorial help for the Spanish kids, who were stuck in crowded classrooms with exhausted teachers among little middle-class achievers" (306). Forbidden to do so by the principal and the Board of Ed., Faith and her friends, "the soft-speaking tough souls of anarchy," simply ignored the voice of authority. "I had Fridays off that year. At about 11 a.m. I'd bypass the principal's office and run up to the fourth floor. I'd take Robert Figueroa to the end of the hall, and we'd work away at storytelling ... Then we would write the beautiful letters of the alphabet invented by smart foreigners long ago to fool time and distance" (307). The slapstick element is gone from the later story, but in both "Friends" and "Faith in a Tree" Faith demonstrates the same commitment to what, in her essays, Paley refers to as "the importance of *not* asking permission" (*Just as I Thought*, 158).

But it is above all in relation to her sons that Faith manifests her self-confident disregard for authority in "Tree." She is "not the least bit ashamed to say that I tie their shoes and I have wiped their backsides well beyond the recommendations of my friends, Ellen and George Hellesbraun, who are psychiatric social workers and appalled" (177). It did not take much to appall the Childrearing Authorities when Paley imagined Faith into life. From her first appearance with two husbands disappointed by eggs, Faith is placed in a world only too ready to blame mother. The imagined world corresponds to the one Paley knew. "In my generation particularly we were really sad a lot because we felt a lot was our fault. The psychology of our life period has enforced that. If there was trouble with the kids and we went to a psychiatrist we were told, 'you're damn right, it's your fault.'"[27] In "Other Mothers" Paley notes the collusion of (male-dominated) literature and psychology in the villainization of the (particularly Jewish) mother: "Science and literature had turned against her. What use was my accumulating affection when the brains of the opposition included her son the doctor and her son the novelist?" (*Just as I Thought*, 38–9).[28] If this was the lot of all (Jewish) mothers, the single mother was viewed as particularly inadequate. Yet despite the loud chorus of blame and disapproval, Faith blithely follows her own maternal instincts. "I kiss those kids forty times a day. I punch them just like a father should." Ignoring the Authorities, and no longer the overwhelmed single mother she describes herself as being in "Living," she relates to her sons in a spirit of energetic loving *camaraderie*. "When I have a date and come home late at night, I wake them with a couple of good hard shakes to complain about the miserable entertainment. When I'm not furiously exhausted from my low-level job and that bedraggled soot-slimy house, I praise God for them" (178). Isaacs' view that Faith's "sexual urges" "undercut" or "conflict" with her "concerns with child raising and PTA-related politics" thus seems off the mark. Faith's sexual energy is part of her full humanity; it informs all areas of her life. Though she has an occasional twinge of sadness at the reminder that her children may indeed be deprived – seeing her son Richard holding the hand of the new man in the park, "which made Richard look like a little boy with a daddy," she reflects, "I could cry when I think that I always treat Richard as though he's about forty-seven" (189) – she enjoys the companionship of her children and remains fundamentally free from inner conflict, as from guilt and worry. Richard may at times be fresh and back-talky, but he is also a buddy and she is not too proud to learn from him at the end. Indeed, one can argue that Faith represents a kind of cultural ideal of quirky, feisty, resilient motherhood, especially single motherhood, rather than a psychologically fully credible character – which is doubtless part of her appeal to many women readers. Not until *Later the Same Day* does Faith begin to experience the anxiety about her children that Paley has acknowledged as so prevalent among Faith's real-life sisters.[29]

At the end of "Faith in a Tree," after narrating that Richard's chalk-written imitation of the peace demonstrators' placards ("WOULD YOU BURN A CHILD? WHEN NECESSARY") marks the moment "when events turned me around," Faith continues, "changing my hairdo, my job uptown, my style of living and telling" (194). Hairdos are regularly ignored in Paley's stories, and we know no more about Faith's current job than that it is "low-level" (178), but the change in Faith's "style of living and telling," particularly the last item, invites reflection. The changed style of living clearly leads into her thinking "more and more every day about the world," thereby implying, as critics have noted, a more focused (if not entirely new) interest in her country's international activities. But her style of telling? Though Paley regularly speaks of writers as storytellers, this does not imply that all storytellers are writers. Although Faith will indeed be revealed as a writer at the end of the last story in this collection, at this point in the construction of her character there is not yet any indication that Faith is more than a writer of private notes and journals (182). But whether we imagine her narrated stories as spoken aloud or only to herself, her style of telling does change after this. Or rather, "Faith in a Tree" is Faith's first and last venture into this kind of rambling, associative, interior monologue that takes precedence over her exchanges with others (though others sometimes respond to her thoughts as though she had spoken them). In subsequent stories, Faith's interactions with others and her recording of their words will play a much larger role, her private interior dramas a much smaller one.

Seeing and Hearing the Other. Slippery Identities

Indeed, in two stories placed after "Faith in a Tree" and (presumably) narrated by Faith, her own role has shrunk considerably. In "Northeast Playground" it is minimal; a somewhat older Faith tells of eleven unwed mothers she meets in the playground, foregrounding her description of them and minimizing her own presence. Her contribution is limited to questioning two depressed mothers about whether they and their babies might be better off mixing with the other mothers and babies and then attempting to relate to these women across a wide cultural divide: "Then I stated: In a way it was like this when my children were little babies. The ladies who once wore *I Like Ike* buttons sat on the south side of the sandbox and the rest of us who were revisionist Communist and revisionist Trotskyite and revisionist Zionist registered Democrats sat on the north side" (225). While her comment helps place the narrator in her time and political culture, her own interest is in the mothers. We learn that Faith has been the narrator of this story only near the end of the subsequent "Long-Distance Runner," when she stops "at the northeast playground where I met a dozen young mothers intelligently handling their little ones. In order to prepare them, meaning no harm, I said, In fifteen years, you girls will be like me, wrong in everything" (256). This statement, together with her narrative approach in "Northeast Playground," reveals a somewhat more chastened Faith, less self-confident about urging her own views, more interested in observing *other* lives. In "The Immigrant Story," her narration takes the form of a dialogue with Jack that ultimately gives way to Jack's monologue, which she simply records without comment. We may infer that the narrator here is Faith because she is juxtaposed with Jack who, from this point on, often appears as Faith's old friend and recurrent lover; but she is never specifically named.

In interviews Paley frequently brings up "The Immigrant Story" as an example of the mysterious process of composition, illustrating her reiterated point that "the form is given by grace."[30] She describes how she had a story in her mind for "maybe twenty-five years" before figuring out "how to tell it"; then one day, going through her drawers, she came upon "two pages of dialogue, rather abstract dialogue ... and I understood how to tell that story."[31] These pages become the opening dialogue between Jack and the narrator (tentatively, Faith) that juxtaposes two ways of looking at the world. Jack, whose head, according to Faith, has "been fermenting with the compost of ten years of gluttonous analysis" (239), views the world psychologically; Faith, "one of [whose] known themes" is the "cruel history of Europe" (238), views it historically.[32] There is also a stark difference in temperament. Jack has grown up "in the shadow of another person's sorrow" (his parents'), while Faith "grew up in the summer sunlight of upward mobility" that "leached out a lot of that dark ancestral grief" (238). Their differences of intellectual orientation and temperament result in totally different explanations of a specific childhood memory of Jack's, his once finding his father sleeping in the crib. Additionally, while Faith and Jack have grown up in the same neighbourhood, their memories of it differ considerably, Faith's being coloured by her family's relative prosperity and her own "rosy temperament" (239), Jack's by his family's poverty and his grim awareness of the suffering around him.

This kind of dialogic conflict of worldviews may be familiar to readers of "A Conversation with My Father," in which a writer-narrator (not Faith, Paley tells us) is challenged by her father when she constructs a happy "open destiny" for a woman in a story she tells him. The ideological conflict between father and daughter here is also an historical, or generational, one. The father represents the Old World view, in which human destinies are determined early, and for life; the writer-daughter, child of the New World, adheres to an ideology in which change is always possible, destinies always open.

But whereas in "A Conversation with My Father" the father's and daughter's points of view seem neatly balanced, with neither antagonist willing – or needing – to concede (allowing of course for the irony of the ailing father's almost already sealed destiny), the dialogue between Faith and Jack in "The Immigrant Story" gives way asymmetrically at the end to an extended monologue. Just before this, it seems that Faith is about to give herself the last – and best – word in their dialogue: "I believe I see the world as clearly as you do ... Rosiness is not a worse windowpane than gloomy gray when viewing the world." Jack's reply, "Yes yes yes yes yes yes yes ... Do you mind? Just listen," then introduces his narration of his parents' heart-rending immigrant tale – his father's emigration from Poland to America ahead of his wife and three sons, his solitary but hopeful life on the Lower East Side, famine in Poland, his father's meeting his wife at the boat when she arrives without the sons. His parents' misery is forever etched in Jack's mind, as his narrative slides from the past, in which they cling to each other in shared sorrow at their unspeakable loss, to a perpetual present, in which "They are sitting at the edge of their chairs. He's leaning forward reading to her in that old bulb light ... he puts the paper down and takes both her hands in his as though they needed warmth ... " and then subtly slips back from present to past, as the darkness of Jack's solitary childhood merges with its haunting memory: "Just beyond the table and their heads, there is the darkness of the kitchen, the bedroom, the dining-room, the shadowy darkness where as a child I ate my supper, did my homework, and went to bed" (240–1). However rosy her temperament, when confronted with the horror of Jack's past – the *reality* of "the cruel history of Europe," which she is so ready to talk about in the abstract – Faith is reduced to silence.

Later Faith stories also juxtapose her more upbeat outlook with Jack's grim surliness. (In "Friends," from *Later the Same Day*, her son Richard, calling long distance, asks, "How's your new boyfriend, did he smile yet?" [305]). While this lends support to our tentative view of Faith as narrator of "The Immigrant Story," such an identification also forces us to recognize a certain slippage between Faith and her author. "Faith in the Afternoon" and "The Long-Distance Runner" both place Faith's childhood roots in Brooklyn; but the narrator of "The Immigrant Story" identifies her childhood home as East 172 Street – not only the Bronx but also the street where Paley herself lived as a girl. Does this mean that we should see the narrator as Paley, rather than Faith? In the case of the first-person narrations of "Debts" and "A Conversation with My Father," Paley has been clear that these are not Faith's stories but "particularly my stories."[33] An additional group of stories draws directly on facts from Paley's life: "Wants," in which the narrator, now married to a second husband, meets her first husband to whom she had been married for twenty-seven years; "Mother" and "In this Country, But in Another Language, My Aunt Refuses to Marry the Men Everyone Wants Her To," in which the facts about the premature death of the narrator's mother and about an aunt's stubborn single status and her warning not to "carry the main flag" in a demonstration because the narrator's seventeen-year-old uncle was killed doing so also correspond to Paley's family experience; and "Love," in which the narrator speaks of her husband's having once been a poet at Harvard, then a shrub buyer for the city, and possessing "north-country fields," all facts that apply to Paley's second husband, Robert Nichols. This is not to imply, of course, that these stories should be understood as literally true (though some of them, like "Mother" may well be) but only that in them Paley is creating her own narrative persona, rather than using a fictional protagonist, like Faith, to do the "work" for her.

In none of Paley's frequent recorded comments on "The Immigrant Story" does she identify its narrator. Viewing the narrator as Paley herself would explain the childhood in the Bronx but creates other problems, for in no other "Paley story" does the narrator interact with fictional characters such as Jack. And unlike Faith, the Paley persona typically relates to husbands rather than lovers (though in "The Immigrant Story," Jack is not clearly the narrator's lover, as he is in the other Faith stories). Our viewing the narrator as Faith enables us to see her interaction with Jack as prototypical of their interactions in the stories that follow; but seeing her as Faith also entails recognizing Paley's kind of metafictional play with her character's identity. This should not overly surprise. The separately published *Enormous Changes at the Last Minute* carries the epigraph "Everyone in this book is imagined into life except the father. No matter what story he has to live in, he's my father, I. Goodside, MD, artist, and storyteller." One father thus lives in three different stories – "A Conversation with My Father," "Faith in the Afternoon," and "Enormous Changes at the Last Minute" – and has, respectively, three different daughters, the Paley persona, Faith Darwin, and Alexandra. By encouraging us to see through the shifting facts of the father's life from story to story to a constant identity, drawn from "real life," Paley is playing with conventions of fictional autonomy and the boundaries between life and fiction, as I am suggesting she is also doing in "The Immigrant Story."[34]

Basic facts about the imagined Jack also seem fluid. If "The Immigrant Story" places his childhood on East 172 Street, in the story immediately following, "The Long-Distance Runner," Faith looks from the window of her former Brooklyn apartment at the "devastation" below to see that the "tenement in which Jack my old and present friend had come to gloomy manhood had been destroyed, first by fire, then by demolition" (251). Jack's childhood moves from Brooklyn back to the Bronx again in "Listening" (*Later the Same Day*), where he describes going with his father, a junk peddler with a pushcart, who "yelled (in Yiddish), Buy old clothes, buy old clothes ... I guess we crawled up and down every street in the Bronx" (384). Jack's father appears very differently from this, however, in "The Story Hearer" (*Later the Same Day*), where his son describes him as "a decent man – your typical nine-to-fiver." His parents' story there is also at odds with the one he tells in "The Immigrant Story." In "The Story Hearer" his mother appears as a sprightly, untraumatized woman who simply walks out on the family one day, kissing her husband and the children (Jack is no longer an only child) goodbye, saying "I'll call you next week, but never did speak to any of us again" (337–8). It is clear, therefore, that while Paley uses many of the same characters from story to story, it would be a mistake to view them as consistent actors in a novel whose transitions have simply been suppressed. Her version of the Balzacian *retour des personnages* allows for far greater liberties, more room for play, than the novelist's. Jack's gloom, like his recurring role in Faith's life, is repeated from story to story; but Paley seems sublimely unconcerned with making the causes for it constant.

Faith is unambiguously identified as the narrator and Jack as her lover in the last story of the second collection, in which she sets off buoyantly in silk shorts and an undershirt, undeterred by being stout and middle-aged, to become "The Long-Distance Runner." But while her neighbour Mrs Raftery refers to Jack as Faith's boyfriend at the beginning of the story, she does so only to observe that he hasn't called. Faith herself does not seem at all concerned by Jack's absence, from which we may infer that she has moved beyond her earlier attitude in "Faith in a Tree," where she is on the lookout and jokingly comments, "I have always required a man to be dependent on, even when it appeared I had one already" (177) – though part of that joke is that she does *not* have a man. Asking Mrs Raftery to look in now and then on her almost grown-up sons, Faith sets off on her run without a thought for the absent Jack. He makes an actual appearance ("looking as grim as ever," 256) only near the end, after the bulk of the story – and Faith's adventure – is over.

Mrs Raftery makes only a cameo appearance in this story; yet her presence is striking because it forges an unexpected link between this Faith story and two earlier stories by Paley that have nothing to do with Faith, in which Mrs Raftery has appeared: "An Interest in Life," from Paley's first collection (*The Little Disturbances of Man*) and "Distance" in the second (*Enormous Changes at the Last Minute*). The link is especially surprising because referring to Mrs Raftery here in "The Long-Distance Runner," Faith casually speaks of "how she got liked by me, loved, invented and endured" (243). In this sudden metafictional move, Faith for the first time clearly suggests her status as a writer, and specifically a writer who is the inventor of her own story(ies) and of other stories by Paley in which Faith herself plays no role. The glimpse Faith offers of her role as both maker and subject is a fleeting one, however, as she quickly leaves Mrs Raftery and her own sons behind to set off on an adventure that is decidedly modest in scope.

After spring training in Connecticut, Faith takes the Independent subway to Brighton Beach and runs through her old neighbourhood. Her interactions with its more recent African-American inhabitants exemplify both the limitations and the strengths of liberal good will. Just when Faith seems to have achieved a friendly rapport with a Girl Scout who accompanies her to her old building, the girl misinterprets Faith's well-intentioned offer of future hospitality as a kidnapping threat and screams for help, causing a terrified Faith to seek refuge in her old apartment from "the large boys" she hears charging up the stairs to the girl's rescue. For three weeks Faith remains in her old apartment with its current inhabitants, Mrs Luddy, her son Donald, and three little baby girls, becoming fearful whenever she contemplates leaving. "Despite my wide geographical love of mankind, I would be attacked by local fears" (250). These fears do not penetrate to the apartment, however, where she is able to forge tenuous bonds of human kinship across the lines of race and class. Paley achieves a delicate balance between Faith's good intentions and genuine affection for the Luddys and the naivety of her judgments and advice. Observing the devastation of the urban landscape she fondly remembers as once having been very different, Faith comments, "Someone ought to clean that up." Mrs Luddy's caustic response shows a more seasoned realism: "Who you got in mind? Mrs Kennedy?" (251). With equal simplicity Faith presumes to advise Mrs Luddy that Donald should go down and "play with the other kids" (252), without reflecting that by keeping him indoors Mrs Luddy is deliberately keeping him out of harm and trouble. Faith's assumption that she should bring Donald "up to reading level at once" is similarly revealed as ill founded, if well intentioned; he turns out to be an experienced reader who goes to his neighbourhood library to bring "some hard books to amuse me" (253) and demonstrates a wonderful gift for composing poetry. Nonetheless, sharing household and childcare tasks, talk of men, children and family, and fears of life outside the apartment, Faith and Mrs Luddy do achieve a limited measure of sisterhood before Mrs Luddy abruptly announces that it's time for Faith to leave.

Despite Faith's proudly described preparations as a long-distance runner at the outset, her actual journey has not taken her much beyond a convenient subway stop. Her departure from home just as her sons are on the verge of manhood has, in fact, led her back to two earlier familiar stages of her domestic life, her childhood in her old apartment and the demanding activities of a single mother of small children (rising at 6:30 to give the babies their bottles, etc.). Back once more in her adult home at the end (in keeping with the surrealistic fantasy element of her experience, she runs all the way home – after three weeks indoors – though her outbound trip had begun with a subway ride), she is unable to communicate her adventure to her uncomprehending sons and the recently returned Jack. After three failed attempts she addresses the reader, summarizing her story in the third person. "A woman inside the steamy energy of middle age runs and runs. She finds the houses and streets where her childhood happened. She lives in them. She learns as though she was still a child what in the world is coming next" (257). Placed at the end of the last story of the collection, this promise encourages us to look forward to Paley's future stories, while it remains tantalizing in its lack of specificity. If Faith has learned from her journey to her geographical and temporal past what the future holds in store, the reader is still left to wonder what that is. In a most literal sense, beyond the transformation of a whole culture into runners, which she also records, "what in the world is coming next" could refer to demographic changes in her city, where many once-Jewish neighbourhoods have become predominantly African-American. It could point, too, to greater future interaction between ethnic groups, perhaps including not only Faith's ready acceptance of the other but maybe also, less comfortingly, their distrust and suspicion of her. On a more personal level it might also promise a newly invigorated Faith, embarking on a more independent stage of life.

What Paley almost certainly did not intend to include in this preview of the future is what we glimpse from the two-page coda that concludes the story. But it too points forward, probably in unanticipated ways, to what is coming. Back home Faith finds Jack and Richard "playing ticktacktoe on the dusty wall" and her younger son, Anthony, about to leave; "Oh yes, I said. Of course. Every Saturday he hurries through breakfast or misses it. He goes to visit his friends in institutions. These are well-known places like Bellevue, Hillside, Rockland State, Central Islip, Manhattan. These visits take him all day and sometimes half the night" (256). Jack sets off on his bike for Central Park, assuming it is closed to cars but open to cyclists. "When he'd been gone about ten minutes Anthony said, It's really open only on Sundays." After expressing annoyance at her son's failure to have communicated this crucial information to Jack, Faith – ever the mother – suggests that Anthony too should get exercise. "I'm too busy, he said. I have to see my friends" (257). Richard hands his brother a note "for Judy, if you get as far as Rockland." Faith makes her first attempt to tell Richard where's she's been. Then "Anthony came home earlier than expected that evening because some people were in shock therapy and someone else had run away" (258). Faith tries twice more to tell her adventure to all three men and then ends with the summary we have already seen.

This coda completes the frame, bringing us back to the apartment and family Faith left behind when she set off at the beginning. But it also introduces a new element that is not only disturbing in itself but somehow tonally at odds with the rest of the story. It is not surprising that while many critics have discussed this story with sensitive appreciation, none has seriously considered this closing episode.[35] For it is not easy to know how to accommodate this kind of black humour in a tale that otherwise treats with comic grace the serious issues of urban blight, changing demographics, relations between Jews and African-Americans and the restorative value of visiting even an altered childhood past. Considered realistically, the image of Anthony, not yet fully out of adolescence, spending every Saturday visiting his friends who are all at mental institutions in and around New York City, too busy to consider exercise or other recreation, is remarkably grim. But despite the horror of the objective situation, we are kept at too great a distance to read this as other than a very funny display of macabre black humour. The irreverence of this kind of humour brings us back to the world of hyperbolic misfortune we saw in Mrs Darwin's tales of disaster in "Faith in the Afternoon." But whereas those stories emphasized the magnitude of the calamities, here the objective plight of Anthony's friends is deliberately understated. Faith's undramatizing narrative mixes information about her son's routine visits with the lighter humour of his ungenerous silence to his mother's boyfriend about the traffic-closing schedule in Central Park. Her deadpan narration and matter-of-fact acceptance of Anthony's regular Saturday activity, her casual listing of no fewer than five well-known institutions, Richard's offhanded passing on of a note to a friend of his as well, and the absolute flatness of her explanation for Anthony's early return preclude any reader involvement in the human dramas taking place off stage.

Nonetheless, if Anthony's friends, like the actors in Mrs Darwin's horror stories, remain out of view, his own visiting routine enters more directly into Faith's world, and hence into ours, since Anthony (Tonto) has been a tangible presence for us since "A Subject of Childhood" in Paley's first collection. We have just seen that potential danger lies in wait for the children in Faith's old neighbourhood. Before meeting Mrs Luddy, who keeps Donald from playing outside, we have met the Girl Scout Cynthia, whose eyes tear over at Faith's mention that her mother is dead, as she immediately imagines how defenceless *she* would be if *her* mother died; "what would I do? She is my protector, she won't let the pushers get me. She hold me tight" (248). Yet the reader is well aware that no amount of mother love can ensure safety for Cynthia or Donald. Paley's world has always been a risky place for children. Her first collection has one story ("In Time Which Made a Monkey of Us All") about a "[kid] who dropped out of sanity even then" (Hulley, "Interview," 41); in her second collection, "A Conversation with My Father" features an adolescent boy who becomes a junkie, though he is fortunately reclaimed, and there are two haunting stories about the terrible, violent deaths of children ("Samuel" and "The Little Girl"). These disasters, however, are kept separate from Faith's world. In this final story of the collection, while Faith's own children remain unscathed, we see one kind of menace threatening children within its pages and another hovering around its edge. In Paley's next and most recent collection of stories, however, the multifold dangers menacing the children become a major undercurrent and enter into the Faith stories in a more immediate way. There, as in "The Long-Distance Runner," passage from childhood to adulthood is revealed as as tricky and perilous as crossing a minefield. Few of the children of Faith's friends, as here none of the friends of Faith's children, succeed in making it safely across.

LATER THE SAME DAY AND "MIDRASH ON HAPPINESS"

A Second Visit. A Jewish Joke

Faith appears in more stories in *Later the Same Day* than in previous collections, and with one exception her appearances have a somewhat different colouration. In some, like "Friends," "Ruthy and Edie," and "Zagrowsky Tells," she is presented as one of a group, with people around her playing more prominent roles. In the last two of these, she is, for the first time, neither the narrator nor a central player. Where she does appear as narrator in "The Story Hearer" and "Listening," one of her main roles, as the titles suggest, is to listen to and tell the stories of others. Indeed, "The Story Hearer" opens with her declaration, "I am trying to curb my cultivated individualism, which seemed for years so sweet. It was my own song in my own world and, of course, it may not be useful in the hard time to come" (337). Many of the stories in which she appears here jump around in time and place and are made up of more separate strands than stories in the previous collections, often seeming more episodic, or mosaic, in structure. Clara Claiborne Park's description of them as a "a web, a tapestry, something woven or embroidered, or a patchwork"[36] is apt, though "patchwork" may obscure the extent to which they are actually tonally more unified and less dissonant than some of the earlier ones we have considered. Moreover, in all of the stories just mentioned, as well as "Anxiety" and "The Expensive Moment," Faith is more consistently politically and socially engaged than previously, involved in causes both local and international. And, as the title of the collection implies, Faith is older, which often means she has witnessed losses even rougher than that of Ricardo's love (though "Living" in *Enormous Changes at the Last Minute* has already recorded the death of a friend).

"Dreamer in a Dead Language" is something of an exception to these generalizations, as a sharply focused third-person narrative in which Faith is indisputably the principal character. To be sure, in keeping with the episodic structure of the later stories, it begins in a tavern with a conversation among Faith, Jack, and Faith's new lover, Philip Mazzano (in "Faith in a Tree," the man in the park who showed greater interest in Faith's friend), then jumps to Faith's kitchen, where she is alone with Philip (now a budding publishing entrepreneur, interested in publishing the poetry of Faith's father, Sid Darwin)[37] and from there to the Children of Judea Home for the Golden Ages, after which it closes with a coda on Brighton Beach. Once the story settles into Faith's visit to Children of Judea, however, it becomes a kind of *reprise* of "Faith in the Afternoon," with the familiar father, mother, and obnoxious Mrs Hegel-Shtein. But Faith is older here, as are her sons who now accompany her, though all three are younger than in "The Long-Distance Runner," which concludes the previous collection. She is also considerably tougher, more self-confident, and makes this visit from a position of relative strength and security, having two lovers in the background. Yet the story itself is considerably darker than "Faith in the Afternoon," where she was frankly miserable. While still comic, it lacks the broad "Jewish humour" provided by Mrs Darwin's grim tales during Faith's earlier visit; and there are continual reminders of the perils and indignities of age, starting with the observant Richard's thrice-posed question, "Is this a hospital?" (269–70), through Faith's glimpse of the sixth-floor ward, where the elevator door once opened by mistake on the "incurables," to Mr Darwin's accounts of how people's brains are disappearing all around him. Although this prompts Faith's outcry, "I can't stand your being here"

(276), she is hardly prepared for her father's confidence that he too feels young and out of place there, wants to leave, and would divorce her mother if not for the thorny problem that they were never properly married, having been "idealists." While close to his Old World Jewish roots in some respects, Mr Darwin is nonetheless now thoroughly American in his sense of entitlement to the pursuit of happiness and his belief (so foreign to the father of "A Conversation with My Father") in the possibility of new beginnings. Having learned that her ex-husband Ricardo has visited her father (like Philip, with an entrepreneurial eye on Mr Darwin's poetry), a horrified Faith suddenly sees the two men as similar male egocentrics; Ricardo too, she scoffs, was "an idealist," who had left her and the children in the belief that "for him somewhere, something perfect existed" (279). Shocking her father with the announcement that she currently has three lovers (the reader can account for only two), Faith hastily collects her sons and leaves.

If her sense of gender identifications seems newly responsible for Faith's feeling of separation from her father here, more familiar generational differences between father and daughter have also made themselves felt earlier in the story. As Mrs Darwin's tales of superlative disaster in "Faith in the Afternoon" exploited a kind of Jewish humour in a linguistic register different from that used by and about Faith, humour functions again in "Dreamer in a Dead Language" as a marker of difference between the generations. Less effortlessly than his wife during Faith's previous visit, Mr Darwin here introduces another, more well meaning example of Jewish humour. He tells a "good joke" about an old Jew who goes to a tourist office in Germany in "maybe '39 or '40," looking for a place to go. Whatever country on the globe the Jew points to, the agent tells him, "Sorry, no, they got finished up with their quota ... Last train left already for there ... absolutely nobody they let in there at the present time ... port is closed ... already too many ... no boats ... So finally the poor Jew, he's thinking he can't go anywhere on the globe, also he can't stay where he is ... He pushes the globe away, disgusted. But he got hope. He says, So this one is used up, Herr Agent. Listen – you got another one?" (271).

This joke is no less an example of Jewish humour than Faith's mother's anecdotes on her previous visit, but the mechanisms at work in it are different; they are far subtler than in Mrs Darwin's stories of calamitous ruin attendant on superlative good fortune. In

Mr Darwin's "joke," catastrophe is already clearly in view at the outset; it will not take anyone by surprise. Instead, the humour here derives from the Jew's linguistic response to it. Although Faith finds none of her mother's stories funny (nor are they intended to be), she is actively repelled by the joke her father tells: "What a terrible thing. What's funny about that? I hate that joke." In fact, the joke functions as a kind of Rorschach test, revealing generational differences, and also personal ones. Faith's older son, Richard, eager to prove his sophistication and impress his grandfather, proudly announces, "I get it ... There is no other globe. Only one globe, Mommy? He had no place to go. On account of that old Hitler." And he asks to have the joke repeated so he can tell his class. The younger Tonto, always more concerned with being supportive of his mother, says, "I don't think it's so funny either" (271). To the American-born Faith, joking about something as catastrophic as the imminent destruction of European Jewry is highly offensive, and all the more so in the light of her family history. For at the end of the story, when she has fled with her sons to Brighton Beach, Faith tells them about her grandfather whom she never knew, who lived way up north on the Baltic Sea and used to skate for miles and miles with a frozen herring in his pocket. "They say he tried to come. There was no boat. It was too late. That's why I never laugh at that story Grandpa tells."

If Faith's response is easy for North American readers to understand, we are still left with Richard's question, "Why does Grandpa laugh?" (282). Paley's own comment on this is tantalizingly sketchy. She observes that a lot of her humour "is Jewish, plain old Jewish humor from around. Where the Jews make these jokes in which they are presumably the butt ... But they're not. Like the joke Faith's father makes in that story where he says, 'Give me another globe.' That's a typical joke, where the Jew says, 'Well, it's probably my fault, but still, give me another globe.'"[38] Paley's point that the Jew only seems to be the butt but is not bears reflection. Our understanding of the joke may vary, depending on how realistic we believe the Jew's retention of hope to be. Jacqueline Taylor appears to recognize that hope is the crux of the matter, but she is somewhat vague about whether the circumstances justify it. "The Jew of this story is in a seemingly hopeless situation and yet he has hope. In one sense he is the butt of the joke, for his request for another globe is absurd. Yet in another sense he gives testimony to the strength of the spirit that has enabled Jewish people to survive through centuries of vicious anti-Semitism."[39] The last part of Taylor's claim is certainly true, and, moreover, those Jews who managed to escape from Hitler's Europe often did so in extraordinary and improbable ways; but it is also true that the Shoah claimed millions of Jewish lives. Ruth Wisse's discussion of Old World Jewish humour as embodied in the *shtetl* figure of the schlemiel may better help us understand this later example of it. "Outrageous and absurd as his innocence may be by the normal guidelines of political reality, the Jew is simply rational within the context of ideal humanism. He is a fool, seriously – maybe even fatally – out of step with the actual march of events. Yet the impulse of the joke, and of shlemiel literature in general, is to use this comical stance as a stage from which to challenge the political and philosophic status quo"[40] Certainly, the political and philosophical status quo is challenged by Mr Darwin's joke, but it does not tell us whether the Jew will become a canny survivor or remain the schlemiel, "the practical loser, winning only an ironic victory of interpretation."[41] Wisse's description of the impulse behind Sholem Aleichem's humour seems apt here: "a solace for people whose situation was so ineluctably unpleasant that they might as well laugh."[42] Particularly helpful is the analysis she cites by Maurice Samuel of the mechanisms at work in the Jews' "trick of converting disaster into a verbal triumph, applying a sort of Talmudic ingenuity of interpretation to events they could not handle in their reality. They turned the tables on their adversaries dialectically, and though their physical disadvantages were not diminished thereby, nor the external situation changed one whit, they emerged with a feeling of victory."[43] Mr Darwin's joke is bound to highlight a profound cultural gap between himself and his daughter, as the Old World Jewish humour of his story of verbal triumph in the face of catastrophe could scarcely be more alien to an American "raised up ... to the true assumption of happiness" (148).

While Faith's anguish in the earlier "Faith in the Afternoon" had been for herself, at the end of this story it is for her parents and, more specifically, her father's newly flowering egocentricity. Once again she is presented as overwhelmed by the circumstances of her life but no longer because of her role as abandoned wife or single mother. As at the conclusion of "Faith in a Tree," at the end of "Dreamer in a Dead Language" her son Richard again calls her to account. "Mom, you have to get them out of there. It's your mother and father. It's your responsibility." In vain she assures him they like it there, then asks, "Why is everything my responsibility, every goddamn thing?"

> It just is, said Richard. Faith looked up and down the beach. She wanted to scream, Help!
>
> Had she been born ten, fifteen years later, she might have done so, screamed and screamed. (283)

The author's frame-breaking flash-forward unexpectedly involves her current-day reader in the plight of her sandwich-generation heroine from an earlier, prefeminist time, before women allowed themselves to scream when demands on them became too overwhelming. Yet if Faith's son fails to provide the sympathy she craves, innocently demanding that she perform the impossible, it is still notable that her children, even here, remain a source of comfort and support. As the story concludes, with Faith lying in the sand, encouraging her sons to bury her, but only partially so that her arms remain free to give them "a good whack every now and then when [they're] too fresh" (283), we are left with the remarkable literary presence of an emotionally balanced, guilt-free mother, who may be filled with worry for her parents but remains lucky in temperament and, unlike her friends in the stories that follow, lucky in her children and her rapport with them.

Grief and Anxiety for the Children

As Faith retreats from her central position in the stories that follow "Dreamer in a Dead Language," parents who have been less fortunate with their children come to the fore. "Friends" is a story doing several things at once. It is sometimes described by Paley as "really about grief for the children,"[44] at other times as memorializing a dying friend and "the whole group of women" friends (of whom Faith is only one) and, at the same time, telling the story of "a kind of quarrel and dissolution of a friendship" between two of them.[45] Since the friends constitute a community of mothers who have shared experiences of childraising from the time their babies first stepped out of the sandbox, their children's fates are inextricable from their own; so the talk on the afternoon of the friends' last visit to the dying Selena in this story is all about their children. No longer isolated in separate stories as in the previous collections, "that beloved generation of our children murdered by cars, lost to war, to drugs, to madness" (303) here enters directly into Faith's world, as is evident in her use of the first-person-plural pronoun, even though her own sons are doing well. We learn on the first page of "Friends" that Abby, Selena's daughter, was found dead one night in a rooming-house in a distant city. Faith acknowledges her own good luck but only to the reader; when Selena asks what Richard is doing, she feigns ignorance: "Who knows where he is? They're all the same"; then she confesses to the reader, "Why did I say that? I knew exactly where he was ... It was only politeness, I think, not to pour my boy's light, noisy face into that dark afternoon" (305).

On the five-hour train ride back to New York City, Faith is verbally attacked for her good fortune by Ann, another mother of "that beloved generation of our children": "Do you realize I don't know where Mickey is? You know, you've been lucky. You always have been." Faith rightly recognizes, "Luck – isn't it something like an insult?" and yet also that "truthfully nothing in my life can compare to hers: a son, a boy of fifteen, who disappears before your very eyes into a darkness or a light behind his own, from which neither hugging nor hitting can bring him back" (308–9). Later in the ride, puncturing the optimism of a younger friend who looks forward to an improved life in two years, Ann comments, "Two years! In two years we'll all be dead"; but Faith reflects, "I know she didn't mean all of us. She meant Mickey. That boy of hers would surely be killed in one of the drugstores or whorehouses of Chicago, New Orleans, San Francisco." In the interim "he'd be picked up for vagrancy, dealing, small thievery, or simply screaming dirty words at night under a citizen's window. Then Ann would fly to the town or not fly to the town to disentangle him, depending on a confluence of financial reality and psychiatric advice" (311). Psychiatric advice is never very helpful in Paley's world. In answer to Selena's question "How did it start?" Ann can reply only with a mother's despair: "Nobody knows, nobody knows anything. Why? Where? Everybody has an idea, theories, and writes articles. Nobody knows" (312). Her calling Faith lucky may have been intended as an insult, but the story does not contradict Ann's judgment. It is, in fact, echoed in Paley's poem "Luck," where the speaker, in a situation remarkably similar to Faith's in relation to Ann, is confronted by a friend who similarly calls her lucky:

... what she means
is her life is hard the man's
far off the boy's mad

The speaker jokes, assures her friend (as Faith does Ann in the story), "there's time for me to be to-/tally wrecked," then tells the reader,

  I grab her grief
jam it into the grief pack between
my shoulders

While the speaker thus, in some sense, bears her friend's grief ("when my head/turns right or left I know it"), it can never truly displace her own good fortune, even if it encroaches on it:

She laughs mentions God throws
Her life up in the sky
In fearful sleep I see it a
Darkness widening among my
Lucky stars (*Begin Again* 171)

Indeed, the worst news Faith has to face when she returns home is that Richard has called collect from Paris. Anthony makes her herbal tea and asks with youthful self-confidence, "How come Selena never realized about Abby?" To which a more seasoned Faith responds, "You don't know yet what their times can do to a person" (314).

The times exert a different kind of toll on the daughter of Faith's friend Ruth from the drugs and madness that have claimed the children of Selena and Ann in "Friends." Like Abby and Mickey there, Ruth's daughter Rachel makes herself felt through her absence in two of the stories that follow. Rachel's absence, however, is tied to her political activism. She first fails to appear at Ruth's fiftieth birthday party in "Ruthy and Edie," a third-person narrative in which Faith, again one of a small group of friends, is an almost invisible narrator who plays an even more limited role than in "Friends." Though the story opens with a childhood episode in the friendship of Ruthy and Edie and then moves to the current birthday party, presenting the women's friendship and their shared history of activism, Ruth's preoccupation with her absent daughter runs through it like a dark undercurrent. To her first expression of worry – "She was supposed to be here last night. She does usually call. Where the hell is she?" – Ann suggests that Rachel is "probably in jail for some stupid little sit-in or something," adding, "You brought her up like that and now you're surprised" (331). When at the end of the story Ruth's other daughter appears with her husband and their child, the granddaughter asks, "Where's my Aunt Rachel? ... She's supposed to be here. Mommy, you promised" (334). "Yes," Ruth concurs. "She is supposed to be here. But where can she be?"

Whatever was "supposed" of Rachel at the time of "Ruthy and Edie," in "The Expensive Moment" Rachel's disappearance from the family circle is presented as being of long standing. Ruth voices appreciation of Jack because "he's the only one who ever asks me anymore about Rachel" (366). But it seems probable that Jack's questions are intended mainly as expressions of sympathetic interest, since Ruth apparently has little direct knowledge of her daughter's whereabouts. "This Rachel of Ruth and Joe's had grown from girl to woman in far absence, making little personal waves from time to time in the newspapers or in rumor which would finally reach her parents on the shores of their always waiting – that is, the office mailbox or the eleven o'clock news" (372). We are never told what Rachel has done to have caused her to go underground, or what deeds are ascribed to her in the newspapers or on the late news. But since we know the times to which she belongs, we draw on our own knowledge and memories of what other earnest if misguided young people were doing then to force them into hiding, thus amplifying the resonance around Ruth's invisible daughter.[46]

Rachel's disappearance is thus less mysterious than the withdrawal to drugs and madness of Abby and Mickey, since it grows out of recognizable political engagement. All the stories in *Later the Same Day*, with the exception of "Dreamer in a Dead Language," contain at least glimpses of the political and social activism of Faith and her friends, from their persistence in tutoring less-privileged children in the face of opposition from the school principal and the Board of Education in "Friends" to their fond recollection of a demonstration in front of the draft board and especially Ruth's courage in standing up to the rearing horses in "The Expensive Moment." In "The Story Hearer" we learn that Faith is a participant in the ongoing lettuce boycott and that in post-narrative time she will abandon her longstanding friendly grocer over Chilean plums. "Listening" opens with Faith mimeographing and collating anti-war pamphlets and leaflets in a church basement, one of which she subsequently passes to a soldier at the Art Foods Deli, and later in the story she leaves Richard and Jack at the kitchen table as she goes out to a meeting. Without ever occupying centre stage, politics is nonetheless a constituent part of the lives of Paley's characters, as of their daily talk.[47] Though Faith and her friends are committed to *non-violent* protest, it is still hardly surprising that their children should, even if less pacifically, be politically engaged. Thus, in "The Expensive Moment," with the example of Rachel in the background, and prompted by a lively political exchange with her son Richard, Faith contemplates – for the first time that the reader sees – the terrifying possibilities that could conceivably be her own child's lot: "Faith thought, what if history should seize him as it had actually taken Ruth's daughter Rachel when her face was still round as an apple; a moment in history, the expensive moment when everyone his age is called but just a few are chosen by conscience or passion or even love of one's own agemates, and they are the ones who smash an important nosecone (as has been recently done) or blow up some buildings full of oppressive money or murderous military plans; but, oh, what if a human creature (maybe rotten to the core but a living person still) is in it?" (370–1). Faith's echoing and reworking of the New Testament phrase "Many are called, but few are chosen" (Matthew 22:14) is only partly ironic. In the New Testament parable, the kingdom of heaven is likened to a king who invites guests to his son's wedding feast. But they fail to come and others are chosen in their stead. In Faith's reformulation, "everyone his age is called," because the evils perpetrated by the US military-industrial complex are clearly manifest, and most of all to members of the younger generation. But "just a few are chosen" – not by religious commitment in the New Testament sense but by a secular equivalent, "conscience or passion or even love of one's own agemates." Faith's generous assessment is able to see through the terrible violence they commit, without condoning it, to the moral passion that unleashed it, capturing at once the folly, idealism, and destructiveness of these young people who earnestly believe they are serving a higher cause. Here, as elsewhere in Faith's thoughts, actions and attitudes are set in their specific historical context. It is this particular "moment in history" (one automatically assumes, the time of the Vietnam War and the domestic anti-war activism it triggered, though this is never specifically mentioned by Paley), when some young people especially sensitive to the violence carried out by their government abroad are led to commit acts of violence at home. The moment is "expensive" because those who are "chosen" will pay dearly for it.[48]

From her imaginings of the terrible violence that her own child or the child of friends might commit (or has committed) and the human impulses behind it, Faith moves to more intimate imaginings of exactly what it would mean to her as a mother if her own child were to be thus seized by history (370–1): "What if they disappear then to live in exile or in the deepest underground and you don't see them for ten years or have to travel to Cuba or Canada or farther to look at their changed faces? Then you think sadly, I could have worked harder at raising that child, the one that was once mine. I could have raised him to become a brilliant economist or finish graduate school or be a lawyer or a doctor maybe. He could have done a lot of good, just as much *that* way, healing or defending the underdog." There is of course much humour in that understated last reflection, but it does not undercut the poignancy of her generous, maternal sympathy.

The same expensive moment has also captivated the interest of Grace Paley's younger contemporary and fellow Jewish-American writer Philip Roth. In his much more extended treatment of a similar situation in *American Pastoral*, Roth also focuses on the point of view of the devastated parents. Meredith ("Merry") Lvov, the "Rimrock Bomber," has blown up a local New Jersey post office and killed a doctor. Her role is akin to that of Ruth's daughter Rachel in Paley's story (though more clearly defined), her disappearance to some shadowy underground existence viewed primarily through its effect on her anguished parents and particularly on her father, the novel's principal subject. "I am thinking of the sixties and of the disorder occasioned by the Vietnam War, of how certain families lost their kids and certain families didn't ... families full of tolerance and kindly, well-intentioned liberal goodwill, and theirs were the kids who went on a rampage, or went to jail, or disappeared underground, or fled to Sweden or Canada. I am thinking of ... how [the father] must have imagined that it was founded on some failure of his own responsibility."[49] While the wider political context evoked by Roth's narrator is recognizably that of Paley's earlier story, his reference to "the kids who went on a rampage" suggests a rather different understanding of it.

Unlike Paley's tight restraint, which relies on the reader to supply the missing information that can contextualize Rachel's disappearance, Roth carefully chronicles the rash of bombings carried out by the disenchanted children of the middle class, conveying a detailed picture of the violence that swept America in the Vietnam years. The more significant difference in their treatments of similar material, however, is Roth's failure to take Meredith's action seriously as political protest. Her action is, in fact, deliberately overdetermined, with political factors seeming to play less of a role than others: she has received an inappropriate kiss from her father, suffers from a stutter, has gotten fat, and, very likely, has sensed something of the tensions in her parents' marriage. Although Meredith is absent from much of the novel, she does finally appear, unlike Rachel, but by that point she has abandoned all political concerns (if she ever truly had any) and become a Jain, a religion presented as conclusive evidence of her "going mad," confirming her father's assessment that "from the moment she had become old enough to think for herself she had been tyrannized ... by the thinking of crackpots."[50] While obviously intent, in some sense, on writing a novel about the politics of the era, Roth chooses to trivialize the political motivation of his terrorist heroine, inviting the reader to share to some extent the complete bafflement of Meredith's non-political father. First presented through the eyes of her unforgiving, censorious uncle, a former classmate and friend of the novel's narrator, Nathan Zuckerman, and then through Zuckerman's own outraged perspective as well as what he imagines to be that of her father, Meredith is repeatedly judged and condemned. Roth's view sees only the unpardonable horror of the terrorist's actions, refusing to acknowledge even a misguided idealism.

In "The Expensive Moment," Faith expresses no condemnation of Rachel (whose deeds are never made explicit), only compassion and sorrow for her mother. Shared concern for the children is an important source of female bonding, constituting a link to another of the story's strands, the Chinese connection. An earlier story in *Later the Same Day*, "Somewhere Else," tells of a trip to China by some of Faith's friends. In "The Expensive Moment" Faith enjoys a vicarious sense of travel through her brief affair with a "famous" and "notably handsome" sinologist; but a more sombre note in the China strand is sounded when Ruth, who has visited China, attends a gathering of Chinese artists in New York and relates to Faith the comments of a Chinese woman who presents the Cultural Revolution from the distinctive – and often overlooked – point of view of a mother. "But she said, well, you can imagine – ... the children ... When the entire working office was sent down to the countryside to dig up stones, she left her daughters with her mother ... It's not so hard to be strong about oneself" (374).[51] Subsequently, Faith meets and befriends this woman, Xie Feng. "She remembered Ruth well. Yes, the lady who hasn't seen her daughter in eight years. Oh, what a sadness. Who would forget that woman. I have known a few" (374). As in "The Long-Distance Runner," and maybe even more easily than there, the two women's shared perspective as mothers cuts through cultural differences. Their friendship, begun in sympathy for Ruth, soon emboldens Xie Feng to ask, "do you notice that in time you love the children more and the man less?" To which Faith first replies, "Yes! But as soon as she said it, she wanted to run home and find Jack and kiss his pink ears and his 243 last hairs, to call out, Old friend, don't worry, you are loved" (375) – a delicately balanced presentation of Faith's ambivalence.

At the end of an afternoon together Xie Feng speaks to Faith more openly about her own life. "Things are a little better now. They get good at home, they get a little bad, then improve. And the men, you know, they were very bad. But now they are better, not all, but some, a few." Then she asks, "do you worry that your older boy is in a political group that isn't liked? What will be his trade? Will he go to university? My eldest is without skills to this day. Her school years happened in the time of great confusion and running about. My youngest studies well" (376). At this point, as Ruth appears in the doorway, Xie Feng begins to ask the harder questions, which may recall the heart-wrenching dilemma expressed by another fictional Chinese woman, Shen Te, in Bertolt Brecht's *Der gute Mensch von Sezuan*. Paley's Xie Feng asks: "Shall we teach them to be straightforward, honorable, kind, brave, maybe shrewd, self-serving a little? What is the best way to help them in the real world? We don't know the best way. You don't want them to be cruel, but you want them to take care of themselves wisely."[52] Like so many mothers, she is filled with self-doubt: "Now my children are nearly grown. Perhaps it's too late. Was I foolish? I didn't know in those years how to do it." Faith first says, "Yes, yes. I know what you mean. Ruthy?" Then, when Ruth remains silent, Faith says "Oh, Xie Feng ... Neither did I" (376–7).

Whether or not Ruth's presence in the background has influenced Faith's expression of uncertainty about her own standards of child-raising, her humility here contrasts sharply with the picture of a somewhat younger and much more self-righteous Faith conveyed in "Zagrowsky Tells." The pharmacist Zagrowsky's narrative may be taken as a darkly comic reflection of the more wrenching stories of madness and destructive political activism that have claimed the children of Faith's friends. The story is told by Zagrowsky to Faith and is not primarily about her.[53] But she plays a crucial role in the history of his daughter Cissy's madness. Cissy's initial breakdown was triggered by the picketing of her father's pharmacy by Faith and her friends in response to Zagrowsky's deliberately slow service to Josie, a Puerto Rican friend of theirs. A week or two after the women have ended their picket, Cissy begins to imitate them, walking up and down with a sandwich board protesting her father's racism. Becoming a grim parody of the political action of Faith and her friends within the story, the crazed Cissy also becomes a grim parody of the political action and madness of the children of Faith's friends throughout the collection. It is only in the figure of Cissy that madness is, albeit parodically, joined with political action (though Paley runs the two together in an interview in which she catalogues the disasters befalling her children's generation).[54]

Making a dark comedy out of Zagrowsky's tale of misfortune, Paley comes closer here than anywhere to the world of Sholem Aleichem, both in the Yiddish inflections of Zagrowsky's oral recitation of his troubles and in his success in making a very bleak tale funny.[55] We are to some extent back in the world of Mrs Darwin's tales of superlative disaster in "Faith in the Afternoon," though we are brought much closer to the sufferings of Zagrowsky and his wife than we were to the subjects in those brief sketches. But this story, unlike Mrs Darwin's tales, takes on, finally, a somewhat idyllic flavour; Zagrowsky's grief is ultimately relieved by the birth of his sunny dark grandson, the child of Cissy and a gardener she has met in the mental institution, "a black man with a green thumb" (360). The optimistically named Emanuel ("God is with us") serves as a moral and spiritual educator for his grandfather and bearer of renewed, brighter life. Yet it will also be a life with unfamiliar difficulties, as Zagrowsky now has to think about where he can live with a grandson who may not be welcome everywhere (as Josie was not welcome in his pharmacy just a short while ago). In listening with generous sympathy to Zagrowsky, the former target of her moral indignation, Faith too emerges as a softer, more compassionate woman than the "Queen of Right" (357) whom he remembers.

Anxiety about the fate awaiting the children makes itself felt in two more stories in the last collection. In the very brief "Anxiety" it assumes a somewhat more impersonal cast than in the stories we have just looked at. An older woman narrator, who we learn only later is Faith, looks out her window at a young father carrying his daughter on his shoulder and warns him, "I must tell you that madmen intend to destroy this beautifully made planet. That the murder of our children by these men has got to become a terror and a sorrow to you, and starting now, it had better interfere with any daily pleasure" (320).[56] The anxiety becomes more immediate in "The Story Hearer," in which Faith is again the narrator. She opens the story with a conversation between Jack and herself and moves from there to a meandering account of her day, her interactions with others, and her listening to their stories. The final scene takes place in the bedroom in the wee hours of the morning and brings us back to the motif of parental anxiety about the disasters looming over the children. Jack cries out in terror, Faith comforts him, then has a nightmare of her own, in which the sympathy she has amply demonstrated for the parents of ill-fated children takes a more personal turn. Faith dreams "that the children had grown all the way up. One had moved to another neighborhood, the other to a distant country. *That* one was never to be seen again, the dream explained, because he had blown up a very bad bank, and in the dream I was the one who'd told him to do it." Her dream brings together the joint fears that her child may do harm and be exposed to harm, and that she, pacifist but also socially conscious mother, will be responsible for both.

Faith's dream frightens her awake, then leads to her improbable announcement that she wants to have a baby. First dismissing her wish because of her age, Jack then suggests a kindred scenario to her dream: "Besides, suppose it worked; I mean suppose a miracle. The kid might be very smart, get a scholarship to MIT, and get caught up in problem solving and godalmighty it could invent something worse than anything us old dodos ever imagined" (344). In this perilous world, Jack reminds her, a socially respectable scientist may be more dangerous than a terrorist who blows up a bank. Pulling the Old Testament out from under her bed to read the story of Abraham and

Sarah "with interlinear intelligence" – that is, with knowledge of how the world has gone since Genesis was composed, Faith has to concede, "There was a lot in what Jack said ... Because you know how that old story ends – Well! With those three monotheistic horsemen of perpetual bossdom and war: Christianity, Judaism, and Islam." But Faith chooses instead to contemplate the promise of "beginnings," which she had discussed with Jack at the beginning of this story: "Just the same ... before all that popular badness wedged its way into the world, there *was first* the little baby Isaac ... looking at Sarah just like all our own old babies – remember the way they practiced their five little senses." Juxtaposed again here with Jack, Faith is, after all, the one who has faith – in the children, in new beginnings, in (maybe) better possibilities. With ecumenical impartiality (perhaps an offshoot of her earlier stated belief in the Diaspora) Faith may dismiss the three monotheistic horsemen of Christianity, Judaism, and Islam. But viewed through a mother's eyes, the story takes on a different coloration. "Oh, Jack, that Isaac, Sarah's boy – before he was old enough to be taken out by his father to get his throat cut, he must have just lain around smiling and making up diphthongs and listening, and the women sang songs to him and wrapped him up in such pretty rugs" (345). A poignant image in any case, and particularly so here, when inevitably given deeper resonance by the stories we have read of Abby, Mickey, Rachel, and Cissy. The end of "that old story" of the "three monotheistic horsemen of perpetual bossdom and war," like the ends of the stories of Faith's friends' children, cannot be ignored; but Faith chooses to end *her* story with the beginning.

"Optimism" and the Place of the Personal

Grace Paley's critics often write with confidence of her "optimism."[57] Of course, Paley's own activism and that of her characters is too marked for anyone to mean this in the simple Panglossian sense that she believes this is the best of all possible worlds or that she subscribes to what Candide comes to describe as "la rage de soutenir que tout est bien quand on est mal."[58] It is only too clear that all is *not* well in Paley's world. Still, the title and some of the contents of her second collection, *Enormous Changes at the Last Minute*, have led many to focus on the promise of sudden change for the better in her stories, as in the middle-aged Alexandra's dramatic reorganization of her life in the title story, or Faith's awakening to greater political consciousness at the end of "Faith in a Tree," or the upbeat story the narrator tells her father in "A Conversation with My Father." "The open destiny of life," which the narrator of "Conversation" holds as an entitlement of "everyone, real and invented," does seem possible for some. But this should not blind us to the fact that Paley's stories also present a number of foreclosed destinies, including that of the dying father who objects to his daughter's view; moreover, as we have seen, children come to bleak and sometimes violent ends, both outside the Faith stories and within them, and the larger world of Paley's stories is increasingly scary, both politically and ecologically.

"Optimism" may not, after all, be quite the right word for the buoyancy and openness we find in much of Paley's writing, which coexist with her irony without being undercut by it, and which her heroine shares. We must distinguish between a personal temperament that is affirmative and life-embracing, and an intellectual awareness that is darker, anxious, and more pessimistic about the world. Both the upbeat temperament and the darker vision coexist in Paley and, increasingly, in Faith. In Paley's interviews she tends to emphasize her darker vision. In one, she refers to "the world – which I happen to think is in incredible hot water right now"; she continues, "I have some very dark views of the world, and I think they've found their way into some funny stories."[59] Justifying her activism, which has taken time she might have spent writing, she says, "I couldn't bear not to respond to the awful things that are. I regret that I haven't written more ... But, I don't know how with my view of how to live in this really *hopeless* world ... how I could have done more." Speaking of her grandchild, she says, "I know she's going to grow up in a world where she may not get to be six years old ... I mean the world may not last."[60] She tells another interviewer, "I always appear very hopeful, but I'm really quite pessimistic about the future of the world."[61] In answer to a question about her "optimism," she replies, "Who said I was optimistic? No, I happen to have a cheerful disposition. But I'm not optimistic. I think we just may kill ourselves ecologically before we kill ourselves with nuclear war, so that's a great piece of anxiety."[62]

In these interviews Paley carefully distinguishes between "a cheerful disposition," which she has, and optimism, which she does not.[63] In her construction of the Faith stories she dramatizes this abiding opposition in several ways. Recurrently, Faith's "rosy temperament" is juxtaposed with a darker view of the world – for example, Jack's "gloomy gray" and the life history that has fostered it in "The Immigrant Story," or the urban blight and dangers she discovers in "The Long-Distance Runner." It is important to remember, too, that the Faith character is not monolithic; she is captured in changing attitudes in different stories. In "Living" we have seen Faith only too aware of both public and private terrors, though her final note is affirmative and celebratory. "Faith in a Tree" balances her personal complaints (both her manlessness and her failure to join her neighbours in their progress of upward mobility) with the ebullience of her spirit and the sense of community and family she enjoys despite – or because of – her single motherhood, until the horrors of American action in Vietnam encroach on the peaceful springtime scene in her neighbourhood playground.

Faith's awareness of wider evils in the world becomes more pronounced in *Later the Same Day*, where its relation to her personal good cheer, which it never really quenches, is an increasing focus of concern. During the visit of Faith and her friends to Selena in "Friends," they talk mainly of their children. But the large political picture is never far from their thoughts. On the train ride back into New York one of the women strikes up a conversation with a man across the aisle, "explaining that the war in Vietnam was not yet over and would not be, as far as she was concerned, until we repaired the dikes we'd bombed and paid for some of the hopeless ecological damage" (312). Intermixed with these observations and her chatty account of their visit to a dying friend, she goes on to "tell that man all our private troubles – the mistake of the World Trade Center, Westway, the decay of the South Bronx, the rage in Williamsburg" (312). The phrase "our private troubles," which ironically distinguishes local from international politics, highlights the extent to which civic involvement is of immediate, personal concern to these women.

The relation between global problems and private concerns comes to the fore in the closing pages of "Friends," after Faith returns home. When, in response to Anthony's query "How come Selena never realized about Abby?" Faith replies, "Basically Abby was OK ... You don't know yet what their times can do to a person," Anthony challenges his mother's generous outlook as an unacceptable form of Pollyannaism. "Here she goes with her good-goodies –

everything is so groovy wonderful far-out terrific. Next thing, you'll say people are darling and the world is *so* nice and round that Union Carbide will never blow it up." The exchange between mother and son can be regarded as a variant of the conflict between rosiness and gloomy gray in "The Immigrant Story." But here, Faith denies the charge of simple Pollyannaism: "I have never said anything as hopeful as that." What is really at issue this time is not simply differences of temperament or outlook but also the very legitimacy of private concerns in a world of active evil. Confronted with so much personal suffering, Faith would like to feel entitled to a respite from the troubles of the world. "Why," she reflects unhappily, "to all our knowledge of that sad day did Tonto at 3 a.m. have to add the fact of the world?" (314).

Faith's account moves from this rhetorical question back to Selena and then to Faith's relationship with Ann. But her closing reflections respond to Anthony's objections as she affirms the legitimacy of both wider public *and* narrower private concerns.

> Anthony's world – poor, dense, defenseless thing – rolls round and round. Living and dying are fastened to its surface and stuffed into its softer parts.
>
> He was right to call my attention to its suffering and danger. He was right to harass my responsible nature. But I was right to invent for my friends and our children a report on these private deaths and the condition of our lifelong attachments. (315)

Faith's casual use here of the verb "invent" suggests again, as she did in "The Long-Distance Runner," her identity as the creative writer of this story, although the emphasis of the sentence falls on the private deaths and conditions of her lifelong attachments. These remain, after all, the main focus of Paley's Faith stories, even though, increasingly, the wider world is visibly present. We have already glanced at "Anxiety," where Faith does seem to foreground the dangers of the world when she warns the young father "that madmen intend to destroy this beautiful planet" and that "the murder of our children by these men has got to become a terror and a sorrow to you, and ... had better interfere with any daily pleasure" (320). But it is unclear even here how much she really wants these dangers to interfere, as her immediate purpose is to get the father to treat his daughter with greater tolerance: "Since those children are such lovely examples of what may well be the last generation of humankind, why don't you start all over again, right from the school door (321)." The possibility for daily pleasure seems, after all, to remain.

In "The Story Hearer" Faith sets the two poles – of private life and the wider world – firmly and clearly in opposition at the outset. Leaving her apartment she sees the *New York Times* on a neighbour's doormat and "could see that it was black with earthquake, war, private murder. Clearly death had been successful everywhere but not – I saw when I stepped out the front door – on our own block. Here it was springtime, partly because of the time of the year and partly because we have a self-involved block-centered street association which has lined us with sycamores and enhanced us with a mountain ash, two ginkgoes, and here and there (because we are part of the whole) ailanthus, city saver" (338). In a wonderful variation on the not-on-my-block disclaimer, Faith finds it hard to embrace with full emotional conviction the ubiquitous reality of death communicated by the *Times* in the face of the immediately perceived beauties of springtime "on our own block." It is, moreover, a springtime determined only partly by the time of year and partly by the work of her public-spirited well-organized neighbours, who have arranged for her street to be lined with the various trees she enumerates individually, with loving specificity. The last mentioned – ailanthus (a ghetto tree but also, literally, tree of the gods) – though planted only "here and there," links her block to the larger city it also benefits, "because we are part of the whole." As a general statement, the last observation would be a hopeless cliché. Applied as it is here, playfully, in a modest parenthesis, to the trees whose benefits spread far beyond their local placements, it not only leads Faith generously outward, beyond her block to her entire city but also, possibly less positively, to the wider world covered in the black headlines she first noted ("black" figuratively, because of the news they chronicle, and also literally, because of the newsprint). The horrors of the wider world are not denied, but they do not extinguish the value of personal experience. Faith's faith – when she has it – may consist in dwelling on the latter, without being blind to the former.[64]

Public political events impinge more directly on personal lives in "The Expensive Moment," we have seen, chiefly through their effect on the lives of the children. In this story, Faith's upbeat affirmative outlook is presented as more deliberate and less spontaneous than earlier. We witness a heated discussion at the dinner table among Faith's sons, Jack, and her temporary sinologist lover – into which Ruth's comments of "a couple of years later" are also tossed – covering the many evils of the world, including Israel's and the USSR's trade with South Africa, Cuba's commercial negotiations with Argentina, China's hasty recognition of Pinochet, Allende's ineptitude. This is followed by a break in spacing and then Faith's thoughts: "But if you think like that forever you can be sad forever. You can be cynical, you can go around saying no hope, you can say import-export, you can mumble all day, World Bank. So she tried thinking: The beauty of trade, the caravans crossing Africa and Asia, the roads to Peru through the terrible forests of Guatemala, and then especially the village markets of underdeveloped countries, plazas behind churches under awnings and tents" (369–70). Faith's "optimism" here is achieved through an act of will; her positive thinking appears as a deliberate choice, made in the face of her lucid awareness of the reasons one could otherwise be "sad forever;" as a response to these reasons, it is in no way simple Pollyannaism. Moreover, she does not have the last word. As so often in Paley's stories, what first seem to be Faith's unspoken thoughts are countered by an interlocutor's rejoinder. "Oh sure, Richard said, the beauty of trade. I'm surprised at you Ma ... those Indians going through Guatemala with leather thongs cutting into their foreheads holding about a ton of beauty on their backs" (370). The presentation, here as elsewhere, is dialogic. There *is* no last word.

In the final story, "Listening," where political events again retreat to the background (entering the story through Faith's printing and distribution of anti-war leaflets), Faith's affirmative attitude toward the world is presented once more as, at least partly, a matter of deliberate choice. And again she is juxtaposed with the more somber Jack, who is overheard at the outset of the story congratulating himself on his unsentimental desire to retain the freedom to commit suicide, as he assumes he "will want to in ten, twenty years" (380). The contrapuntal opposition of their temperaments and outlooks here, as at the end of "The Story Hearer," is triggered by Faith's late-life desire to have another child. Questioning her wish, Jack asks, "Haven't we agreed often, haven't we said that it had become noticeable that life is short and sorrowful? Haven't we said the words 'gone' and 'where'? Haven't we sometimes in the last few years used the word 'terrible' and we mean to include in it the word 'terror'?" Then, with a barb apparently directed at Faith, he adds,

"Everyone knows this about life. Though of course some fools never stop singing its praises." Faith's response captures both her instinctive life-affirming outlook and her recognition of the objective truth of Jack's view. "But they're right. Yes, and this is in order to encourage the young whom we have after all, brought into the world – they must not be abandoned. We must, I said, continue pointing out simple and worthwhile sights such as – in the countryside, hills folding into one another in light-green spring or white winter, the sky which is always astonishing." What first appears as merely a tactical argument to encourage the young for whom we are responsible quickly becomes a loving song of praise for the real beauties of nature, from which Faith then moves on to "our own beloved city," whose vitality she paints with similar appreciative detail. She concludes, "It's very important to emphasize what is good or beautiful so as not to have a gloomy face when you meet some youngster who has begun to guess" (381–2). Her final sentence manages to affirm in one breath both the objective validity of what is good or beautiful and the recognition of a terrible, sorrowful dimension to life, which, ultimately, the young too will begin to guess.

Not only is Faith, then, repeatedly placed in contexts that call into question any claim for her creator's clear-cut "optimism"; Faith's own rosy temperament and life-embracing attitude are increasingly qualified by her awareness of suffering and death, and they come to require a certain underpinning of deliberate will. In two moments in the late stories, moreover, she is forced into a posture of direct self-questioning. The first occurs at the end of "Listening," the last story of Paley's most recently published collection of stories. With her sons more or less on their own, and Jack "off to Arizona for a year to clear his lungs and sinuses and also to have, hopefully, one last love affair," Faith watches a man cross the street and voices to her friend Cassie her "homesickness" for the "sentimental and carnal … everyday life" that seems to have slipped out of her grasp (385). Turning on Faith with impatience, the lesbian Cassie attacks Faith's selective, exclusively heterosexual view of "everyday life" and the fact that Faith has omitted *her* from her stories. Cassie's accusation is striking on several counts. First, this is one of the few indications the reader gets that Faith is in fact the writer of the stories we have just finished reading. We have already noted Faith's fleeting reference to how Mrs Raftery got "liked by me, loved, invented and endured" (243) in the last story of Paley's previous collection and her re-use of the verb "invent" at the end of "Friends" (*Later the Same Day*) to indicate the fictionality of the story she has just related and her own role as storymaker, while teasingly suggesting at the same time the fundamental reality of the deaths and attachments her story reports. ("I was right to invent for my friends and our children a report on these private deaths and the conditions of our lifelong attachments.") In neither earlier story, however, does Faith highlight her identity as a writer, as she does in "Listening."

The elusiveness with which Paley treats this aspect of Faith's identity prior to the last story of her last collection encourages me to indulge in a slight digression here on the intriguing question of Faith's work – her occupation – or, perhaps better, her *other* work, in addition to the work she does for Paley. In the early "Used-Boy Raisers," the married Faith appears to have no work outside the home. In the companion piece, "A Subject of Childhood" (*The Little Disturbances of Man*), as a single mother she describes herself as having "raised these kids, with one hand typing behind my back to earn a living" (91). In "Faith in the Afternoon," she even considers "taking a master's degree in education in order to exult at last in a profession and get out of the horseshit trades of this lofty land" (147). She still seems stuck in them, however, in "Faith in a Tree," where she refers to her "low-level job" (178) and the fact that, unlike other members of her building, she is not "on the way up through the affluent society" (182). At the end of that story she changes her "job uptown," but we are told neither what it has been nor what she changes it to. Paley's decision to keep Faith's employment obscurely in the background in the first two collections may reflect both Faith's prefeminist and her bohemian culture, in which women were not expected to have significant careers, and often neither were men; during her marriage to Ricardo, Faith felt called upon to explain, when queuing in the A&P, "that odd jobs were a splendid way of making out if you had together agreed on a substandard way of life" (150). But even if Faith's "yellow-dog contract with Bohemia, such as it survives" (91), keeps her from being defined by her work, her father nonetheless asks for her opinion when he reads her his poem in "Faith in the Afternoon," since he knows that she knows "a whole bunch of artists and writers" (158). (In "Enormous Changes at the Last Minute," 208, Dennis affirms, "I drive a cab but I am not a cabdriver." Rather he is a songmaker, a poet.) In the surrealistic "Long-Distance Runner," no mundane question of work interferes with Faith's prolonged journey to her old neighbourhood, though she is only forty-two years old and so can hardly be retired.

Things begin to change in *Later the Same Day*. In "Dreamer in a Dead Language," Faith tells her mother that she's buying a new typewriter and wants to work at home. "It's a big investment," she explains, "like going into business" (272). Whether this makes her a freelance typist or a writer, or both, is unclear. But when, at the beginning of "The Story Hearer," Jack asks her, "What did you do today with your year off?" (337) the unavoidable inference is that she has now become a college professor – like her creator (who also worked as a typist in her time); who else gets a year off? In that story, too, she displays a full-blown writerly interest in language, its varied cadences ("wheat and chaff ... its widening pool of foreign genes," 338), its uses and abuses, which constitutes an important focus of the story. In "The Expensive Moment" she meets Xie Feng at a meeting of women's governmental organizations sponsored by the UN, though nothing is said about what Faith has done to get there. Paley's refusal to specify a clear occupation for her heroine is not only intriguing in itself but may also be understood as a realistic aspect of Faith's American identity, demonstrating what the narrator of "A Conversation with My Father" argues, namely that possibilities do – at least for some – remain open in America. (By contrast, we know from "The Expensive Moment" that her friend Jack has a discount furniture store and is a serious reader and writer. He publishes in a journal called *The Social Ordure* and is shown giving a paper at the Other Historian Meeting. There is also the clear suggestion in "The Immigrant Story" that he was "wiped out of [his] profession during the McCarthy inquisitions" [204].)

Cassie's revelation that Faith is a writer, who, moreover, has written most of the stories we have just finished reading (though certainly not Zagrowsky's), most of which she has narrated, may be understood, like her earlier references to inventing her stories, as a "post-modern" move. It is also a time-honoured pattern in autobiographical narratives, including Wordsworth's *Prelude*, Dickens's *David Copperfield*, and Proust's *À la recherche du temps perdu*, in which the narration includes the story of the narrative's own genesis. Here, Cassie's revelation constitutes both the impetus for the story in which it is presented and the premise for Faith's autocritique, which now becomes indistinguishable from Cassie's criticism.

Cassie reproaches her friend first by asking why Faith hasn't told her story when she has told "everybody's story but mine." She quickly modifies this demand, however, saying, "I don't even mean my whole story, that's my job. You probably can't." But she criticizes Faith severely for omitting her from the other stories when "I was there ... And it's not even sensible, because we *are* friends, we work together and you even care about me at least as much as you do Ruthy and Louise and Ann. You let them in all the time; it's really strange, why have you left me out of everybody's life?" (385–6).[65] Faith accepts the justice of Cassie's reproach with understanding and self-criticism. "I don't understand it either ... It must feel for you like a great absence of yourself. How could I allow it." First appealing, like Zagrowsky – "I did what everyone did" (353) – to the fact that "it's not me alone, it's them too," she then acknowledges, "Oh, but it *is* my fault" and asks Cassie, "How can you forgive me?" (386).

Cassie's criticism is directed at Faith, but Paley has not previously intervened in the Faith stories or elsewhere to acknowledge Cassie's existence. Paley's decision to end her last published story collection on this note of personal self-reproach should be seen in the context of her reiterated belief that her writing about ordinary life, especially women's lives, was a political act, even though it took her some time before she understood this: "I think that sometimes things are political that people don't think of as political. At the time I began writing about women's lives, it was really very political. I didn't know it ... I was just part of that political movement without even knowing it was a movement. I think it often happens that people write politically without thinking that they are."[66] Or again, "I would say that my interest in ordinary life and how people live is a very political one ... That's politics. But I can't say that I thought, Oh, I'm going to write this political story ... I just thought I'm going to write about this woman and this man and how they live."[67] If writing about the daily lives of ordinary women and men is political, so is the exclusion of Cassie and other gay and lesbian friends from those stories. Faith's admission "I don't understand it either" suggests that her generous tolerance and sympathy – and that of the author she works for – are in advance of her ability to deal artistically with certain kinds of material, however many other constraints she has successfully overcome. The most powerful taboos are the ones we are not conscious of observing. Cassie feels personally betrayed by her friend and, at the same time, makes us all reflect how quintessentially political is the silent exclusion of the other, the rendering invisible of what is. The prominence of this exchange, on which Paley's last collected story closes, not only highlights the way in which the personal is the political but also constitutes a kind of homage and reparation to the previously invisible Cassie.

At the end of the last story of Paley's previous collection, Faith reflects on her journey to "the houses and streets where her childhood happened" and on how, by living in them, "she learns as though she were still a child what in the world is coming next" (258). Glancing simultaneously backward and forward, Faith thus also whets the reader's curiosity about what Paley will go on to write. The ending of "Listening" similarly arouses our expectations for Paley's future work and the greater inclusiveness it may demonstrate. Responding to Faith's "How can you forgive me?" Cassie has the last word: "You are my friend, I know that Faith, but I promise you, I won't forgive you ... From now on, I'll watch you like a hawk" (386).

Since *Later the Same Day*, Paley has published three books but, to date, no further literary collections of stories. Instead, there have been two collections of more directly political, occasional, or autobiographical prose, and poetry, *Long Walks and Intimate Talks* and *Just as I Thought*, and her collected poems, *Begin Again*. Of the pieces in *Long Walks*, Paley specifically identifies only two, "Midrash on Happiness" and "Three Days and a Question," which she considers "really full stories" and would use in a collection of stories.[68] It would seem that Paley has yet to publish any new story that might slacken Cassie's vigilance. *Just as I Thought*, however, does contain an eloquent memorial tribute to Barbara Demming, a fellow writer and political and social activist, who "became a fine artist who suffered because she was unable to fully use the one unchangeable fact of her life – that she was a woman who loved women" (239), a sad reminder, as in "Listening," of the taboos that have constrained the work of even radical writers.

Faith appears in only one of the two brief stories that Paley considers "really full stories" in *Long Walks and Intimate Talks*, "Midrash on Happiness." When she subsequently republished this as the first of three pieces she put together under the title "Like All the Other Nations" in *Just as I Thought*, she prefaced it with the comment, "I don't think this is really a midrash, but I called it that"

(44). In keeping with the tradition to which it refers, midrash – "the rabbinic term for biblical exegesis"– is itself susceptible of multiple definitions. Citing many of these in the *Anchor Bible Dictionary*, Gary G. Porton summarizes its meaning thus: "Midrash is a type of literature, oral or written, which has its starting point in a fixed canonical text, considered the revealed word of God by the midrashist and his audience, and in which this original verse is explicitly cited or clearly alluded to."[69] The use of the word midrash can often be somewhat looser, referring to commentary, interpretation or the retelling of the story to make the original more contemporary and relevant.[70] Through her admittedly playful title, "Midrash on Happiness," Paley aligns herself with the time-honoured Jewish tradition of exegesis, but in place of a canonical text considered to be the revealed word of God she puts "happiness," the quintessentially American object of pursuit and reverence. One might argue, in fact, that the ideal of "happiness" does indeed allude to a canonical text, though the text is not the Hebrew scriptures but the Declaration of Independence, specifically, the climax of its best-known phrase.[71] In "Faith in the Afternoon" (*Enormous Changes at the Last Minute*), Paley affirms her heroine's American identity, we have seen, by pointing to the fact that Faith "was raised up like everyone else to the true assumption of happiness" (148). In "Midrash on Happiness" Paley once again uses Faith to highlight the cultural mix of Jewish and American traditions. In the later story, however, she not only deconstructs this "true assumption" but also demonstrates the evolution and translation of what was once solely the Hebrew canon to include the secular authority of Jefferson's New World text.

"Midrash on Happiness" thus establishes its continuity with the more explicitly Jewish context of Paley's earlier stories, "Goodbye and Good Luck," "the Contest," and "The Loudest Voice," in which Faith plays no role, as well as "The Used-Boy Raisers" (all in *The Little Disturbances of Man*) where we have seen her tell her two Catholic husbands, "I believe in the Diaspora" and express the hope that Jews will remain "a splinter in the toe of civilizations ... to aggravate the conscience," and the two stories in subsequent collections that show Faith's visits to her parents in the Children of Judea retirement home. With Paley's development, the Jewish note becomes more muted. "Midrash on Happiness" suggests, however, that it is still present in Paley's later stories, though now chiefly visible through the greater social consciousness and social and political activism that characterize Faith and her friends, in keeping with Paley's own experience and that of many of her generation of Jewish Americans.[72]

The story presents a dialogue between Faith and Ruth, as they are walking together somewhere on Manhattan's Upper West Side, in which Faith expounds on the meaning of happiness, and Ruth, more briefly, replies. Faith proceeds by a process of definition and commentary, in which the terms of definition themselves are then further glossed and defined. "What she meant by happiness," it starts off, is "having (or having had) (or continuing to have) everything. By everything, she meant, first, the children, then a dear person to live with, preferably a man, but not necessarily." Faith's sensitivity to Cassie's criticism is evident in her "but not necessarily," which was added subsequent to the story's initial publication in the *TriQuarterly*. Faith then adds a series of additional demands, first among which are "three or four best women friends to whom she could tell every personal fact and then discuss on the widest deepest and most hopeless level the economy, the constant, unbeatable, cruel war economy, the slavery of the American worker to the idea of that economy, the complicity of male people in the whole structure." Apparent from the outset are the foregrounding of the personal and yet the presence of wider social concerns and a clear feminist perspective. After further explicating and amplifying each term, Faith adds the requirement of "work to do in this world and bread on the table. By work to do she included the important work of raising children righteously up. By righteously she meant that along with being useful and speaking truth to the community, they must do no harm." What started as a definition of the narcissistic-sounding term "happiness," a term that in "Faith in the Afternoon" related only to Faith's immediate personal situation, is now shown to include a network of obligations and commitments to others, in which friendship and responsible motherhood play crucial roles. Then the sight of lovers strolling along Riverside Park suddenly makes Faith remember: "Oh I forgot ... Ruthy I think I would die without love," and "love" then becomes the subject of her further explorations (*Long Walks* 6–8).

Though much of Faith's exegesis has the ring of wisdom, she is once again not given the last word. Picking up on Faith's disquisition on love, Ruth acknowledges that she sometimes thinks as Faith does, but: "Nowadays it seems like pride, I mean overweening pride, when you look at the children and think we don't have time to do much (by time Ruth meant both her personal time and the planet's time). When I read the papers and hear all this boom boom bellicosity, the guys out-daring each other, I see we have to change it all – the world – without killing it absolutely ... Until that begins, I don't understand happiness – what you mean by it" (8). Ruth's reflections focus the tension between the personal and the global that runs through Paley's later stories. In gentler, more sympathetic tones, and with a mildly feminist slant, she echoes objections we have seen from Jack, Richard, and Anthony. Ruth's appeal to the wider world makes Faith "ashamed to have wanted so much and so little – to be so easily personally satisfied in this terrible place, when everywhere vast public suffering rose in reeling waves from the round earth's nation states ... Of course, Faith said, I know all that. I do, but sometimes walking with a friend I forget the world" (9). Echoing Donne, implicitly evoking Jefferson and explicitly the tradition of Jewish exegesis, Paley presents us once again with a Faith who, as in the earlier "Afternoon," is "ashamed" – this time, however, not of any personal unhappiness, but rather for having wanted so much and so little, for being so easily personally satisfied in a world of so much suffering. The product of a complex heritage – Jewish, American, late-twentieth-century feminist – Faith works for Paley to affirm the value of the quotidian and the personal, even "in this terrible place," and even if Faith's view is increasingly qualified by some version of Ruth's reservations. Paley never allows her reader, any more than her heroine, to forget the world for long; but in Faith's company we are also privileged to share her humanity, her buoyancy, and her commitment to personal possibility.

Notes

INTRODUCTION

1 Woolf, "Professions for Women," 62.
2 For the echoes of Lily Briscoe in Anna Banti's *Artemisia*, see below, pp. 65–6.
3 Woolf, *Between the Acts*, 88, 189.
4 In another of Munro's collections, *Who Do You Think You Are* (published as *The Beggar Maid* in the US and Britain), the protagonist is also a performer, in this case an actress. She is successful enough to make a living at it, but here too, as with the opera singer in *Friend of My Youth*, no enormous claims are made for her talent, nor does her profession significantly distinguish her predicament from that of other women in the text.
5 To be sure, Munro refers to her *Lives of Girls and Women* as a novel; yet Paley has shrewdly observed of this book, "but it's all stories" (Batt, Noelle, "An Interview with Grace Paley," 125).
6 Munro, *Selected Stories*, xi.
7 Conway, Celeste, et al., "Grace Paley Interview," 11.
8 Taylor, "Grace Paley on Storytelling and Story Hearing," 175.
9 Munro, "Everything Here Is Touchable and Mysterious."
10 Michaels, "Conversation with Grace Paley," 28; Hulley, "Interview with Grace Paley," 50.
11 Eliot, *Daniel Deronda*, 694 (ch. 51).
12 Banti, *Artemisia*, 134. As in my chapter on Banti's novel, the citations are to the Italian edition and the translations are mine. The novel has been translated into English by Shirley D'Ardia Coracciolo (see Works

Cited). Here, however, the crucial phrase disappears entirely in Caracciolo's translation: "In my bosom lies a heart of gold" (106).

13 *Bolletino d'arte* (1916), 51.

CHAPTER ONE

1 Moers, *Literary Women*, 173–4 for the citation, 173–211 for her discussion of *Corinne* and its influence.

2 Herold, *Mistress to an Age*, 232.

3 Gutwirth, "Madame de Staël," 101.

4 Corinne's defeat itself, of course, has never been in question, but explanations for it vary – from the view of Corinne's death as expressing simple pessimism regarding the fate of the exceptional woman in a world unreceptive to her claims, to Madelyn Gutwirth's suggestion that it reflects Mme de Staël's guilt over her own transgression of the limits placed on female achievement by a patriarchal society and by her own father in particular. This view informs Gutwirth's important full length study of *Corinne*, *Madame de Staël, Novelist,* 154–310; see especially 157, 207–8, 224–7. While I am in broad sympathy with Gutwirth's argument, I shall argue here that in Mme de Staël's presentation of Corinne's death – its inner logic as well as Corinne's own active role – and in her attempt to transmute tragedy into a victory so powerful as virtually to annihilate its tragic aspects, the novelist has internalized more values destructive to women, and with less self-awareness, than has generally been acknowledged. On Corinne's willed death also see Starobinski, "Suicide et mélancolie chez Mme de Staël."

5 While the pattern is too familiar to require examples, the "Prelude" to George Eliot's *Middlemarch* succinctly states the conflict as "a certain spiritual grandeur ill-matched with the meanness of opportunity."

6 All citations to *Corinne* are to the French edition edited by Simone Balayé. This edition reproduces the spelling of the third edition of 1807. The translations are mine. Recent English translations have been done by Avriel Goldberger and Sylvia Raphael and are listed in the Works Cited.

7 Balayé, *Madame de Staël,* 137.

8 The status of Staël's "Italy," which had an enormous impact on subsequent nineteenth-century representations of that country, has been the subject of extensive commentary. Moers, *Literary Women*, and Gutworth, *Madame de Staël, Novelist*, in particular discuss Staël's construction of Italy as a land uniquely favourable to female possibility,

and Hogsett discusses parallels between Staël's Italy and women, *The Literary Existence of Germaine de Staël*, 117–22.

9 Because Gutwirth refers to Corinne's "[living] freely, taking and leaving lovers" (*Madame de Staël, Novelist*, 162), I have dwelt on the extreme care Staël takes to clarify the unconsummated nature of the love between Oswald and Corinne and the latter's unimpugned "virtue." The corollary of this is that the term "lovers" can be applied to the men in Corinne's life only if we understand it in its nineteenth-century sense – roughly equivalent to "suitors."

10 One may be reminded here of Racine's Phèdre or Richardson's Clarissa, who also bring about their own deaths as a means of regaining or achieving heroic stature after the consequences of their feelings and judgment threaten to leave them irrevocably compromised. The pattern is a familiar one, though the circumstances and complex of meanings surrounding each heroine's death vary from text to text.

11 For example, Simone Balayé, in the introduction to her recent edition of the novel, while reminding us that "Mme de Staël n'est jamais tout entière chez l'un ou l'autre des protagonistes," goes only so far as to add, "on la trouve un peu partout même chez d'Erfeuil. Lui, Corinne et Oswald, dans leurs dissemblances, représentent des moments de Mme de Staël" (22) – ignoring Mme d'Arbigny entirely. Goldberger's introduction to the American edition does mention Mme d'Arbigny but only in passing, as "one of the three characters who represent France in the novel [she ignores M. de Maltigues] ... a product of the Parisian society that has corrupted her ability to be honest" (xxxii). Similarly, Gutwirth's extensive discussion of *Corinne* makes only the briefest passing reference to Mme d'Arbigny, uncritically accepting Oswald's view of his first beloved and all but dismissing her as a kind of villainess preying on innocence (*Madame de Staël, Novelist*, 162, 224, 235, and, by implication, 196). In her discussion of *Corinne* in *Lumières et Liberté*, Balayé also makes only the briefest passing reference to Mme d'Arbigny ("une femme ... intrigante et fausse"), relating this +episode in Oswald's past to the situation of Constant's Adolphe in Germany, 149. Hogsett discusses various autobiographical elements in *Corinne* in *The Literary Existence of Germaine de Staël* but never mentions Mme d'Arbigny. This dismissive assessment of Mme d'Arbigny possibly owes something to Sainte-Beuve's early identification of her as a "portrait" based on a real-life model – Mme de Flahaut (*Portraits de Femmes*, 155), a reminder that is picked up by Geneviève Gennari

when she dismisses Mme d'Arbigny as a "peinture assez conventionnelle de l'hypocrisie mondaine" (*Le Premier Voyage*, 123).

12 Jean Rhys's *Wide Sargasso Sea* offers the classic revisionist view of *Jane Eyre*'s mad Mrs Rochester. The literary critical equivalent of this can be found in Sandra Gilbert and Susan Gubar's *The Madwoman in the Attic*, which has called our attention to suppressed bonds of kinship among unlikely literary and fictional women.

13 See Gutwirth, *Madame de Staël, Novelist*, 237–45 and Goldberger, "Introduction," *Corinne*, xl-xlii. Sensitively arguing that "the sisters represent ... the divided part of what ought to be a unity" (241), Gutwirth nonetheless ignores Mme d'Arbigny completely when she asserts, "Mme de Staël always ends by embracing another woman's plight imaginatively" (245). Goldberger, who also praises the vision of sisterhood conveyed in the bond between "the dark woman and the fair lady," refers to Lucile without qualification as "the 'other woman' in the novel" (xl).

14 See Goldberger, *Corinne*, xli-xlii; Gutwirth, *Madame de Staël, Novelist* 251–7; Moers, *Literary Women*, 175.

15 See Moers, *Literary Women*; Jean Starobinski, "Suicide e mélancolie chez Mme de Staël"; Gutwirth, *Madame de Staël, Novelist*; George Poulet, "'Corinne' ét 'Adolphe': deux romans conjugés."

16 Although the full extent of *Corinne*'s influence is beyond the scope of this study, that influence is most famously apparent in both the life and work of Elizabeth Barrett Browning, whose own escape to Italy (nicely memorialized in Virginia Woolf's *Flush*), owes at least something to the model of Corinne, and in George Sand's *Consuelo* and *La Comtesse de Rudolstadt*; these novels, along with Barrett Browning's *Aurora Leigh*, have been regarded as reworkings of *Corinne*. See Lewis, *Germaine de Staël*, 13–64, 99–134. Moers also discusses *Corinne*'s influence on *Aurora Leigh* and, much more briefly, on Sand in *Literary Women*, 201–7, 263. Cora Kaplan's "Introduction" to *Aurora Leigh* carefully compares the similarities and differences between that poem and Mme de Staël's novel, 15–23. For the debt of another woman intellectual to *Corinne*, see Blanchard, "*Corinne* and the 'Yankee Corinna.'" Male writers were also responsive to Corinne's legacy. Nathaniel Hawthorne shows the influence of *Corinne* in *The Marble Faun*, when he places his American woman artist heroine, Hilde, in Rome, where she can enjoy freedoms not easily imaginable in her native New England. While this may in part reflect social realities for American women artists in Italy, his other heroine, Miriam, shares with Corinne her Italian-English parentage

(though Hawthorne complicates this by giving her an admixture of "Jewish blood" [429] and inverting the gender/national identities of the parents of Corinne – and Aurora Leigh: Miriam's mother is English and her father Italian). Moreover, Miriam self-consciously echoes Staël's heroine when she seeks to re-enact the scene of Corinne's recognition of her lover by seeing the reflection of his face in the Trevi fountain (*Marble Faun*, 146). In Henry James's *The Portrait of a Lady*, we learn that Gilbert Osmond's deceased mother, "who had bristled with pretensions to elegant learning and published descriptive poems ... had liked to be called the American Corinne" (305), a designation repeated several times (385, 483), which may also hint at a certain lack of moral rigour.

17 In keeping with the quite separate roles envisioned for men and women, Oswald is loved by three women in the novel without *his* taking the least pains to please any of them; nor would any reader accuse him of being excessively *agréable*. Indeed, Corinne loves him precisely for his tortured, melancholy reserve, in which he distinguishes himself from her more ingratiating Continental admirers, whose deficiency, articulated by the British M. Edgermond, is tacitly confirmed by Corinne's love for Oswald (204): "Les hommes en Italie n'ont rien à faire qu'à plaire aux femmes" (Men in Italy have nothing to do but to please women). This correspondence can also be seen as part of a more general correlation suggested by the novel between the position of women and Italy (or Italians) with regard to their shared lack of political power.

18 Dickens, *Great Expectations*, 411, ch. 49.

CHAPTER TWO

1 "Women in France: Madame de Sablé," in Eliot, *Essays*, 55. Ellen Moers cites the first part of the sentence to establish Eliot's admiration for Staël; *Literary Women*, 173–4. Linda M. Lewis cites Eliot's praise for both Sand and Staël; *Germaine de Staël*, 13.

2 For a discussion of *Corinne*'s influence on the novels of Sand and on Barrett Browning's epic poem, see my chapter 1, note 16. Lewis argues, moreover, that there is a "tenuous bond" between George Eliot and Staël "in their sibylline authority" (by this she means between Eliot and the character of Corinne), and that Eliot also owes a debt to Staël (though "to a lesser degree" than to Sand) in the creation of "her monumental female characters." With greater confidence she argues that Eliot's heroines are "influenced by Staël and Sand – and in some instances by Barrett Browning as well – in that multiple mythic sibyls

and goddesses are invoked in their creation" (*Germaine de Staël*, 141–3). In a less-appreciative vein, indeed, with an almost deliberate perversity, Moers argues (*Literary Women*, 194) that "like Mme de Staël, George Eliot was always concerned with the superior large-souled woman whose distinction resides not in her deeds but in her capacity to attract attention and arouse admiration."

3 Eliot, *The Mill on the Floss*, 332 (Bk 6, ch. 4).

4 Eliot, *Middlemarch*, 167 (Bk 2).

5 There is, to be sure, the singer Caterina Sarti in the early story, "Mr Gilfil's Love-Story (*Scenes of Clerical Life*), but she is not a professional. The eponymous heroine of Eliot's dramatic poem *Armgart* is also a singer; but my focus here is on Eliot's novels.

6 Eliot, *Daniel Deronda*, 84. Subsequent references to this novel will be included in my text.

7 The importance of such a "corporate existence that raises man above the otherwise more respectable and innocent brute" is treated in Eliot's essay, "The Modern Hep! Hep! Hep!": "Not only the nobleness of a nation depends on the presence of this national consciousness, but also the nobleness of each individual citizen" (*Impressions of Theophrastus Such*, 144, 147–8).

8 Nancy Henry has recently argued, however, that the novel actually "incorporates a critically self-conscious attitude toward the myth of the empty land" that Daniel and Mordecai somewhat naïvely accept. *George Eliot and the British Empire*, 121.

9 Rosenberg, *From Shylock to Svengali*, 173.

10 A muted authorial caution is expressed by the description of the princess's speech as "a piece of what may be called sincere acting: this woman's nature was one in which all feeling – and all the more when it was tragic as well as real – immediately became matter of conscious representation: experience immediately passed into drama, and she acted her own emotions." The narrator adds, however: "It would not be true to say that she felt less because of this double consciousness (691)." Although this authorial intervention does to a limited extent mediate the princess's indisputable eloquence, it hardly undercuts it.

11 Leavis, *The Great Tradition*, especially 82–5.

12 A nice summary of postcolonial treatments of *Daniel Deronda* from Edward Said on is given by Henry, along with her rebuttal of this approach (*George Eliot and the British Empire*, 113–27).

13 Leavis, *The Great Tradition*, 85.

14 Beer, *George Eliot*, 180–1.

15 Eliot, *Letters* II, 396 (1857). See also *Letters* V, 58 (1869): "I feel too deeply the difficult complications that beset every measure likely to affect the position of women and also I feel too imperfect a sympathy with many women who have put themselves forward in connection with such measures, to give any practical adhesion to them. There is no subject on which I am more inclined to hold my peace and learn, than on the 'Women Question.' It seems to overhang abysses of which even prostitution is not the worst ... But on one point I have a strong conviction ... And that is, that women ought to have the same fund of truth placed within their reach as men have."

16 Eliot, *Letters* II, 86 (1853).

17 Eliot, *Letters* VIII, 402 (1867). She qualifies this statement somewhat by adding, "I do not trust very confidently to my own impressions on this subject. The peculiarities of my own lot may have caused me to have idiosyncrasies rather than an average judgment."

18 The questioning of such uniformity is a major motif in *Middlemarch*, initially sounded in the "Prelude" (26): "If there were one level of feminine incompetence as strict as the ability to count three and no more, the social lot of women might be treated with scientific certitude. Meanwhile the indefiniteness remains, and the limits of variation are really much wider than anyone would imagine ..."

19 Eliot, *Letters* IV, 298 (1866).

CHAPTER THREE

1 Banti, *Artemisia*, 3. All citations to *Artemisia* are to the Italian Mondadori edition (1974) and future page references will be included in the text. The translations are mine. For a published English version, readers are referred to the translation by Shirley D'Ardia Caracciolo.

2 Elizabeth S. Cohen's "The Trials of Artemisia Gentileschi: A Rape as History," which considers the meaning and significance of rape in Artemisia's culture, provides an overview of historical writings on Artemisia Gentileschi. Recent fictional treatments include a Canadian play and docudrama, a French feature film, and two historically based novels (one in French by Alexandra Lapierre, 1998, now translated into English, the other by the American Susan Vreeland, 2002). Mary D. Garrard's major full-length study, *Artemisia Gentileschi: The Image of the Female Hero in Italian Baroque Art*, written in part to rectify the "extraordinary fact" (4) that no monograph on the painter had previously appeared, met with considerable acclaim in the United States and

Britain when it was published in 1989. In an earlier article ("Artemisia Gentileschi: The Artist's Autograph," 91) Garrard asserts: "Artemisia Gentileschi is today widely regarded as the most creative and most significant woman artist of the premodern era." R. Ward Bissel's more recent book, *Artemisia Gentileschi and the Authority of Art: Critical Reading and Catalogue Raisonné*, describes the seventeenth-century painter on the front jacket flap as "arguably the most forcefully expressive and influential woman painter in history." In *Women Artists: 1550–1950*, Ann Sutherland Harrris and Linda Nochlin write, "Artemisia Gentileschi is the first woman in the history of Western art to make a significant and undeniably important contribution to the art of her time," 118. In Germaine Greer's *The Obstacle Race*, Gentileschi is the only woman painter to receive a full chapter to herself ("The Magnificent Exception," 189–208). In 2002 a major exhibition of paintings by Artemisia Gentileschi and her father, Orazio Gentileschi, was held at the Museo del Palazzo di Venezia, Rome, and subsequently at the Metropolitan Museum of Art in New York, and then at the Saint Louis Art Museum (see the catalogue, *Orazio and Artemisia Gentileschi*, edited by Keith Christiansen and Judith W. Mann). A smaller exhibition of Artemisia Gentileschi's paintings was held at the Casa Buonarroti in Florence, Italy, in 1991 (see the catalogue, *Artemisia*, a cura di Roberto Contini e Gianni Papi con un saggio di Luciano Berti).

3 See Longhi, "Gentileschi padre e figlia," 253, and Bissell, "Artemisia Gentileschi,"153.

4 Bissel, "Artemisia Gentileschi," 156.

5 See Greer, *The Obstacle Race*, 102. Bissell ("Artemisia Gentileschi," 153) in fact puts the word "rape" in sneer quotes. (His recent monograph, *Artemisia Gentileschi and the Authority of Art*, however, offers a rueful recantation of his earlier treatment of Artemisia's rape.) Something of this attitude is evident even in Longhi who, writing of Artemisia, seems quite ready to accept Tassi's self-serving countercharges: "She must have been very precocious in everything – one should consult, in this regard, the record of Tassi's trial – and thus too in painting, if, around 1612, at the age of fifteen, when Tassi was teaching her, among other things, perspective, she was painting the portrait of a child" ("Gentileschi padre e figlia," 254). Less ceremoniously, Rudolf and Margot Wittkower, largely on the basis of Tassi's own defence, blithely refer to Artemisia as "a lascivious and precocious girl," while at the same time they write: "The list of Tassi's 'escapades' is impressive: it includes rape, incest, sodomy, lech-

ery, and possibly homicide" (*Born under Saturn*, 163, 164). An account of – predominantly English – treatments of Artemisia Gentileschi by male historians and scholars over several centuries can be found in Garrard, "Artemisia and Susannah," 164.

6 See Garrard, "Artemisia and Susannah," 163–4, and Greer, *The Obstacle Race*, 192, where she speaks specifically of the *nozze di riparazione*, pointing out that marriages of reparation are still considered an acceptable sequel to rape in Southern Italy today; Garrard makes the same point about Sicily.

7 Woolf, *A Room of One's Own*, 74.

8 Ibid., 66.

9 Bissel, "Artemisia Gentileschi," 154.

10 Barthes, *Le Texte et l'image*," 95.

11 Garrard's fascinating discussion (*Artemisia Gentileschi*, 298–9) of Gentileschi's four Judith paintings (the one described in Banti's novel as well as the others) makes plain that the figure of Judith's maidservant Abra was typically present in the Judith paintings of other artists of the period. Garrard observes, however, that Gentileschi's presentation of Abra as a *young* woman – in Garrard's reading, as "a double of Judith" – is one of Gentileschi's important innovations in her distinctive treatment of this charged subject. Ibid., 310–13.

12 Garrard, "Artemisia and Susannah," 165.

13 Artemisia refers to works by a daughter in two letters, separated by some thirteen and a half years: 11 October 1635, A.M. Crinò, "More Letters from Orazio and Artemisia Gentileschi," 264, and 13 di Marzo 1649, *Bollettino d'arte* (1916), 49. Bissell argues persuasively that these must be two different daughters ("Artemisia Gentileschi – A New Documented Chronology," 158). Greer interprets Bissell's additional data in a way that would suggest Artemisia had at least three daughters (*The Obstacle Race*, 195).

14 *Bolletino d'arte*, 51.

15 As I pointed out in my introduction, note 12, the phrase disappears entirely in Caracciolo's English translation: "In my bosom lies a heart of gold" (106).

16 See Bottari and Ticozzi, *Raccolta di lettere sulla pittura, scultura ed architettura*, 353: "Sia servita darmi nuova della vita o morte di mio marito."

17 Garrard's full-length study also considers Artemisia Gentileschi's collaborations with Massimo Stanzione and Viviano Codazzi (*Artemisia Gentileschi* 97–9, 101).

18 See Levey, "Notes on the Royal Collection – II: Artemisia Gentileschi's 'Self-Portrait' at Hampton Court"; Garrard, "Artemisia Gentileschi's Self-Portrait as the Allegory of Painting" and *Artemisia Gentileschi* 337–71; Parker and Pollock, *Old Mistresses*, 25–6; and Greer, *The Obstacle Race*, 201.

19 Notable exceptions to this pattern are the many self-portraits by Sofonisba Anguissola (1532/35–1625); see Harris and Nochlin, *Women Artists*, 27–8, 106–8, and Parker and Pollock, *Old Mistresses*, 18, 84–6. Parker and Pollock also suggest as a "precedent for ... [the] image of a woman artist dishevelled and absorbed in work" an anonymous portrait medallion of the Bolognese painter Lavinia Fontana (though it is not a self-portrait); at the same time, they contrast this view of a woman artist "seized by some strange form of lunacy and ecstasy" with "Gentileschi's quiet, serious and dignified realism" (ibid., 25). Some delightful early self-portraits of women artists are included in Fox, *The Medieval Woman: Illuminated Book of Days*, 19–24 March, 19–24 May, 13–18 November.

20 For example, during her "honeymoon" with Vronsky in Italy, Tolstoy's Anna Karenina sits for portraits by both her lover and a resident Russian artist. And she is considerably more successful in her role of model than she will be later in the novel when she turns to creative endeavours in her own right; her work on a children's book in the increasingly strained final period of her liaison with Vronsky is presented as a desperate piece of busywork, tending chiefly to emphasize her tragic alienation from society and, ironically, her inadequacies as a mother to both her legitimate son and illegitimate daughter. In George Eliot's *Middlemarch*, Dorothea Brooke Casaubon, also on a honeymoon in Italy, serves as inspirational model for a portrait by a German artist friend of Will Ladislaw. However, with the exception of her early plans for tenant cottages, Dorothea never turns to creative work herself; when she later speculates on the possibility of Will's becoming a poet, asserting that she herself could never produce a poem, Will counters, "You *are* a poem" (256, ch. 22).

21 Both Jane Austen's Emma Woodhouse and Flaubert's Emma Bovary have learned to dabble at sketching as part of their proper young lady's education, and the reader of both novels gets amusing glimpses of their scarcely impressive work. As a governess, Charlotte Brontë's Jane Eyre both teaches and practices drawing and painting; but while she is more truly accomplished than either the French or English Emma, even her haunting watercolour paintings, which are described in some detail, are important only for what they tell us about her sensibility and imagination. Theodor

Fontane's eponymous Effi Briest and Kate Chopin's Edna Pontellier (*The Awakening*) both turn to sketching and painting with relative earnestness in the interval between their estrangement from their husbands and the death that inevitably seals the fate of adulterous heroines in nineteenth-century fiction. But both women are presented as having the wisdom and good grace not to take their artistic activity too seriously, and neither novelist bothers to say much about the content of either heroine's work.

22 Woolf, *To the Lighthouse*, 216.

23 We know only that a purple triangle represents Mrs Ramsay sitting with her son and that "a light there needed a shadow there" (ibid., 238).

CHAPTER FOUR

1 All references to Alice Munro's stories will be included in my text. Unless otherwise specified, the page numbers refer to *Friend of My Youth*.

2 On metamorphosis, change, and fluid boundaries, see Lorna Irving, who treats these as properties of *female* nature in "'Changing Is the Word I Want.'" On Munro's refusal of definitive closure, also see David Crouse, "Resisting Reduction: Closure in Richard Ford's *Rock Springs* and Alice Munro's *Friend of My Youth*," and Helen Hoy, "Alice Munro: 'Unforgettable, Indigestible Messages,'" 18–19. A number of critics observe that the self in Munro is shifting and multiple. E.g. see Blodget, *Alice Munro*, 12, 68, and passim; Thacker, "'So Shocking a Verdict in Real Life,'" 156; Stead, "The Twinkling of an 'I'," 151–3; Hoy, "Alice Munro," 17.

3 Munro, "Real Material," 21. Speaking of her mother in another interview, Munro says of "The Peace of Utrecht," "The first real story I ever wrote was about her" ("Alice Munro," 215).

4 See also Carrington, *Controlling the Uncontrollable*, 187–8; and Stead, "The Twinkling of an 'I,'" 156. Earlier in "Friend of My Youth," the narrator writes of her mother's becoming "busy with her own life and finally a prisoner in it" (19).

5 See also Stead, "Twinkling," 156 and Redekop, *Mothers and Other Clowns*, 215.

6 This fear would fit nicely into Carrington's thesis that "the most central and creative paradox of Munro's fiction is its repeated ... attempt to control what is uncontrollable" (*Controlling the Uncontrollable*, 5).

7 Carol Shields, "In Ontario," 22. Dermot McCarthy writes of the mother's affirming "her own impenetrable otherness" ("The Woman Out Back: Alice Munro's 'Meneseteung,'" 12).

8 This suggests more radical doubt than is implied by the question in "Winter Wind," "How am I to know what I claim to know?" (*Something I've Been Meaning to Tell You*, 201), or than "the difficulty of getting to the truth," which W.R. Martin has described as a focus of *Lives of Girls and Women* and "The Progress of Love" (*Alice Munro: Paradox and Parallel*, 179). It leads into "the vexatious question of the nature of reality" (Hoy, "Alice Munro," 12) and of Munro's relation to postmodernism and metafiction, which have been treated with increasing frequency by critics. Linda Hutcheon, for example, identifies Munro as a "postmodern metafiction writer" (*The Canadian Postmodern*, 45 and *passim*), while Stephen Regan comments on her willingness "to harbour intense doubts about the representational value of fiction and yet to persevere in the creation of something that is true to life" ("'The Presence of the Past,'" 124–5).

9 Also see "The Peace of Utrecht" (*Dance of the Happy Shades*, 195, 199).

10 Katherine J. Mayberry ("Narrative Strategies of Liberation in Alice Munro," 59) discusses the development of the "communal cooperative narrative" in *The Moons of Jupiter* (though she locates it first at the end of *The Lives of Girls and Women*). The kind of collaborative narrative that I am describing in *Friend of My Youth* is similar, but not identical, to the narrative cooperation that she describes in the earlier books; our view of the impulse behind such narratives also differs somewhat. In a parenthetical remark (64), Mayberry does mention "Friend of My Youth" as an example of this "new configuration of narrative," but she does not elaborate.

11 Munro's rejection of anything like "a traditional plot" has become a basic premise of Munro criticism. See, for example, Mathews, "*Who Do You Think You Are?* Alice Munro's Art of Disarrangement."

12 For example, Rose in *Who Do You Think You Are?* and Isabel in "White Dump" in *The Progress of Love*. The situation recurs in "The Children Stay" and "Jakarta," in *The Love of a Good Woman*.

13 Woolf, *A Room of One's Own*, 96.

14 McCarthy, "The Woman Out Back," 1, and Redekop, *Mothers and Other Clowns*, 227, also speak of Almeda as foremother and offer various Canadian examples of this kind of recovery.

15 See McCarthy ("The Woman Out Back," 4): "The 'plot' of the story is the project of freeing this imaginative ancestor from the patriarchal stereotype."

16 McCarthy, "The Woman Out Back," 20; Redekop, *Mothers*, 255; and Stead, "Twinkling," 159, all see "wrath" in Almeda's last name, Roth. Perhaps we can also see the Early Middle English "ruth," whose first definition in the Shorter OED is "the quality of being compassionate; pitifulness; compassion, pity."

17 McCarthy, "Woman," 7. For Redekop, "this body is a parody of Mother Earth" (*Mothers*, 224).

18 See also Stead, "Twinkling," 161.

19 In Charlotte Perkins Gilman's *The Yellow Wallpaper*, the heroine obsessively watches movements behind the wallpaper, seeing there a woman behind bars struggling to get out. After "helping" the kindred woman by ripping off wide swaths of the wallpaper, she imaginatively merges with this phantom as she seeks her own escape.

20 More than thirty years ago, Munro wrote of the "short river the Indians called the Menesetung [*sic*] and the first settlers ... called the Maitland," which flowed past her father's land. Rising in spring to cover the flats, thus earning the nickname "the Flood," "shallow and tropical" in summer, and filled with myriad varieties of plants and fish, it offered a comprehensive image of the variegated abundance of ordinary experience: "We believed there were deep holes in the river ... I am still partly convinced that this river – not even the whole river, but this little stretch of it – will provide whatever myths you want, whatever adventures. I name the plants, I name the fish, and every name seems to me triumphant, every leaf and quick fish remarkably valuable. This ordinary place is sufficient, everything here is touchable and mysterious" ("Everything Here Is Touchable and Mysterious").

21 While this scene has rightly been viewed as echoing the end of "The Stone in the Field" in *The Moons of Jupiter*, it may be more instructive to contrast the narrator's passionate "scrabbling" in "Meneseteung" with the narrator's rational decision in "The Stone in the Field" not to bother walking over to the rock-pile.

CHAPTER FIVE

1 Grace Paley, *The Collected Stories*, 81. All future citations of the three volumes of Paley's stories are to this edition and page references are included in my text. References to collections of Paley's essays and occasional pieces (*Just as I Thought* and *Long Walks and Intimate Talks*) are also included in my text, with appropriate identification.

2 Batt and Rocard, "An Interview with Grace Paley," 235.
3 Lidoff, "Clearing Her Throat," 79.
4 Paley, "The Value of Not Understanding Everything," in *Just as I Thought*, 186.
5 Remnick, "Grace Paley, Voice from the Village," 134, and Bonetti, "An Interview with Grace Paley, 179.
6 Batt and Rocard, "An Interview," 134, 5.
7 For studies of Faith that treat her as a consistent psychological character see, for example, Baba, "Faith Darwin as Writer Heroine," and Mandel, "Keeping Up with Faith" For Faith as the embodiment of Paley's "philosophy," see Gelfant, "Grace Paley: Fragments for a Portrait in Collage" (59): "This sense of the value of life – and of every individual life and of life as process and change – may be exactly what we mean by faith; and Paley's heroine, who pops in and out of her stories, growing older and treasuring both past and future, is well named."
8 In an interview more than twenty years after the publication of this story, Paley observes, "People have always blamed everything on that poor egg ... Society has told you that your egg is responsible for the child and that you yourself are responsible for the life of the child, for what happens to the kid" (Burns and Sugnet, "Grace Paley," 16, 18).
9 Baba, "Faith Darwin as Writer Heroine," 42–3, Mandel, "Keeping Up With Faith," 91, and Kamel, "To Aggrevate the Conscience," 38, all praise the image that, Kamel writes, "embodies the bonding-bondage encompassing single parenthood." (Why only single?) Neil D. Isaacs writes, "Tonto climbs into her lap, forming a living statue of a *Pietà*" (*Grace Paley: A Study of the Short Fiction*, 27). But the essence of the *pietà* is the *dead* son, whereas this one is very much alive.
10 Conway et. al., "Grace Paley Interview," 5.
11 While Paley refuses to speculate on the literal meaning of her heroine's name, the word "grace" recurs in her interviews, used, in a secularized version of its Christian meaning, to designate the serendipitous mystery by which a writer finds the proper form. "The form, the vessel, has to be given to you, and that's by grace" (Conway, "Grace Paley Interview," 6); "the form is given by grace ... it descends on you ... it's like gifts that do come from outside" (Hulley, "Interview with Grace Paley," 37). "And the form, I don't know how it's gotten; I consider it received, like grace" (Lidoff, "Clearing Her Throat," 86).
12 We could speculate even further on Paley's sense of play by toying with the notion that Charles Darwin's nineteenth-century scientific theory of evolution can be regarded as a subversion of William Paley's

eighteenth-century theological argument from design, but the impact of the Darwin family name is strong enough without recourse to the author's married one.

13 While some critics haven written of Jack (from the later Faith stories) as Faith's husband (Baba, "Faith Darwin as Writer Heroine," 47; Arcana, "Truth in Mothering," 206, and "*Grace Paley's Life Stories*, 165; Cronin, "Melodramas of Beset Womanhood," 144), the more compelling evidence is that Jack is, rather, a longstanding but not always present lover of Faith's. One critic, observing Faith's husbandless status in the later stories, also describes her as "twice-abandoned" (Mandel, "Keeping Up with Faith," 85). But there is no evidence for this, unless one feels a compulsion to impose an artificial consistency on the persona of Faith from one collection to another.

14 My understanding of this sentence is helped by my own mother's description of *her* grandmother, who "lived in Yorkville in the days when Jews thought they were Germans."

15 DeKoven, "Mrs Hegel-Shtein's Tears," 220–2.

16 Mandel, "Keeping Up With Faith," 92.

17 Baba, "Faith Darwin as Writer Heroine, 44.

18 Aarons, "Talking Lives," 32.

19 Aeschylus, *Agamemnon*, ll. 463–6.

20 Issacs, who judges this as "perhaps the least fulfilled as a story," surprisingly asserts it is "almost entirely explication" (*Grace Paley*, 41).

21 In *Just as I Thought* (1998), the story is followed by a statement locating this piece as having been written before the AIDS epidemic.

22 Isaacs, *Grace Paley*, 47.

23 See Burns, "Grace Paley," 22, 23; Perry, "Grace Paley," 99; Kaplan, "Grace Paley Talking with Cora Kaplan," 151; Taylor, "Grace Paley on Storytelling and Story Hearing," 169; Bonetti, "An Interview with Grace Paley," 184.

24 Barbara Eckstein ("Grace Paley's Community,"132) credits this reading, with which she concurs, to Mandel, though Mandel herself is actually somewhat less reductionist.

25 Perry, "Grace Paley," 99.

26 Kaplan, "Grace Paley Talking," 152.

27 Burns, "Grace Paley," 18–19.

28 "I'm a woman and that makes a big difference. It separates me a lot from Bellow and Roth and all those guys. There's such a distortion in their writing sometimes, the kind of stuff that gives men a bad name" (Remnick, "Grace Paley," 134).

29 Commenting on her characters' lack of guilt, Paley says, "I think I made a mistake in some ways because although they don't feel guilty in there, just because they're fictional characters, a couple of them should!" She points out, for example, that although Faith "refuses guilt" when her lover Clifford accuses her of not raising the children right, "a lot of her sisters accepted" it "because they were so involved in psychology. I have spent time with women going around to psychiatrists about their children, and everything, everything, was always their fault!" (Batt and Rocard, "Interview," 136).

30 For Grace Paley's frequent use of the term "grace," see note 11 above. Elsewhere Paley speaks of "the discovery of form – which the Lord gives you sometimes, and sometimes he don't" (Michaels, "Conversation with Grace Paley," 31).

31 Hulley, "Interview with Grace Paley, 37; Conway, "Grace Paley Interview, 6; Michaels, "Conversation with Grace Paley, 31; Silesky, "Grace Paley: A Conversation," 141. She makes essentially the same points in all these interviews, though the gestation period she gives for the story varies, from the low of twenty (told to Silesky in 1985) to the high of twenty-five, thirty (told to Michaels, 1980).

32 Despite the distinction in this story, in later stories it is Jack who is (or becomes) the historian. In "The Story Hearer" (*Later the Same Day*), Jack writes for a magazine called *The Social Ordure* (340, 343), and in "The Expensive Moment" (also in *Later the Same Day*), where he is described as "reading reading reading, thinking writing grieving all night the bad world-ending politics," we see a picture of him giving a paper at the Other Historian meeting (375). However, Paley seems happily ready to shift many details of her characters' lives, as I shall show.

33 Taylor, "Grace Paley on Story Telling," 173.

34 Paley's metafictional play becomes more apparent and has been frequently noted in *Later the Same Day*, where, in "Love," the narrator's husband mentions Dotty Wasserman (a main character in "The Contest," *Little Disturbances of Man*, and the offstage girlfriend of Ricardo in "Faith in a Tree," *Enormous Changes at the Last Minute*) as a former girlfriend. The narrator – a writer, the Paley persona – dismisses his claim, pointing out that Dotty was "made up, just plain invented in the late fifties" (262). But he stubbornly clings to his story.

35 Eckstein, however, writes, somewhat puzzlingly, "Faith returns home where her sons, now grown, engage in nononsense political activity" ("Grace Paley's Community," 132).

36 Park, Clara Claiborne, "Faith, Grace and Love," 486.

37 In the separately published collections, as several critics have noted, Faith's parents have one set of first names in "Faith in the Afternoon" (Gersh and Gittel) and another set in "Dreamer in a Dead Language" (Sid and Celia). In the more recent one-volume *Collected Stories*, however, Paley harmonizes the names, making the parents Sid and Celia in the earlier story as well, and turning Mrs Hegel-Shtein, who had originally been named Celia, into Gittel. Similarly, Philip's name, which had had two l's when "Faith in a Tree" appeared in the separately published *Enormous Changes at the Last Minute* becomes Philip with one l when that story is republished in *Collected Stories*, harmonizing him with Philip in "Dreamer," who always had a single l. In "Dreamer" Philip is identified as "the guy who dumped" Anita Franklin (268), suggesting some slippage between him and the Arthur Mazzano of Mrs Darwin's story in "Faith in the Afternoon." Clara Claiborne Park asserts that Arthur Mazzano "definitely" becomes Phillip in volume three ("Faith, Grace, and Love," 486); I prefer to call this slippage rather than identity, not only because "Philip" is different from "Arthur" but also because it is hard to reconcile the Harvard scholar with "maybe two PhD's" whom we hear about in "Afternoon" with the somewhat itinerant Philip we meet in "Tree," who has children in Chicago and describes himself as having been a teacher and worked for the State Department but now wants to be a comedian (despite the fact that he's not funny). Paley's response to an interviewer who comments on the "fun" it is "trying to keep up with these characters and all their connections," is telling: "Well, sometimes it gets all mixed up ... So I decided not to worry about it. I just want to pretty generally imply the connections, but it doesn't have to be exactly right" (Taylor, "Grace Paley on Storytelling," 173).

38 Ibid., 174.

39 Ibid., 60.

40 Wisse, *The Schlemiel as Modern Hero*, 3.

41 Ibid., 22.

42 Ibid., 44.

43 Samuel, "The Tribune of the Golus," 54; cited in Wisse, *The Schlemiel*, 44.

44 Hulley, "Interview with Grace Paley," 41.

45 Bonetti, Kay, "An Interview with Grace Paley," 183, 190, 184.

46 A reader's immediate assumption here will be that Rachel has participated in violent action of the kind carried out by young anti-war

activists during the time of the Vietnam War. That conflict, however, also had a protracted afterlife. See note 48.

47 "A lot of political writing ... is about leaders and big shots ... my interest ... is in writing about ordinary political people [.] I think they've been abandoned in many ways, as though they don't exist. The fact that there are a lot of people who are just normally political is a hidden fact in this country. Nobody wants to know it, and they try to pretend that there is only private life, and that people don't even talk politics, which they really do" (Kaplan, "Grace Paley Talking with Cora Kaplan," 147).

48 The fact that the Vietnam War is never specifically mentioned by Paley may have more than literary causes, as the "moment" was, in fact, a protracted one. In an interview Paley has said, "I often think of those kids in the Brinks case. If they had been born four years later, five years earlier ... It really was that particular moment: they were called. In one of the new stories ['Friends'], I talk about that whole beloved generation of our children who were really wrecked" (Smith, "PW Interviews Grace Paley," 128). Two policemen and one security guard were killed in the Brinks robbery attempt, which, notably, occurred in 1981, six years *after* the end of the Vietnam War; the tangled motivation of some of its participants, however, goes back to their wartime political engagement. One of "those kids," Kathy Boudin (then 38 years old), had spent more than eleven years underground, between the memorable explosion of the Greenwich Village townhouse in March 1970, the result of a bombmaking project gone awry, and the failed robbery getaway. Paley's creation of the fictional Rachel may well owe something to the experience of Kathy Boudin and her parents, Greenwich Village neighbours of Paley's. Boudin's parole hearing in August 2001, after twenty years in prison, was the occasion for a flurry of journalistic accounts of her case. See Kolbert's *New Yorker* article and the *New York Times* reports, 20 and 23 August 2001; when she was finally granted parole two years later, the news was on the front page of the *New York Times* (21 August 2003). A book about Kathy Boudin and her family was published in the same year (*Family Circle: The Boudins and the Aristocracy of the Left*, by Susan Braudy).

49 Roth, *American Pastoral*, 88.

50 Ibid., 246, 241.

51 Presenting a mother's view of the Cultural Revolution may remind us of Paley's praise of Elsa Morante's novel *History: A Novel*, which charts the Second World War from the point of view of a mother of two sons,

trying to survive in Rome. Paley refers to this as "another great book that really no man could write" (Fromkorth and Opfermann, "Grace Paley," 254). See also Lidoff, "Clearing Her Throat," 93.

52 If Xie Feng's moral dilemma, and the childlike simplicity and directness of language with which she expresses it, recall Brecht's Shen Te, however, the world faced by Brecht's compassionate mother-to-be appears more non-negotiably Manichean. Whereas Xie Feng still thinks some moral accommodation may be possible, Shen Te well knows that only on "Nimmerleinstag" (never-to-be day) "zahlt die Güte sich aus/Und die Schlechtigkeit kostet den Hals" (Brecht, *Der gute Mensch*, 65–6: is good rewarded and does bad cost you your neck), and that she can save her unborn child from want and evil only by "doubling" herself in the persona of her ruthless cousin, Shui Ta. As she confesses to the gods in anguish and perplexity at the end of the play (98–9):

Euer einstiger Befehl
Gut zu sein und doch zu leben
Zerriß mich wie ein Blitz in zwei Hälften. Ich
Weiß nicht, wie es kam: gut sein zu andern
Und zu mir konnte ich nicht zugleich.
Andern und mir zu helfen, war mir zu schwer.
Ach, eure Welt is schwierig! ...
... Wer den Verlorenen hilft
Ist selbst verloren!

(Your former command to be good and yet to live split me in two halves like a bolt of lightning. I don't know how it happened: I couldn't be good to others and to myself at the same time. Ah, your world is difficult ... Whoever helps the lost ones is lost himself.) All translations from the German, including that in note 64 below, are mine.

53 Paley has described how she had originally planned to have Faith tell this story, then realized it was impossible – "she didn't know the first damn thing about him" – and the story had to be told by Zagrowsky (Bonetti, "An Interview with Grace Paley," 185).

54 See Paley's reference to "those kids in the Brinks case" in note 48. After saying of them, "It really was that particular moment: they were called," she refers to one of the new stories where she talks "about that whole beloved generation of our children who were really wrecked." The interviewer inserts "Friends" in brackets here, but although Faith comments in that story on "that beloved generation of our children murdered by cars, lost to war, to drugs, to madness," it actually treats only those children lost to drugs and madness, not to war. In this

interview, in fact, Paley may be referring to two stories at once, "Friends" and "The Expensive Moment." Following her comment about "the generation of children who were really wrecked," Paley adds: "I mean, I lived through the Second World War, and I only knew one person in my generation who died. My children, who are in their early thirties, I can't tell you the number of people they know who have died or gone mad. They're a wonderful generation though: thoughtful, idealistic, self-giving and honorable. They really gave" (Smith, "PW Interviews Grace Paley," 128).

55 Victoria Aarons, who stresses Paley's debt to Sholom Aleichem, is on firmest ground here. "As the tellers of their own tales, Paley's characters resemble the monologists in Sholom Aleichem's early stories of ordinary *shtetl* Jews, Jews who relate their troubles, their complaints to the writer Sholem Aleichem" (*A Measure of Memory*, 126). Also see Aarons "A Perfect Marginality," 39. In fact, few of Paley's characters are actually monologists in the sense that Zagrowsky and Rosie Lieber ("Goodbye and Good Luck") are, and Zagrowsky's story is not exactly ordinary. Murray Baumgarten also mentions the example of Sholem Aleichem in his discussion of Grace Paley ("Urban Rites and Civic Premises," 410).

56 We know this is Faith because at the end of "The Story Hearer," the narrator, who has been identified as Mrs A. by her grocer, is talking to Jack and reflects, "The day had been too long and I hadn't said one word about the New Young Fathers or my meeting with Zagrowsky the Pharmacist" (343).

57 For example, Aarons speaks of Paley's "unwavering optimism" (*A Measure of Memory*, 168), Arcana of her "insistent optimism" ("Truth in Mothering," 204), and Taylor of her "irrepressible optimism" (*Grace Paley*, 55). A corollary of this is the critics' insistence on Paley's "chronic hopefulness" (Taylor, *Grace Paley*, 55); "Truth plus hope is Paley's formula" (Arcana, "Truth," 204).

58 Voltaire, *Candide ou l'Optimisme*, 183, ch. 19.

59 Michaels, "Conversation," 30–1.

60 Hulley, "Interview with Grace Paley," 39, 46.

61 Bonetti, "An Interview with Grace Paley," 191.

62 Wachtel, "An Interview with Grace Paley," 210.

63 In one place where Paley refers to "my disposition, which tends to crude optimism" (*Just as I Thought*, 289), it is clear that she is writing of her temperament, not her intellectual outlook. Similarly, in an interview describing a local victory preventing the city from pushing a road

through Washington Square Park, she says, "We fought that and we won; in fact, having won, my friends and I had a kind of optimism for the next 20 years that we might win something else by luck." The interviewer then reports, "She laughs, as amused by her chronic optimism as she is convinced of its necessity" (Smith, "PW Interviews Grace Paley," 128). While Paley continues to act as though one can make a difference in the world, her words and laugh here seem rather to point to an ironic estimation of the "kind of optimism" she had in the wake of this success and hardly justify the interviewer's broad inferences.

64 One might be tempted to compare this to the contrary view expressed in Brecht's lines from "An die Nachgeborenen" (To Posterity) in *Hundert Gedichte* (305):
Was sind das für Zeiten, wo
Ein Gespräch über Bäume fast ein Verbrechen ist
Weil es ein Schweigen über so viele Untaten einschließt!
(What kind of times are these, where speaking of trees is almost a crime because it implies silence about so many horrible deeds?)

65 Cassie's criticism is limited to Faith's sin of omission; she does not look back to her friend's earlier reflection in "Faith in a Tree," where, with little visible evidence, Faith assumes that the overtures of a handsome man to her friend Lynn are those of a "weekend queer, talking her into the possibilities of a neighbourhood threesome" (182). Faith and her author have clearly come a long way from that earlier story.

66 Silesky, "Grace Paley," 136.

67 Marchant and Robertson, "A Conversation with Grace Paley," 121. See also Pearlman, "Grace Paley. Listen to Their Voices," 228.

68 Fromkorth and Opfermann, "Grace Paley," 258.

69 Porton, "Midrash," 818, 19.

70 I am indebted to my colleague Barrie Wilson for this looser definition.

71 "We hold these truths to be self-evident, that all men are created equal, that they are endowed by their Creator with certain inalienable Rights, and among these are Life, Liberty and the pursuit of Happiness" (Jefferson, "The Declaration of Independence," 307).

72 In interviews Paley frequently talks about her Jewishness, linking it to both her irony and her social consciousness: "I really felt having an identity of some kind with a people who had been seriously, severely oppressed for a couple of thousand years, not just last week, not since the Holocaust, but for a long, long time really gave me a very powerful and active feeling for other people ... I liked very much ... the social tradition of the Jewish family of very deep charity toward others and a

feeling … that they really had of helping other people, of sympathy, of empathy … and a strong social consciousness" (Satz, "Looking at Disparities," 196, 7). In the section following this midrash in "*Just As I Thought*" Paley describes the effect of her upbringing: even after she "got over" her childhood assumption "that to be Jewish was to be a socialist" (48), she still "had this idea that Jews were supposed to be better. I'm not saying they were, but they were *supposed* to be; and it seemed to me on my block that they often were. I don't see any reason in being in this world actually if you can't in some way be better, repair it somehow" (49).

Works Cited

Aarons, Victoria. *A Measure of Memory: Storytelling and Identity in American Jewish Fiction*. Athens: University of Georgia Press, 1996.

– "A Perfect Marginality: Public and Private Telling in the Stories of Grace Paley." *Studies in Short Fiction* 27, no. 1 (Winter 1990): 35–43.

– "Selves and 'Other Shadows': Grace Paley's Ironic Fictions." In *Speaking the Other Self: American Women Writers*, edited by Jeanne Campbell Reesman, 185–98.

– "Talking Lives: Storytelling and Renewal in Grace Paley's Short Fiction." *Studies in American Jewish Fiction* 9 (1990): 20–36.

Aeschylus, *Agamemnon*. Translated by Richard Latimore. *Greek Tragedies Vol. 1*. Edited by David Grene and Richard Lattimore. Chicago: University of Chicago Press, 1953.

Arcana, Judith. "Truth in Mothering: Grace Paley's Stories." In *Narrating Mothers: Theorizing Maternal Subjectivities*, edited by Brenda O. Daley and Maureen T. Reddy, 195–209.

– *Grace Paley's Life Stories: A Literary Biography*. Urbana: University of Illinois Press, 1993.

Austen, Jane. *Emma*. 1816. Introduction by Lionel Trilling. Boston: Houghton Mifflin, 1957.

Baba, Minako. "Faith Darwin as Writer Heroine: A Study of Grace Paley's Short Stories." *Studies in American Jewish Literature* 7 (Spring 1988): 40–55.

Bach, Gerhard, and Blaine Hall, eds. *Conversations with Grace Paley*. Jackson: University Press of Mississippi, 1997.

Balayé, Simone. *Madame de Staël: Lumières et Liberté*. Paris: Editions Klincksieck, 1979.

Banti, Anna. *Artemisia*. 1947. N.P. (Italy): Mondadori, 1974.

– *Artemisia*. Translated by Shirley D'Ardia Caracciolo. Lincoln: University of Nebraska Press, 1988.

Barthes, Roland. *Le Texte et l'image*. Paris: Edition Paris Musées, 1986.

Batt, Noelle, and Marcienne Rocard. "An Interview with Grace Paley." *Caliban* 25 (1988): 119–38.

Baumgarten, Murray. "Urban Rites and Civic Premises in the Fiction of Saul Bellow, Grace Paley, and Sandra Schor." *Contemporary Literature* 34:3 (1993): 395–425.

Beer, Gillian. *George Eliot*. Bloomington: Indiana University Press, 1986.

Binder, Wolfgang, and Helmbrecht Breinig, eds. *American Contradictions: Interviews with Nine American Writers*. Hanover: University Press of New England, 1995.

Bissel, R. Ward. *Artemisia Gentileschi and the Authority of Art: Critical Reading and Catalogue Raisonné*. University Park Pennsylvania: Pennsylvania University Press, 1999.

– "Artemisia Gentileschi – A New Documented Chronology." *Art Bulletin* 50, no. 2 (1968): 153–68.

Blanchard, Paula. "*Corinne* and the 'Yankee Corinna': Madame de Staël and Margaret Fuller." In *Woman as Mediatrix: Essays on Nineteenth-Century European Women Writers*, edited by Avriel H. Goldberger, 39–47. Westport, CT: Greenwood, 1987.

Blodget, E.D. *Alice Munro*. Boston: Twayne, 1988.

Bollettino d'arte (Rome 1916): 46–53.

Bonetti, Kay. "An Interview with Grace Paley." Audiocassette. *The American Audio Prose Library*. 1986. Reprinted in *Conversations with Grace Paley*, edited by Gerhard Bach and Blaine Hall, 177–92.

Bottari, Giovanni Gaetano, and Stefano Ticozzi. *Raccolta di lettere sulla pittura, scultura ed architettura scritta da' più celebri personaggi dai secoli XV, XVI, XVII*. 1822. 8 vols. Vol. 1, 349–55. Hildesheim and New York: Georg Olms Verlag, 1976.

Bradley, Sculley, Richard Croom Beatly, E. Hudson Long, and George Perkins, eds. *The American Tradition in Literature*. 4th ed. N.p.: Grosset and Dunlap, 1974.

Brecht, Bertolt. *Der gute Mensch von Sezuan*. Berlin: Aufbau-Verlag, 1960.

– *Hundert Gedichte: 1918–1950*. Berlin: Aufbau-Verlag, 1959.

Brontë, Charlotte. *Jane Eyre*. 1847. Edited by Q.D. Leavis. Harmondsworth, England: Penguin, 1966.

Browning, Elizabeth Barret. *Aurora Leigh and Other Poems*. Edited with an introduction by Cora Kaplan. London: The Women's Press, 1978.

– *Aurora Leigh*. 1859. Edited by Margaret Reynolds. New York: W.W. Norton and Company, 1996.

Burns, Alan, and Charles Sugnet. "Grace Paley." In *The Imagination on Trial: British and American Writers Discuss Their Working Methods*, 121–32. London: Allison and Busby, 1978. Reprinted in *Conversations with Grace Paley*, edited by Gerhard Bach and Blaine Hall, 14–26.

Carrington, Ildikó de Papp. *Controlling the Uncontrollable: The Fiction of Alice Munro*. DeKalb, IL: Northern Illinois University Press, 1989.

Chamberlain, Mary, ed. *Writing Lives: Conversations between Women Writers*. London: Virago, 1988.

Chopin, Kate. *The Awakening*. 1899. Edited by Margaret Culley. New York: W.W. Norton, 1976.

Christiansen, Keith, and Judith W. Mann, eds. *Orazio and Artemisia Gentileschi*. New Haven and London: The Metropolitan Museum and Yale University Press, 2001.

Cohen, Elizabeth S. "The Trials of Artemisia Gentileschi: A Rape as History." *Sixteenth Century Journal* 31, no. 1 (2001). 47–75.

Contini, Roberto, and Gianni Papi, eds. *Artemisia*. Con un saggio di Luciano Berti. Rome: Leonardo ~ DeLuca Editori s.r.l, 1991.

Conway, Celeste, Elizabeth Innes-Brown, Laura Levine, Keith Monley, and MarkTeich. "Grace Paley Interview." *Columbia: A Magazine of Poetry and Prose* 2 (1978): 29–39. Reprinted in *Conversations with Grace Paley*, edited by Gerhard Bach and Blaine Hall, 3–14.

Crinò, Anna Maria. "More Letters from Orazio and Artemisia Gentileschi." *The Burlington Magazine* 102 (1960): 264–5. In Italian.

Cronin, Gloria L. "Melodramas of Beset Womanhood: Resistance, Subversion, and Survival in the Fiction of Grace Paley." *Studies in American Jewish Literature*. 11 (1992): 140–50.

Crouse, David. "Resisting Reduction: Closure in Richard Ford's *Rock Springs* and Alice Munro's *Friend of My Youth*." *Canadian Literature* 146 (1995): 51–64.

Daley, Brenda O., and Maureen T. Reddy, eds. *Narrating Mothers: Theorizing Maternal Subjectivities*. Knoxville: University of Tennessee Press, 1991.

DeKoven, Marianne. "Mrs Hegel-Shtein's Tears." *Partisan Review* 48 (1981): 217–23.

Dickens, Charles. *Great Expectations*. 1861. Edited by Angus Calder. Harmondsworth: Penguin, 1977.

Eckstein, Barbara. "Grace Paley's Community: Gradual Epiphanies in the Meantime." In *Politics and the Muse: Studies in the Politics of Recent*

American Literature, edited by Adam J. Sorkin, 124–61. Bowling Green, OH: Bowling Green State University Popular Press, 1989.

Eliot, George. *Adam Bede*. 1859. Edited by Stephen Gill. London: Penguin, 1985.

– *Daniel Deronda*. 1876. Edited by Barbara Hardy. Harmondsworth: Penguin, 1976.

– *Essays of George Eliot*. Edited by Thomas Pinney. London: Routledge and Kegan Paul, 1963.

– *The George Eliot Letters II, IV, V, VIII*. Edited by Gordon Haight. New Haven: Yale University Press, 1954, 1955, 1978.

– *Impressions of Theophrastus Such*. Edited by Nancy Henry. London: William Pickering, 1994.

– *Middlemarch*. 1871–72. Edited by W.J. Harvey. London: Penguin, 1985.

– *The Mill on the Floss*. 1860. Edited by Gordon S. Haight. Oxford: Oxford University Press, 1998.

– "The Modern Hep! Hep! Hep!" In George Eliot. *Impressions of Theophrastus Such*, 143–67.

– *Romola*. 1863. Edited by Andrew Sanders. Harmondsworth: Penguin, 1980.

Flaubert, Gustave. *Madame Bovary: Moeurs de Province*. 1857. Avec introduction, notes et variantes par Édouard Maynial. Paris: Garnier Frères, n.d.

Fontane, Theodor. *Effi Briest*. 1894. Leipzig: Friedrich Rothbart, 1938.

Fox, Sally, ed. *The Medieval Woman: Illuminated Book of Days*. Toronto: Key Porter Books, 1985. First published in the US as a New York Graphic Society book by Little, Brown, 1985.

Fromkorth, Birgit, and Susanne Opfermann. "Grace Paley." In *American Contradictions: Interviews with Nine American Writers*, edited by Wolfgang Binder and Helmbrecht Breinig, 78–100. Reprinted in *Conversations with Grace Paley*, edited by Gerhard Bach and Blaine Hall, 249–69.

Garrard, Mary D. *Artemisia Gentileschi: The Image of the Female Hero in Italian Baroque Art*. Princeton: Princeton University Press, 1989.

– "Artemisia and Susannah." In *Feminism and Art History: Questioning the Litany*, edited by Norma Broude and Mary D. Garrard, 147–73. New York: Harper and Row, 1982.

– "Artemisia Gentileschi: The Artist's Autograph in Letters and Paintings." In *The Female Autograph*, edited by Donna C. Stanton and Jeanine Parisier Plottel, 91–106. New York: New York Literary Forum, 1984.

– "Artemisia Gentileschi's Self-Portrait as the Allegory of Painting." *Art Bulletin* 62, no. 1 (1980): 97–112.

Gelfant, Blanche H. "Grace Paley: Fragments for a Portrait in Collage." *Women Writing in America,* 11–29. Hanover: University Press of New England, 1984. Reprinted in *Conversations with Grace Paley,* edited by Gerhard Bach and Blaine Hall, 56–72

Gennari, Geneviève. *Le Premier Voyage de Madame de Staël en Italie et la Genèse de Corinne.* Paris: Boivin, 1947.

Gilbert, Sandra M., and Susan Gubar. *The Madwoman in the Attic.* New Haven: Yale University Press, 1979.

Gilman, Charlotte Perkins. *The Yellow Wallpaper.* 1892. New York: The Feminist Press, 1973.

Goldberger, Avriel H., ed. *Woman as Mediatrix: Essays on Nineteenth-Century European Women Writers.* Westport, CT: Greenwood, 1987.

Greer, Germaine. "The Magnificent Exception." In Germaine Greer. *The Obstacle Race: The Fortunes of Women Painters and Their Work,* 189–208.

– *The Obstacle Race: The Fortunes of Women Painters and Their Work.* London: Picador, 1981.

Gutwirth, Madelyn. *Madame de Staël, Novelist: The Emergence of the Artist as Woman.* Urbana: University of Illinois Press, 1978.

– "Madame de Staël, Rousseau, and the Woman Question," *Publications of the Modern Language Association* 86 (1971): 100–9.

Hancock, Geoff. *Canadian Writers at Work: Interviews with Geoff Hancock,* 187–225. Toronto: Oxford University Press, 1987.

– "Alice Munro." In Geoff Hancock. *Canadian Writers at Work: Interviews with Geoff Hancock,* 187–225.

Harris, Ann Sutherland, and Linda Nochlin. "Artemisia Gentileschi." In Ann Sutherland Harris and Linda Nochlin. *Women Artists: 1550–1950,* 118–25.

– *Women Artists: 1550–1950.* New York: Knopf, 1981.

Hawthorne, Nathaniel. *The Marble Faun.* 1860. With Introduction and Notes by Richard H. Brodhead. New York: Penguin Books, 1990.

Henry, Nancy. *George Eliot and the British Empire.* Cambridge: Cambridge University Press, 2002.

Herold, J. Christopher. *Mistress to an Age: A Life of Mme de Staël.* London: Hamish Hamilton, 1959.

Hogsett, Charlotte. *The Literary Existence of Germaine de Staël.* Carbondale: Southern Illinois University Press, 1987.

Howells, Coral A., and Lynett Hunter, eds. *Narrative Strategies in Canadian Literature.* Milton Keynes, Philadelphia: Open University Press, 1991.

Hoy, Helen. "Alice Munro: 'Unforgettable, Indigestible Messages.'" *Journal of Canadian Studies/Revue d'études canadiennes* 26, no. 1 (1991): 5–22.

Hulley, Kathleen. "Interview with Grace Paley." *Delta: Revue du Centre d'Étude et de Recherche sur les Écrivains du Sud aux États-Unis* 14 (1982): 19–40. Reprinted in *Conversations with Grace Paley*, edited by Gerhard Bach and Blaine Hall, 36–56.

Hutcheon, Linda. *The Canadian Postmodern*. Toronto Oxford: Oxford University Press, 1988.

Isaacs, Neil D. *Grace Paley: A Study of the Short Fiction*. Boston: G.K. Hall, 1990.

Irving, Lorna. "'Changing Is the Word I Want.'" In *Probable Fictions: Alice Munro's Narrative Acts*," edited by Louis K. MacKendrick, 99–112.

James, Henry. *The Portrait of a Lady*. 1881. With Introduction and Notes by Nicola Bradbury. Oxford, New York: Oxford University Press, 1995.

Jaumain, Serge, and Marc Maufort, eds. *The Crises of Canadian Diversity/Les Masques de la diversité canadienne*. Amsterdam, Atlanta: Rodopi, 1995.

Jefferson, Thomas. "The Declaration of Independence." In *The American Tradition in Literature*, edited by Sculley Bradley et al., 307–10.

Kamel, Rose. "To Aggravate the Conscience: Grace Paley's Loud Voice." *Journal of Ethnic Studies* 11 (1983): 29–49.

Kaplan, Cora. "Grace Paley Talking with Cora Kaplan." In *Writing Lives: Conversations between Women Writers*, edited by Mary Chamberlain, 181–90. Reprinted in *Conversations with Grace Paley*, edited by Gerhard Bach and Blaine Hall, 146–53.

Kolbert, Elizabeth. "The Prisoner." *The New Yorker* (16 July 2001): 44–58.

Lapierre, Alexandra. *Artemisia: A Novel*. Translated by Liz Heron. New York: Grove Press. 2000.

Leavis, F.R. *The Great Tradition*. 1948. London: Chatto and Windus, 1960.

Lewis, Linda M. *Germaine de Staël, George Sand, and the Victorian Woman Artist*. Columbia, MO: University of Missouri Press, 2003.

Levey, Michael. "Notes on the Royal Collection – II: Artemisia Gentileschi's 'Self-Portrait' at Hampton Court." *The Burlington Magazine* 104 (1962): 79–80.

Lidoff, Joan. "Clearing Her Throat," *Shenandoah: The Washington and Lee Review* 32, no. 3 (1981) 3–26. Reprinted in *Conversations with Grace Paley*, edited by Gerhard Bach and Blaine Hall, 72–94.

Longhi, Roberto. "Gentileschi padre e figlia." *L'Arte* 19 (1916): 245–314. Reprint. *Scritti Giovanili: 1912–1922*. 2 vols. Vol. 1, 219–83. *Opere Complete di Roberto Longhi*. Florence: Sansoni, 1961.

MacKendrick, Louis K., ed. *Probable Fictions: Alice Munro's Narrative Acts*. Downsview, ON: ECW Press, 1983.

Mandel, Dena. "Keeping Up with Faith: Grace Paley's Sturdy American Jewess." *Studies in American Jewish Literature* 4 (1983): 85–98.

Marchant, Peter, and Mary Elsie Robertson. "A Conversation with Grace Paley." *Massachusetts Review* 26, no. 4 (1985): 606–14. Reprinted in *Conversations with Grace Paley*, edited by Gerhard Bach and Blaine Hall, 117–26.

Martin, W.R. *Alice Munro: Paradox and Parallel*. Edmonton: Canada: The University of Alberta Press, 1987.

Mathews, Lawrence. "*Who Do You Think You Are?* Alice Munro's Art of Disarrangement." In *Probable Fictions*, edited by Louis K. MacKendrick, 181–93.

Mayberry, Katherine J. "Narrative Strategies of Liberation in Alice Munro." *Studies in Canadian Literature/Études en littérature canadienne* 19, no. 2 (1994): 57–66.

McCarthy, Dermot. "The Woman Out Back: Alice Munro's 'Meneseteung.'" *Studies in Canadian Literature/Études en littérature canadienne* 19, no. 1 (1994): 1–20.

Menzio, Eva, ed. *Artemisia Gentileschi / Agostino Tassi: Atti di un processo per stupro*. Milan: Edizioni delle Donne, 1981.

Michaels, Leonard. "Conversation with Grace Paley." *Threepenny Review* 3 (1980): 4–6. Reprinted in *Conversations with Grace Paley*, edited by Gerhard Bach and Blaine Hall, 26–36.

Moers, Ellen. *Literary Women*. New York: Doubleday, 1976.

Munro, Alice. *Dance of the Happy Shades*. Toronto: McGraw-Hill Ryerson, 1968. Reprint. Toronto: McGraw-Hill, 1988.

– "Everything Here Is Touchable and Mysterious." *Weekend Magazine* (supplement to the *Globe and Mail*), 11 May 1974, 33.

– *Friend of My Youth*. 1990. Toronto: Penguin Books, 1991.

– "Introduction." *Selected Stories*, ix–xvii. Toronto: Penguin, 1998.

– *The Love of a Good Woman*. Toronto: McClelland and Stewart, 1998.

– *The Moons of Jupiter*. 1982. Toronto: Penguin, 1986.

– *The Progress of Love*. 1986. Toronto: Penguin, 1986.

– "The Real Material: An Interview with Alice Munro." With J.R. (Tim) Struthers. *Probable Fictions: Alice Munro's Narrative Acts*, edited by Louis K. MacKendrick, 5–37.

– *Something I've Been Meaning to Tell You*. 1974. Toronto: Penguin, 1990.

– *Who Do You Think You Are?* 1978. Toronto: Penguin, 1991.

Paley, Grace. *The Collected Stories* New York: Farrar Straus Giroux, 1994.
– *Enormous Changes at the Last Minute*. New York: Farrar Straus Giroux, 1974.
– *Later the Same Day*. 1985. New York: Penguin Books, 1986.
– *The Little Disturbances of Man*. 1959. New York: New American Library, 1973.
– *Begin Again: Collected Poems*. New York: Farrar Straus Giroux, 2000.
– *Just as I Thought*. New York: Farrar, Straus and Giroux, 1998.
– & Paintings by Vera B. Williams. *Long Walks and Intimate Talks*. New York: The Feminist Press, 1991.
– "Midrash on Happiness." *TriQuarterly* 65 (1986): 151–3.

Park, Clara Claiborne. "Faith, Grace, and Love." *Hudson Review* 38, no. 3 (1985): 481–8.

Parker, Rozsika, and Griselda Pollock. *Old Mistresses: Women, Art and Ideology*. London and Henley: Routledge and Kegan Paul, 1981.

Pearlman, Mickey. "Grace Paley. Listen to Their Voices." In Mickey Pearlman. *Twenty Interviews with Women Who Write*, 23–35. Reprinted in *Conversations with Grace Paley*, edited by Gerhard Bach and Blaine Hall, 226–235.
– Twenty Interviews with Women Who Write, New York: Norton, 1993.

Perry, Ruth. "Grace Paley." In *Women Writers Talking*, edited by Janet Todd, 34–56. Reprinted in *Conversations with Grace Paley*, edited by Gerhard Bach and Blaine Hall, 95–117.

Porton, Gary G. "Midrash." In *Anchor Bible Dictonary*, edited by David Noel Freedman, vol. 4, 818–22. New York: Doubleday, 1992.

Poulet, George. "'Corinne' et 'Adolphe': deux romans conjugués." *Revue d'histoire littéraire de la France* (1978): 580–97.

Redekop, Magdalene. *Mothers and Other Clowns*. London and New York: Routledge, 1992.

Reesman, Jeanne Campbell, ed. *Speaking the Other Self: American Women Writers*. Athens and London: University of Georgia Press, 1997.

Regan, Stephen. "'The Presence of the Past': Modernism and Postmodernism in Canadian Short Fiction." In *Narrative Strategies in Canadian Literature*, edited by Coral A. Howells and Lynett Hunter, 108–34.

Remnick, David. "Grace Paley, Voice from the Village." *Washington Post*, 14 April 1985, 71–2. Reprinted in *Conversations with Grace Paley*, edited by Gerhard Bach and Blaine Hall, 131–5.

Rhys, Jean. *Wide Sargasso Sea*, 1966. Introduction by Francis Wyndham. Harmondsworth, England: Penguin, 1975.

Roth, Philip. *American Pastoral*. New York: Vintage, 1998.

Rosenberg, Edgar. *From Shylock to Svengali: Jewish Stereotypes in English Fiction*. Stanford: Stanford University Press, 1960.

Ross, Catherine Sheldrick. "'At least part legend': The Fiction of Alice Munro." In *Probable Fictions*, edited by Louis K. MacKendrick, 112–27.

Sainte-Beuve, Charles Augustin. *Portraits de Femmes*. Paris: Garnier, 1947.

Samuel, Maurice. "The Tribune of the Golus." *Jewish Book Annual* 25 (1967–68): 54.

Satz, Martha. "Looking at Disparities: An Interview with Grace Paley." *Southwest Review* 72, no. 4 (1987). Reprinted in *Conversations with Grace Paley*, edited by Gerhard Bach and Blaine Hall, 192–204.

Shields, Carol. "In Ontario." *London Review of Books* (7 February 1991): 22–3.

Sholem Aleichem. "The Enchanted Tailor." In *The Collected Stories of Sholem Aleichem*, 93–138.

– *The Collected Stories of Sholem Aleichem: The Old Country*. Translated by Julius and Frances Butwin. New York: Crown Publisher, 1956.

Silesky, Barry, Robin Hemley, and Sharon Solwitz. "Grace Paley: A Conversation." *Another Chicago Magazine* 14 (1985): 100–14. Reprinted in *Conversations with Grace Paley*, edited by Gerhard Bach and Blaine Hall, 135–46.

Smith, Wendy. "PW Interviews Grace Paley." *Publisher's Weekly* (5 April 1985): 71–2. Reprinted in *Conversations with Grace Paley*, edited by Gerhard Bach and Blaine Hall, 126–31.

Spalding, Linda, and Michael Ondaatje, eds. *The Brick Reader*. Toronto: Coach House Press, 1991.

Staël, Germaine de. *Corinne ou l'Italie*. 1807. Edited by Simone Balayé. France: Gallimard, 1985.

– *Corinne, or Italy*. Translated and edited by Avriel Goldberger. New Brunswick: Rutgers University Press, 1987.

– *Corinne, or Italy*. Translated and edited by Sylvia Raphael. New York: Oxford University Press, 1998.

Starobinski, Jean. "Suicide et mélancolie chez Mme de Staël," *Madame de Staël et l'Europe: Colloque de Coppet*. Paris: Editions Klincksieck, 1970.

Stead, Kit. "The Twinkling of an 'I': Alice Munro's *Friend of My Youth*." In *The Guises of Canadian Diversity/ Les masques de la diversité canadienne*, edited by Serge Jaumain and Marc Maufort, 151–65.

Strich, K.P., ed. *Reflections: Autobiography and Canadian Literature*. Ottawa: University of Ottawa Press, 1988.

Struthers, J.R. (Tim). "The Real Material: An Interview with Alice Munro." In *Probable Fictions*, edited by Louis K. Mackendrick, 5–37.

Taylor, Jacqueline. *Grace Paley: Illuminating the Dark Lives*. Austin: University of Texas Press, 1990.

– "Grace Paley on Storytelling and Story Hearing." *Literature and Performance* 7, no. 2 (1987): 46–58. Reprinted in *Conversations with Grace Paley*, edited by Gerhard Bach and Blaine Hall, 163–77.

Thacker, Robert. "'So Shocking a Verdict in Real life': Autobiography in Alice Munro's Stories." In *Reflections: Autobiography and Canadian Literature*, edited by K.P. Strich, 153–63.

Todd, Janet, ed. *Women Writers Talking*. New York: Holmes and Meier, 1983.

Tolstoy, Leo. *Anna Karenina*. 1878. New York: Penguin, 2002.

Voltaire. *Candide ou l'Optimisme*. *Romans et Contes*. 1759. Paris: Garnier Frères, 1960.

Vreeland, Susan. *The Passion of Artemisia*. New York: Viking, 2002.

Wachtel, Eleanor. "An Interview with Grace Paley." In *The Brick Reader*, edited by Linda Spalding and Michael Ondaatje, 185–91. Reprinted in *Conversations with Grace Paley*, edited by Gerhard Bach and Blaine Hall, 204–13.

Wisse, Ruth R. *The Schlemiel as Modern Hero*. Chicago: University of Chicago Press, 1971.

Wittkower, Rudolf, and Margot Wittkower. "Agostino Tassi – the Seducer of Artemisia Gentileschi." In Rudolf Wittkower and Margot Wittkower. *Born under Saturn*, 162–5.

– *Born under Saturn*. London: Weidenfeld and Nicholson, 1963.

Woolf, Virginia. *A Room of One's Own*. 1928. Harmondsworth, Middlesex: Penguin Books, 1972.

– *Between the Acts*. 1941. Oxford New York, Toronto: Oxford University Press, 1992.

– *Flush: A Biography*. 1933. Introduction by Trekkie Ritchie. San Diego, New York, London: Harcourt Brace Jovanovich, 1983.

– *Orlando: A Biography*. 1928. Edited with an introduction by Rachel Bowlby. Oxford, New York, Toronto: Oxford University Press, 1992.

– "Professions for Women." In Virginia Woolf. *Virginia Woolf and Writing*, introduced by Michèle Barrett, 57–64.

– *To the Lighthouse*. 1927. Edited with an introduction by Margaret Drabble. Oxford, New York, Toronto: Oxford University Press, 1992.

– *Virginia Woolf and Writing*. Introduced by Michèle Barrett. London: The Woman's Press, 1979.

Index